Lecture Notes in Computer Science　　　13763

Founding Editors

Gerhard Goos
Juris Hartmanis

Editorial Board Members

The series Lecture Notes in Computer Science (LNCS), including its subseries Lecture Notes in Artificial Intelligence (LNAI) and Lecture Notes in Bioinformatics (LNBI), has established itself as a medium for the publication of new developments in computer science and information technology research, teaching, and education.

LNCS enjoys close cooperation with the computer science R & D community, the series counts many renowned academics among its volume editors and paper authors, and collaborates with prestigious societies. Its mission is to serve this international community by providing an invaluable service, mainly focused on the publication of conference and workshop proceedings and postproceedings. LNCS commenced publication in 1973.

Han Wang · Wei Lin · Paul Manoranjan ·
Guobao Xiao · Kap Luk Chan · Xiaonan Wang ·
Guiju Ping · Haoge Jiang

Editors

Image and Video Technology

10th Pacific-Rim Symposium, PSIVT 2022
Virtual Event, November 12–14, 2022
Proceedings

Springer

Editors
Han Wang ⓘD
Xiamen University Malaysia
Sepang, Malaysia

Paul Manoranjan ⓘD
Charles Sturt University
Bathurst, NSW, Australia

Kap Luk Chan
Yau Lee Holdings Ltd.
Hong Kong, Hong Kong

Guiju Ping
Nanyang Technological University
Singapore, Singapore

Wei Lin ⓘD
Singapore Institute of Manufacturing
Technology
Singapore, Singapore

Guobao Xiao ⓘD
Minjiang University
Fuzhou, China

Xiaonan Wang ⓘD
Tsinghua University
Beijing, China

Haoge Jiang
Nanyang Technological University
Singapore, Singapore

ISSN 0302-9743   ISSN 1611-3349 (electronic)
Lecture Notes in Computer Science
ISBN 978-3-031-26430-6   ISBN 978-3-031-26431-3 (eBook)
https://doi.org/10.1007/978-3-031-26431-3

This Springer imprint is published by the registered company Springer Nature Switzerland AG
The registered company address is: Gewerbestrasse 11, 6330 Cham, Switzerland

Preface

This is the proceedings of the 10th Pacific-Rim Symposium on Image and Video Technology (PSIVT2022). The series provides a forum for researchers and practitioners who are involved in or contribute to theoretical advances or practical implementations for image and video technology.The sequence of events is Hsinchu, Taiwan (2006), Santiago, Chile (2007), Tokyo, Japan (2009), Gwangju, South Korea (2011), Singapore (2010), Guanajuato, Mexico (2013), Auckland, New Zealand (2015), Wuhan, China (2017), and Sydney, Australia (2019). Due to the pandemic, the most recent PSIVT was delayed for a year and took place on November 26, 2022 online.

Eighteen papers were submitted. Each paper received two reviews, and the review time was 60 days, using double-blind review. Finally 15 papers were accepted. The acceptance rate of ca. 2/3 was due to the high quality of the papers, fulfilling the PSIVT standards. The conference was organized into one keynote speech, followed by 4 main sessions. Each paper presentation lasted 20 minutes, with 15 minutes for the talk and then 5 minutes Q&A. It was nice that all speakers could attend the presentations despite the time differences with Europe and South America.

I strongly believed the conference would bring researchers and entrepreneurs together by pooling their knowledge and resources, and this event was enjoyable and fruitful for all participants. I would like to thank the program committee for their diligent work, specially Wei Lin for his dedication in the programme organization; Guiju Ping and Haoge Jiang who patiently handled all the conference details including web page and paper review organization; Kap Luk Chan for his care in handling all the finance details; and finally Xiaonan Wang who helped organize the final proceedings.

Finally, we'd like to pay our final respects to the founder of this conference series, Reinhard Klette, for his friendship, and unfailing encouragement in the field of video and image development.

November 2022   Han Wang

Organization

General Chair

Han Wang — Xiamen University Malaysia, Malaysia

Program Chairs

Wei Lin — Simtech, Singapore
Paul Manoranjan — Charles Sturt University, Australia
Guobao Xiao — Minjiang University, China

Publicity Chair

Young Woon Woo — Dong-Eui University, Korea

Tutorial Chair

Weisi Lin — Nanyang Technological University, Singapore

Regional Chairs

Anwaar Ul-Haq — Charles Sturt University, Australia
Bok-Suk Shin — Korea Polytechnic, Korea
Christian Laugier — Inria, France
Domingo Mery — Universidad Católica de Chile, Chile
Fawzi Nashashibi — Inria, France
Guilin Yang — NIIT, CAS, China
Jason Gu — Dalhousie University, Canada
Kai-Kuang Ma — Nanyang Technological University, Singapore
Michael Yu Wang — HKUST, China
Philippe Martinet — Inria, France
Shiping Wang — Fuzhou University, China
Wei Qi Yan — Auckland University of Technology, New Zealand
Marcelo H. Ang Jr. — NUS, Singapore

Minh Nguyen	Auckland University of Technology, New Zealand
Nevrez İmamoğlu	AIST, Japan
Tsung-Jung Liu	National Chung Hsing University, Taiwan
Jinjian Wu	Xidian University, China
Lichen Fu	National Taiwan University, Taiwan
Zijun Wang	UESTC, China

Finance Chairs

Kap Luk Chan	Yau Lee Holdings, Singapore
Wei-Yun Yau	I2R-A*STAR, Singapore

Publication Chairs

Xiaonan Wang	NUS, Singapore
Lihong Zheng	Charles Sturt University, Australia

Steering Committee

Kap Luk Chan	Yau Lee Holdings Limited, Singapore
Yo-Sung Ho	Gwangju Institute of Science and Technology, South Korea
Wen-Nung Lie	National Chung Cheng University, Taiwan
Paul Manoranjan	Charles Sturt University, Australia
Domingo Mery	Pontificia Universidad Católica, Chile
Mariano Rivera	Centro de Investigacion en Matematicas, Mexico
Akihiro Sugimoto	National Institute of Informatics, Japan
Han Wang	Xiamen University Malaysia, Malaysia
Xinguo Yu	Central China Normal University, China

Contents

Waste Classification from Digital Images Using ConvNeXt

Jianchun Qi, Minh Nguyen, and Wei Qi Yan[(✉)]

Auckland University of Technology, Auckland 1010, New Zealand
weiqi.yan@aut.ac.nz

Abstract. In this paper, ConvNeXt is selected as a model for waste classification from digital images. ConvNeXt is a CNN-based backbone network that has been proposed to further improve the performance of models for visual tasks, following the various types of research work that have been generated based on Transformer. In this paper, we take ConvNeXt as the backbone to obtain an efficient waste classification model. In our experiments, we categorized waste into four classes based on predefined classification criteria. We have collected 1,660 labeled images for model training. By using ConvNeXt, we observed that the best experimental result in this paper was from ConvNeXt, which has achieved an accuracy 79.88% in the waste classification. In order to evaluate the model, we consider AP and mAP for waste classification. Our experimental results show that using Mask R-CNN network with ConvNeXt as the backbone outperforms the existing methods for waste classification.

Keywords: ConvNeXt · Mask R-CNN · Waste detection · Waste classification · Object detection

1 Introduction

An increasing amount of waste products are being consumed every day [3]. The disposal and recycling of wastes is a problem that should be considered in the process of protecting the environment. For waste classification, it should be grouped into categories according to its components, properties, value, and impact on the environment, depending on the type of disposal. In general, according to the characteristics of wastes, we group wastes into four major categories, namely hazardous waste, recyclable waste, wet waste, and dry waste. For example, after the waste is efficiently classified into the four classes and then transported to the waste treatment plant, the hazardous waste will be disposed to protect our environment. Recyclable waste will be sent to various resource recycling factories where it is recycled to save resources. Then, wet waste is tackled in the factory to produce biogas, which in turn helps to generate electricity and save electricity resources. The recycling of dry waste by incinerating it, can produce fuel for clean energy. If the waste is not classified and both dry waste and wet waste are treated at the same time, they are mixed and incinerated to produce significantly higher levels of carcinogenic substances, increasing the risk of secondary pollution to the environment [4]. We see that

H. Wang et al. (Eds.): PSIVT 2022, LNCS 13763, pp. 1–13, 2023.
https://doi.org/10.1007/978-3-031-26431-3_1

garbage classification is of great significance for resource utilization and environmental protection.

At this stage, there are still many challenges in household waste classification, such as the lack of waste classification and the shortage of basic infrastructure for waste disposal. Therefore, an automatic waste classification method is of great value and significance to society. With the development of deep learning [11, 12, 14], it has become possible to improve the automated waste classification, realize the treatment and effective utilization of garbage [13, 21]. This provides a good chance for promoting the development of the municipal domestic waste treatment industry.

At present, a plethora of deep learning algorithms have achieved excellent results in waste classification [6, 28]. However, the characteristics of waste make the task of waste classification more difficult. For example, nut shells need to be classified into two classes: Dry garbage and wet garbage. Chestnuts need to be classified as wet waste, while walnut shells are dry waste. However, the similarity between the two types of nut shells is relatively high. During the experiment, we see that the two types of nut shells are very easily confused in the classifications.

Therefore, we aim to find a model that is much suitable for the task of garbage classification as a way to improve the accuracy of waste classification and save the classification costs. Furthermore, the collection of waste data is a major challenge due to the diversity of household waste, it is also a significant goal for us to collect waste images into a comprehensive, accurate, and diverse waste dataset. Overall, the main contributions of this paper are as follows:

(1) The training results of ConvNeXt model in waste classification have been conducted. The mAP of classification 79.88% was reached.
(2) Accurate waste images among a large number of waste images are found, a dataset with four classes of waste is constructed: Hazardous waste, dry waste, wet waste, and recyclable waste.
(3) The development of convolutional neural networks has a slew of advantages compared to attention mechanisms.

In this paper, we show our related work in Sect. 2, our methodology is depicted in Sect. 3, the result analysis is stated in Sect. 4, and our conclusion will be drawn in Sect. 5.

2   Related Work

Convolutional Neural Networks (CNN or ConvNet) is a deep neural network with a convolutional architecture, which has the ability of representation learning [38]. It is usually composed of three parts. The first part is the input layer, the second is composed of multiple pooling layers and sampling layers, where the two types of layers, pooling and convolutional, are usually alternating, and the depth of each filter increases sequentially from left to right. The final part then consists of one or more fully connected classifiers [39]. Among these, CNN has three critical operations, namely, local receptive fields, shared weights, and pooling layers, where CNNs have the advantage of reducing the number of network parameters and avoiding model overfitting [15, 16, 25].

Specifically, a convolutional layer of CNN contains a number of feature maps, each layer comprises a number of neurons. A neuron is only connected to the neurons in the adjacent layer and forms a rectangular arrangement of states [32, 37]. Neurons in the same layer then share the same weights. The convolutional kernel is initialized in the form of a random matrix, the weights are continuously trained during the training process for feature extraction. Besides, the pooling layer also has two forms: Average pooling and max pooling. This allows the complexity of the proposed model to be significantly simplified and the parameters of the model to be reduced.

Owing to the apparent advantages of convolutional neural networks, it has applications in face recognition, automatic speech recognition, gesture recognition, and natural language processing [30, 33]. Moreover, the performance of CNNs is even much outstanding for visual object recognition from digital images, as it allows images to be directly employed as the input to the network, and automatically extracts visual features, such as color and texture. Moreover, it avoids complex feature extraction and has excellent robustness and computational efficiency.

The depth of early CNN algorithms is critical to model performance, capable of extracting visual features. An increase in the number of network layers means that the network can extract more abundant features. Theoretically, the more layers a network has, the better the results will be. However, simply network leads to the vanishing and exploding gradient problem [22, 23, 37], which prevents the backpropagation process from effectively updating the gradients, resulting in the parameters not fully being updated. Currently, batch normalization can solve this problem [24, 31], which normalizes scattered data to prevent the gradient from vanishing in the process of backpropagation, so that the number of model layers can reach a level of dozens.

However, the increase in the number of network layers brings another problem, the degradation problem, in which the accuracy of network training saturates, and even performance degrade [9]. ResNet is also a relatively mainstream CNN algorithm at present. It introduces the residual network and makes use of a sliding window model to extract visual features and outputs a multilayer pyramidal feature map, which is ideal for a variety of downstream tasks. ResNet adds a shortcut [7] between every two layers of the network, forming a residual network. All residual blocks do not have a pooling layer, and directly use the convolution with stride 2 for downsampling. This residual network structure allows each layer of the neural network to fully learn the residuals of the previous layers' output and preserve the integrity of the information.

Besides ResNet, there are a consortium of CNN-based models, such as Mask R-CNN [8] and YOLO series [1]. Mask R-CNN is a two-stage model. The first stage generates proposals, the second stage generates masks and bounding boxes. However, the backbone network of Mask R-CNN is ResNet-50, a Feature Pyramid Network (FPN) is introduced so that the feature map of each layer can be fused to extract the features of each layer. Moreover, Mask R-CNN also introduces a mask branch. As a result, Mask R-CNN has the advantage of both high speed and high accuracy. There are a series of YOLO models, the latest one is YOLOv7 [35]. YOLO is a one-stage model [19, 20, 26, 36], which do not show the step of generating proposals and directly take use of regression method for detection.

Transformer is the first deep learning model that is based entirely on attention mechanism to improve the speed of model training [34], which is primarily proffered in the field of natural language processing (NLP) [27]. It is structured by using encoder and decoder. Among them, self-attention layer and multihead attention mechanism are the key parts of this model. Therefore, its advantage is that it can be efficiently parallelized. After that, the attention mechanism was gradually developed, the attention-based models in the field of vision have been proposed, such as Vision Transformer [5], Swin Transformer [17], and DERT [2].

CNN has a slew of advantages for extracting visual features, such as detecting the boundary of visual objects and other basic visual elements. However, because attention-based models have an attention mechanism, they are able to capture global contextual information, which has a larger receptive field and substantial model representation capabilities. We see that attention-based models are much more effective in dealing with high-level visual effects.

Therefore, we speculate that the combination of the two advantages of CNN model and the attention-based model may have better development prospects. This is also one of the purposes of this paper to prob the newly proposed ConvNeXt network.

3 Our Method

In the last two years, attention-based models have become mainstream research, such as Swin Transformer. Although Swin Transformer has achieved remarkable achievements for various vision tasks and successfully solved the problem of substantial computational cost, there is still room for improvement. For example, its calculations based on sliding windows are much complex, which makes it challenging to be deployed. With recent findings, the depthwise convolution appears to be equivalent to the self-attention mechanism. In particular, the performance of depthwise convolution is deeper than that of Swin Transformer in the case of smaller parameters.

Hence, pertaining to waste classification, we concentrate our research intention on the newly proposed ConvNeXt net [18], which outperforms Swin Transformer to explore the most suitable algorithm for waste classification.

ConvNeXt outperforms Swin Transformer in terms of not only accuracy but also performance and simplicity. ConvNeXt is based on ResNet structure and improves the model in five main ways:

(1) Macro design replaces the stem cell layer of ResNet with a Patchify layer and adjusts the computational ratio to approximately 1:1:3:1.
(2) In ResNeXt, depthwise convolution [4] is employed, the network width is set to 96.
(3) Related to inverted bottleneck, the inverted bottleneck in the Transformer block is adopted.
(4) With very large kernel size, a larger convolution kernel is taken.
(5) Under the assistance of various layer-wise micro designs, ReLU was replaced with GELU. Furthermore, fewer activation functions and fewer layer normalization were used.

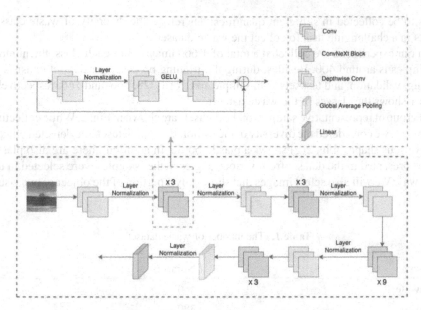

Fig. 1. The framework of our model.

The network structure of ConvNeXt is shown in Fig. 1. We combine ConvNeXt with Mask R-CNN. Mask R-CNN is chosen because it has an excellent performance in downstream tasks which is a very flexible framework that can add multiple branches to accomplish various tasks, such as instance segmentation, semantic segmentation, and human pose recognition. In ConvNeXt, stride is 4. The numbers of channels are 96, 192, 384, and 768, which correspond to the numbers of blocks stacked in each stage, i.e., 3, 3, 9, and 3. After that, layer normalization and GELU are added to the net. Finally, drop path is adopted to prevent overfitting and improve performance.

In Mask R-CNN, five loss functions are employed, which contain two loss functions for the RPN network [8], two loss functions for classification, and one loss function for the mask branch. The first four loss functions are as same as the loss function of Faster R-CNN [29], the final mask loss function adopts the mask branch with Km^2 output for each ROI. By using a per-pixel sigmoid, the average binary cross-entropy loss is obtained for the pixels. In this way, the model only needs to detect which class the ROI is, which only calculates for one branch and avoids the competition among classes.

4 Result Analysis

4.1 Our Dataset

There are various types of domestic wastes, which are classifiered into four main classes according to the waste classification criteria, namely, dry waste, wet waste, hazardous waste, and recyclable waste. Within each class, there is a consortium of subcategories. For example, recyclable waste includes cardboard, glass, and plastic bottles. The hazardous waste includes batteries, nail polish bottles, and medicine bottles. Each of these classes needs to be collected in sufficient quantities. Therefore, the diversity of waste classes results in a challenging task to collect the waste dataset.

In our experiment, we collected a total of 1,660 images. For each class, the number of samples is around 400. Besides, during the training process, our dataset consists of training, validation, and test sets with sample sizes of 1,328, 166, and 166, respectively. Table 1 shows the classes of the waste dataset.

A group of representative samples of the datasets are shown in Fig. 2. While collecting waste data, we considered the diversity of the samples. In our dataset, the detected objects have various shapes, Fig. 2(g) shows a plastic bottle. In addition, there are also plastic bottles presented in the dataset from various angles. Other samples were selected in the same way. We will also select images that show only a portion of the object as our visual data.

Table 1. The number of waste dataset

Classes	Numbers
Dry waste	460
Wet waste	380
Hazardous waste	450
Recyclable waste	370
TOTAL	1,660

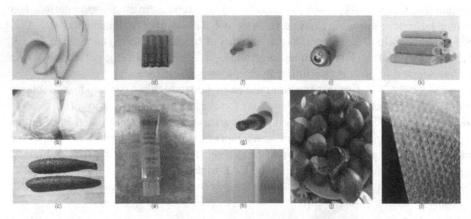

Fig. 2. The samples of the waste dataset. (a), (b), (c), and (j) are banana peel, cabbage, cucumber, and chestnut shell, respectively, which belong to wet class. (d) and (e) are battery and ointment shell, respectively, which are classified to hazardous class. (f), (g), (h), and (i) are a plastic bottle, glass bottle, cardboard, and can, respectively, which are grouped to recyclable class. (k) and (l) are rag and bubble film, respectively, are identified as dry class.

After the data had been collected, we annotated each sample by using the labeling software LabelMe. Our annotations follow the JSON file format of the COCO dataset. Then, we labelled the four types of images as "Hazardous", "Dry", "Wet", and "Recyclable", respectively. Finally, we save the images in JPG format.

4.2 Evaluation Methods

In order to better improve the model, we need to evaluate its performance of the model. According to our experimental purpose, we choose to use average precision (AP) and mean average precision (mAP).

Accuracy is a popular evaluation metric, which is a number of correctly selected samples divided by using the number of all samples. General speaking, the higher the accuracy rate, the better the classifier. Equation (1) shows the algorithm for accuracy.

$$\textbf{Accuracy} = (TP + TN)/(TP + FP + TN + FN) \qquad (1)$$

where TP, TN, FP, and FN are true positive, true negative, false positive, and false negative. Positive and negative represent the predicted results, positive samples are predicted to be positive, and negative samples are predicted to be negative. True or false indicates the ground truth of samples, positive or negative refers to the test results. $TP + TN$ is the sum of all correctly predicted positive samples and negative samples, $TP + TN + FP + FN$ is the total number of samples.

Besides, precision measures the probability of a classifier judging a positive sample to be a true positive sample. AP is the area under the curve, and mAP refers to the average of multiple classes of precisions. The calculation method of precision is shown in Eq. (2).

$$\textbf{Precision} = TP/(TP + FP) \qquad (2)$$

4.3 Result Analysis

Figure 3 shows us an example of our waste detection results. We see that there are various classes of waste samples in the image, each class has the colored bounding box and label.

In Fig. 4, we see that AP rates of the four classes: Dry, wet, recyclable, and hazardous, are 59.90%, 81.51%, 95.50%, and 82.61%, respectively. Hence, Fig. 5 shows the mAP rate is 79.88%.

We quantitatively compare our model with other models by using our own dataset. Table 2 shows the comparison results. The accuracy of Swin Transformer is 0.78, which is slightly lower than that of the ConvNeXt by 0.02. The accuracy rates of YOLOv3 and ResNet-50 are 0.77 and 0.75, respectively. It is only 0.05 different from ConvNeXt most. This means that the ConvNeXt model is currently the better performing model, but could be further improved.

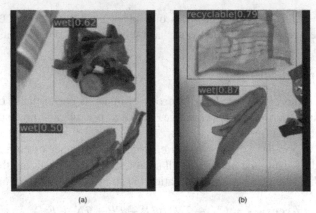

(a)   (b)

Fig. 3. ConvNeXt-based classification results from digital videos. (a) The results of classifying green onion leaves and cucumber peel are classified to the class wet. (b) The classification results of banana peel and waste paper, which are classified to class wet and class recyclable, respectively.

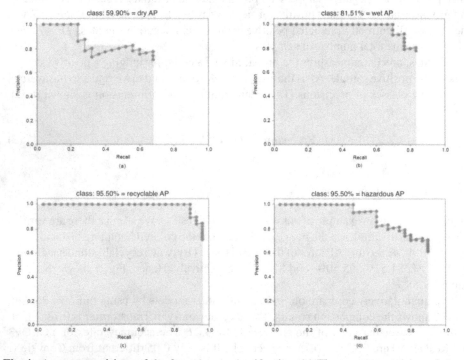

Fig. 4. Average precisions of the four classes classification. (a) The average precision of class dry. (b) The average precision of class wet. (c) The average precision of class recyclable. (d) The average precision of class hazardous.

Furthermore, we kept the ConvNeXt as the backbone network approach to whether Mask R-CNN was the best performing model when combined with ConvNeXt. As shown

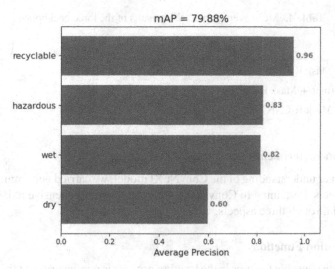

Fig. 5. Mean average precisions of the four classes.

Table 2. Mean average precision results between four models

Dataset	ConvNeXt	Swin Transformer	YOLOv3	ResNet-50
Recyclable waste	0.96	0.91	0.81	0.83
Hazardous waste	0.83	0.80	0.72	0.79
Dry waste	0.60	0.65	0.67	0.58
Wet waste	0.82	0.76	0.88	0.80
AVERAGE	**0.80**	**0.78**	**0.77**	**0.75**

Table 3. Mean average precision results between the three algorithms

Model	mAPs
ConvNeXt + Mask R-CNN0.80	0.80
ConvNeXt + Cascade Mask R-CNN	0.79
ConvNeXt + Faster R-CNN	0.76

in Table 3, by using Cascade Mask R-CNN in combination with ConvNeXt, the mAP dropped 0.01. After replacing Mask R-CNN with Faster R-CNN, the mAP was the lowest one, up to 0.76.

Finally, we experimented with other backbone networks instead of ConvNeXt and obtained Table 4. After substituting the backbone network with Swin Transformer and ResNet-50, the mAP values dropped by 0.02, and 0.07 to 0.78 and 0.73, respectively. With this experiment, we see that the ConvNeXt model has the most stable performance.

Table 4. Mean average precision results of the three backbones

Model	mAPs
ConvNeXt + Mask R-CNN	0.80
Swin Transformer + Mask R-CNN	0.78
ResNet-50 + Mask R-CNN	0.73

4.4 Ablation Experiments

To gain a deeper understanding of the ConvNeXt model, we carried out a number of ablation experiments. Pertaining to ConvNeXt, we conduct comprehensive ablation studies on the model through three aspects.

4.4.1 Activation Functions

One of the indispensable features in the training process is nonlinearity. At the same time, for the generalization ability of the model, random regularization, such as dropout, needs to be added. Activation functions play an essential role for the proposed models. The nonlinear properties are introduced into the network which solves problems that cannot be solved by linear models. GELU [10] introduced the idea of random regularization and outperformed ReLU experimentally. Therefore, in the ConvNeXt net, the ReLU activation function was replaced by the GELU activation function in the ConvNeXt Block. However, ConvNeXt harnesses only one GELU activation function in each block.

Hence, in our experiments, we added a GELU to the convolutional layer in ConvNeXt Block as a way to investigate the effect of the number of GELU activation functions on the model. In Table 5, we see that after changed the number of GELU to two, the AP value of the model drops by 0.50 to 0.68, which shows that not the more activation functions are, the better the model performance is.

Table 5. Influence of activation function on average precision values

GELU	AP	AP_{50}	AP_{75}	AP_S	AP_M	AP_L
× 1	0.73	0.74	0.69	0.28	0.56	0.76
× 2	0.68	0.71	0.62	0.25	0.50	0.72

4.4.2 Batch Normalization

In convolutional neural networks, normalization has an important significance in preventing gradient disappearance and gradient explosion. At present, Batch Normalization (BN) is widely employed, while ConvNeXt makes use of Layer Normalization (LN). Hence, we investigate the impact of batch normalization on the performance of the model. As shown in Table 6, we see that replacing LN with BN is an imperfect solution, which results in a slight decrease of 0.02 in AP value from 0.73 to 0.71.

Table 6. Impact of Batch Normalization on average precision rates

LN	BN	AP	AP_{50}	AP_{75}	AP_S	AP_M	AP_L
×	√	0.71	0.73	0.65	0.26	0.52	0.75
√	×	0.73	0.74	0.69	0.28	0.56	0.76

4.4.3 Layer Normalization

Previously, we replaced layer normalization with batch normalization and received the result that the value of AP dropped. We investigated the number of LN again. In ConvNeXt, only one layer normalization is employed in the block. In Table 7, we have experimented with two-layer normalizations and three-layer normalizations, respectively, the results show that the more layer normalizations are, the smaller the AP value is. However, the AP value decreases slightly; it seems that the number of layer normalizations does not significantly affect the model performance.

Table 7. Influence of Layer Normalization on average precision rates

LN	AP	AP_{50}	AP_{75}	AP_S	AP_M	AP_L
× 1	0.73	0.74	0.69	0.28	0.56	0.76
× 2	0.71	0.73	0.67	0.26	0.55	0.76
× 3	0.71	0.72	0.64	0.25	0.54	0.75

Based on these three ablation experiments, we see that the number of activation functions has significant impact on the performance of ConvNeXt. The AP rates differed substantially from the increase of the GELU. Conversely, the effect of changing the number of LNs on the model performance is insignificant. These indicate that the activation function plays a decisive role in the performance of the ConvNeXt.

The experimental results show that the algorithm has stable performance, the design of model structure is much simpler than that of Swin Transformer. ConvNeXt combines the excellent components of high-performance neural network models, improves the performance of CNN to 87.8%, and creates inspiration for our research outcomes based on the attention-based models.

5   Conclusion

In this paper, we propose to utilize a network based on ConvNeXt as the backbone network for waste classification. It was constructed to conduct an efficient waste classification by using deep learning method. Overall, 1,660 images were collected as the waste dataset. We manually annotated these images. The experimental results show that the accuracy of ConvNeXt is 79.88%, which has a better performance compared to other peer models.

We see that in the process of the rapid development of attention mechanism, there is also a room for the exploration of convolutional neural network. Further research work on convolutional neural networks is needed. It is also indispensable to improve the accuracy and efficiency of waste classification. Finally, the collected waste dataset needs to be updated.

References

1. Bochkovskiy, A., Wang, C.Y., Liao, M.Y.: YOLOv4: optimal speed and accuracy of object detection. arXiv (2020)
2. Carion, N., Massa, F., Synnaeve, G., Usunier, N., Kirillov, A., Zagoruyko, S.: End-to-End object detection with transformers. In: Vedaldi, A., Bischof, H., Brox, T., Frahm, J.-M. (eds.) ECCV 2020. LNCS, vol. 12346, pp. 213–229. Springer, Cham (2020). https://doi.org/10.1007/978-3-030-58452-8_13
3. Chen, S.S., et al.: Carbon emissions under different domestic waste treatment modes induced by garbage classification: case study in pilot communities in Shanghai, China. Sci. Total Environ. **717**, 137193 (2020)
4. Chollet, F.: Xception: deep learning with depthwise separable convolutions. In: IEEE Conference on Computer Vision and Pattern Recognition (2017)
5. Dosovitskiy, A., et al.: An image is worth 16x16 words: transformers for image recognition at scale. arXiv (2020)
6. Funch, O.L., Marhaug, R., Kohtala, S., Steinert, M.: Detecting glass and metal in consumer trash bags during waste collection using convolutional neural networks. Waste Manag. **119**, 30–38 (2021)
7. Geirhos, R., et al.: Shortcut learning in deep neural networks. Nat. Mach. Intell. **2**(11), 665–673 (2020)
8. He, K.M., Gkioxari, G., Dollár, P., Girshick, R.: Mask R-CNN. IEEE ICCV, pp. 2961–2969 (2017)
9. He, K.M., Zhang, X.Y., Ren, S.Q., Sun, J.: Deep residual learning for image recognition. In: IEEE CVPR, pp. 770–778 (2016)
10. Hendrycks, D., Gimpel, K.: Gaussian error linear units (GELUs). arXiv (2016)
11. Ji, H., Liu, Z., Yan, W.Q., Klette, R.: Early diagnosis of Alzheimer's disease based on selective kernel network with spatial attention. In: Palaiahnakote, S., Sanniti di Baja, G., Wang, L., Yan, W. (eds.) Pattern Recognition. ACPR 2019. LNCS, vol. 12047, pp. 503–515. Springer, Cham (2020). https://doi.org/10.1007/978-3-030-41299-9_39
12. Ji, H., Liu, Z., Yan, W., Klette, R.: Early diagnosis of Alzheimer's disease using deep learning. ACM ICCCV (2019)
13. Kang, Z., Yang, J., Li, G.L., Zhang, Z.Y.: An automatic garbage classification system based on deep learning. IEEE Access. **8**, 140019–140029 (2020)
14. Krizhevsky, A., Sutskever, I., Hinton, G.E.: ImageNet classification with deep convolutional neural networks. Commun. ACM **60**, 84–90 (2017)
15. Liang, S., Yan, W.: A hybrid CTC+Attention model based on end-to-end framework for multilingual speech recognition. Multimed. Tools Appl. **81**, 41295–41308 (2022)
16. Liu, X., Neuyen, M., Yan, W.Q.: Vehicle-related scene understanding using deep learning. In: Cree, M., Huang, F., Yuan, J., Yan, W. (eds.) Pattern Recognition. ACPR 2019. Communications in Computer and Information Science, vol. 1180, pp. 61–73. Springer, Singapore (2020). https://doi.org/10.1007/978-981-15-3651-9_7
17. Liu, Z., et al.: Swin transformer: hierarchical vision transformer using shifted windows. In: IEEE ICCV, pp. 10012–10022 (2021)

18. Liu, Z., Mao, H.Z., Wu, C.Y., Feichtenhofer, C., Darrell, T., Xie, S.N.: A ConvNet for the 2020s. arXiv (2022)
19. Luo, Z., Nguyen, M., Yan, W.: Kayak and sailboat detection based on the improved YOLO with transformer. ACM ICCCV (2022)
20. Luo, Z., Nguyen, M., Yan,W.: Sailboat detection based on automated search attention mechanism and deep learning models. IEEE IVCNZ (2021)
21. Nie, Z.F., Duan, W.J., Li, X.D.: Domestic garbage recognition and detection based on Faster R-CNN. J. Phys. Conf. Ser. **1738**(1), 012089 (2021). https://doi.org/10.1088/1742-6596/1738/1/012089
22. Nixon, M., Aguado, A.: Feature Extraction and Image Processing for Computer Vision. Academic Press, Cambridge (2019)
23. Pan, C., Yan, W.Q.: Object detection based on saturation of visual perception. Multimed. Tools Appl. **79**(27–28), 19925–19944 (2020). https://doi.org/10.1007/s11042-020-08866-x
24. Pan, C., Liu, J., Yan, W., et al.: Salient object detection based on visual perceptual saturation and two-stream hybrid networks. IEEE Trans. Image Process. **30**, 4773–4787 (2022)
25. Pan, C., Yan, W.: A learning-based positive feedback in salient object detection. In: IVCNZ, pp. 311–317 (2018)
26. Prince, S.J.: Computer Vision: Models, Learning, and Inference. Cambridge University Press, Cambridge (2012)
27. Radford, A., Wu, J., Child, R., Luan, D., Amodei, D., Sutskever, I.: Language models are unsupervised multitask learners. OpenAI **1**(8), 9 (2019)
28. Redmon, J., Divvala, S., Girshick, R., Farhadi, A.: You only look once: unified, real - time object detection. In: IEEE CVPR, pp. 779–788 (2016)
29. Ren, S., He, K., Girshick, R., Sun, J.: Faster R-CNN: towards real-time object detection with region proposal networks. NIPS 28 (2015)
30. Sakalle, A., Tomar, P., Bhardwaj, H., Acharya, D., Bhardwaj, A.: A LSTM based deep learning network for recognizing emotions using wireless brainwave driven system. Expert Syst. Appl. **173**, 114516 (2021)
31. Shen, D., Xin, C., Nguyen, M., Yan, W.: Flame detection using deep learning. In: International Conference on Control, Automation and Robotics (2018)
32. Simonyan, K., Zisserman, A.: Very deep convolutional networks for large-scale image recognition. arXiv (2014)
33. Srivastava, N., Geoffrey, H., Alex, K., Ilya, S., Ruslan, S.: Dropout: a simple way to prevent neural networks from overfitting. J. Mac. Lear. **15**, 1929–1958 (2014)
34. Vaswani, A., et al.: Attention is all you need. Adv. Neural Inf. Process. Syst. (2019)
35. Wang, C.Y., Bochkovskiy, A., Liao, H.Y.: YOLOv7: trainable bag-of-freebies sets new state-of-the-art for real-time object detectors. arXiv (2022)
36. Xiao, B., Nguyen, M., Yan, W.Q.: Apple ripeness identification using deep learning. In: Nguyen, M., Yan, W.Q., Ho, H. (eds.) Geometry and Vision. ISGV 2021. Communications in Computer and Information Science, vol. 1386, pp. 53–67. Springer, Cham (2021). https://doi.org/10.1007/978-3-030-72073-5_5
37. Xin, C., Nguyen, M., Yan, W.: Multiple flames recognition using deep learning. In: Handbook of Research on Multimedia Cyber Security, pp. 296–307 (2020)
38. Yan, W.Q.: Computational Methods for Deep Learning - Theoretic. Practice and Applications. Springer, Heidelberg (2021). https://doi.org/10.1007/978-3-030-61081-4
39. Yan, W.Q.: Introduction to Intelligent Surveillance - Surveillance Data Capture, Transmission, and Analytics, 3rd edn. Springer, Heidelberg (2019). https://doi.org/10.1007/978-3-030-10713-0

A Federated Learning Approach for Text Classification Using NLP

Mynul Islam$^{(\boxtimes)}$, Shahriar Iqbal, Sohanoor Rahman, Surid Imam Khan Sur,
Md Humaion Kabir Mehedi, and Annajiat Alim Rasel

Department of Computer Science and Engineering, Brac University,
66 Mohakhali, Dhaka 1212, Bangladesh
{mynul.islam,shahriar.iqbal,sohanoor.rahman,surid.imam.khan.sur,
humaion.kabir.mehedi}@g.bracu.ac.bd

Abstract. Text classification is important in many aspects of natural language processing (NLP), such as word semantic categorization, emotion analysis, question answering, and conversation management. Law, health, and marketing are just a few of the professions that have made use of it throughout the last century. We focused on emotion analysis in this research, which includes categories like happiness, sadness, and more. We investigated the precision of three alternative models for assessing the emotional tone of written text. Deep learning models like GRU (Gated Recurrent Unit) and CNN (Convolutional Neural Network) are used in conjunction with the Bi-LSTM (Bidirectional LSTM) model. These three major deep learning architectures have been extensively studied for classification applications. Finally, the model with the greatest accuracy on the dataset was trained using federated learning (FL). Using the FL approach, more data has to be collected, eliminating data gaps and ensuring data security. The focus of this research is to increase the model's accuracy by collaborating with FL approaches while maintaining data confidentiality.

Keywords: NLP · Federated · Deep learning · CNN · GRU · Bi-LSTM

1 Introduction

Text can be categorized using a variety of approaches, such as the number of words in a paragraph or the genre of the text. It is possible to employ text classification for a variety of natural language processing (NLP) tasks, such as sentiment analysis, question answering, and subject identification. A text classification issue is often broken down into four stages: dimension reduction, text preparation, text classification, and text assessment. Text categorization may be useful in NLP tasks including sentiment analysis, question answering, and topic labeling. Text classification problems often include four-step processes: dimension reduction, text preparation, classification, and evaluation. However,

H. Wang et al. (Eds.): PSIVT 2022, LNCS 13763, pp. 14–23, 2023.
https://doi.org/10.1007/978-3-031-26431-3_2

the main issue is uploading or sharing text data in order to improve model performance, which has previously been achieved utilizing deep learning models. It is not always practicable because of the various privacy concerns of the customers. It is done with the help of a sophisticated deep learning model. Despite the fact that deep learning models have already attained the highest levels of performance in text categorization, uploading and sharing text data is still a significant barrier. This method is implemented via the usage of a pre-trained deep learning model. One way to keep text classification private is to use federated learning (FL). With the introduction of Google's federated learning in 2016, service providers may benefit from models that have access to private data without needing to access such data or aggregate all the information into a single dataset. If many devices were trained together, the model would be distributed to each device for additional refinement and improvement [1]. There are numerous clients working together to solve a machine learning problem under the direction of one central server or service provider in the federated learning model. Training machines via federated learning is a decentralized method. No third party receives any of the raw data from any of the clients. The framework's database was used to train local models. When the central server has acquired gradients from all platforms and has completed collecting them, a global model update is generally done. Once this procedure is complete, a new set of parameters is transmitted to each platform for the next round of modeling training.

2 Related Work

Muthukumar [1] used a few-shot learning architecture for text classification in an FL environment. Few-shot learning works with federated datasets with minimal data on each device. Federated learning offers training models on users' devices so service providers may access private data. Various architectures and methodologies may be used to train and merge peripheral models. This document reports some of their experiments and their findings. In one experiment, each node is trained using an IN, while in another, fine-tuned examples are used. All experiments were conducted using the Amazon Review dataset. Each node was categorized and trained separately. In the first experiment, IN SoTA was compared against zero-shot learning with BART models. They trained ML models to predict infant domain probability distributions. Natural language inference was taught using BART-MNLI. 10 instances per labeling criterion were used to fine-tune each model (5 positive and 5 negative). Hugging Face's BART-MNLI-large predicted the second sentence's entailment probability. On another development set, hyperparameters were manually tweaked. All settings are fine-tuned over 10+4 epochs. Using information from before training, the BART model does better than the baseline with 30 instances and 100 epochs.

Liu and Miller [2] presented the federated pre-training and fine-tuning of the BERT model using clinical data. They were the first ones who used the federated settings for a large transformer model. In a federated manner, they trained the clinical corpus with both pre-training and fine-tuning methods while using multiple silos of data. Even though the original BERT model was trained on books and Wikipedia, they did it on clinical data using MIMIC-III discharge summary in a federated manner, for which they conducted 6 different experiments.

Leroy et al. [3] proposed in their paper a realistic technique for dealing with out-of-domain issues utilizing continuous speech-based models like wake word detectors. Precision is more critical since the model may be utilized at any time. An embedded wake word detector is used to investigate the usage of federated learning. They offer a stochastic gradient descent optimization method that uses both local and global per-coordinate gradient scaling to increase convergence. How to train a wake word detector with entirely decentralized user data will be the subject of the first section of this article. Next, they talked about federated optimization and how to replace its global averaging with an adaptive averaging algorithm inspired by Adam.

In the paper by Basaldella et al. [4], federated learning uses client devices to train a neural network model, which is then delivered back to the machine. The learning model's owner is the server. The server compiles these models into a single global model and delivers it back. We repeat this until the global model reaches our desired accuracy. Any transaction and model data in FL is stored on the server. The records and models stored on the server will be lost or destroyed if it is damaged or malfunctioned. If this happens, the model will need to be retrained.

Ge et al. [5] presented a framework where the server usually coordinates multiple clients for the purpose of local model updating and global model sharing. Basically, here the clients are different medical platforms, and they are used to train their local models with the data that is stored privately. FedNer is also implemented in different places like Dataset and Experimental Settings, Experimental Results, Influence of Training Data Size, Model Decomposition Strategy, Influence of Overlapped Entity Number, and Generalization of the FedNer Framework.

3 Proposed Methodology

3.1 Dataset Description

The dataset we are using it is collected from Kaggle [6]. Our dataset contains six classes: happy, sadness, anger, fear, love and surprise. We have used deep learning models to classify this dataset into above mentioned six classes. The dataset comprises of 21450 unique data points of multi-class emotions. Our dataset contains more than simply sentiment classification; there is more to a sentence's sentiment than just positive, negative, and neutral sentiment. We were trying to figure out what was going on in the mind of the person who wrote the words. Happy, sadness, anger, fear, love and surprise are just a few of the emotions represented in this multi-class data collection. We chose to create a csv file from all of the text files since arranging the data from a text file is very time-consuming and difficult. The csv file has 2 columns and they are text and emotions. The Emotions column has a number of different categories, ranging from happy to sadness, to love and fear. For more clarity some data are shown in Table 1.

Table 1. Sample data of the dataset.

Text	Emotion
i didn't feel humiliated	sadness
i can go from feeling so hopeless to so damned	sadness
i'm grabbing a minute to post i feel greedy wrong	anger
I am ever feeling nostalgic about the fireplace	love
i am feeling grouch	anger

3.2   Data Pre-processing

We have previously processed the data before delving into the model's work. This data processing will allow the models to operate more effectively and with fewer mistakes. To begin, we eliminated the emoji symbols from each sentence in the dataset so that the models could only deal with text. After that, we removed any URLs from the texts. We do not require the URL in our dataset since it does not indicate any kind of emotion. Unnecessary punctuation marks may appear in the text. Unnecessary punctuation may lead us to wrong evaluation, so we eliminated all unnecessary punctuation. We divided the data into three sets: the training dataset (which contains about 70% of the whole dataset), validation dataset (which contains about 20% of the whole dataset) and the test dataset (which contains 10% of the total dataset). We will use the training dataset to train the models, while the testing dataset will be used to assess the model's accuracy after training. Finally, we ran the dataset through the tokenization algorithm. Tokenization is the process of breaking down a phrase, sentence, or text document into smaller pieces, such as individual words.

3.3   GRU

GRUs are a gating mechanism that is used in RNN [7]. There is a problem with short-term memory in RNN. When a sequence becomes large enough, they face difficulty sending information to later time steps from earlier ones. RNNs may leave out essential information at the start when attempting to predict anything from a paragraph of text. During back propagation, the vanishing gradient problem impacts recurrent neural networks. To update a neural network's weights, gradients are used, which are actually values. The vanishing gradient problem occurs when a gradient decreases as it propagates backwards in time. If a gradient value goes below a fixed level for learning, it will not be useful after that. In recurrent neural networks, layers that get a minor gradient update cease learning. Those are often the first layers to show up. RNNs may forget what they have watched in longer sequences since these layers do not learn, resulting in a short-term memory. GRUs were created to address the issue of short-term memory percentage accuracy.

3.4   Fed Averaging

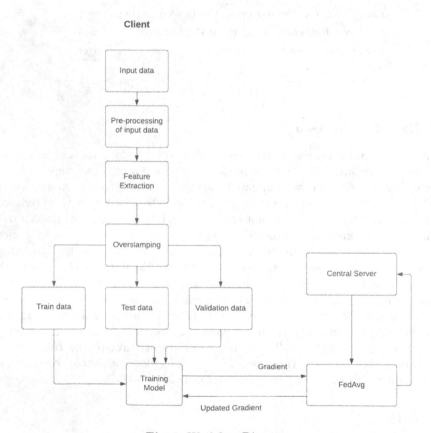

Fig. 1. Workflow Diagram

Our research workflow is shown in Fig. 1. Our planned study on federated learning would include numerous clients, however, we are only displaying data for one.

Initial processing will be performed on the supplied data. The pre-processed data is then used for the extraction of features. The extracted featured data is separated into three sets, and these sets are fetched into the training model. FedAvg, an algorithm used in the federated learning technique, is fed the gradient of the learned model. The gradient is sent to the central server. Each server transmits an epoch for a particular time to the central server. The central server updates gradients and sends them back to client-servers using the Fed Average Algorithm. Local servers provide data to the central one, resulting in a federated learning paradigm.

3.5 Bi-LSTM

The extraordinary capacity of LSTM to extract complex text information is crucial in text classification [8]. Variable-length sequences benefit from the attention mechanism as well as a more even distribution of weight. We employed Word2vec weights that had been pre-trained with a large corpus, guaranteeing that the model was more accurate. The model's accuracy was evaluated using precision, recall, and the F1-score. For NLP applications, the LSTM model plus a CNN proved to be unexpectedly successful. An increasing number of research have proven that sequence-based sentiment categorization may be achieved using LSTMs [9]. The LSTM's accuracy is further hindered by its inability to distinguish between different relationships between document components. To solve this problem, we have used data preprocessing. Before being input into the model, the text was preprocessed. This includes, among other things, removing whitespace and unneeded words, converting other words to approximations, and minimizing duplicate words.

3.6 CNN

Another proposed framework for our research is based on convolutional neural network. ConV1D layer, GlobalMaxPooling layer, and fully connected layer make up our CNN model. Convolutional layers receive the word from the embedding layer. Pooling layers help minimizing computation in the network and control overfitting issue by convolve the input.

Our model was implemented on a Tensorflow sequential model to extract features. In general, we know CNN [10] has three different layers: the Conv Layer, the pooling layer, and the fully connected layer. So after the addition of our embedding layer, we had our 1D conv layer, which has 128 of filter size and 3 of kernel size. Next we have our pooling layer. We used GlobalMaxPooling as our pooling layer. It minimizes and down samples the features in the feature map. Then a dropout layer is used to prevent overfitting issues. At the end, a fully connected layer of 6 units was added.

Figure 2 describes the overall architecture of our CNN model that used here. We have also used two activion fuction in our model, which are ReLu and sigmoid.

```
Layer (type)                    Output Shape              Param #
==================================================================
embedding (Embedding)           (None, 40, 64)            1280064

conv1d (Conv1D)                 (None, 38, 128)           24704

global_max_pooling1d (Globa     (None, 128)               0
lMaxPooling1D)

dropout (Dropout)               (None, 128)               0

dense (Dense)                   (None, 6)                 774

==================================================================
Total params: 1,305,542
Trainable params: 1,305,542
Non-trainable params: 0
```

Fig. 2. Model summary of CNN model

In the end to compile our model, we also used adam optimizer with the learning rate of 0.001 to optimize the algorithm.

4 Experiments and Results

As previously stated, we have applied three distinct models to our dataset. The performance of all models is rather satisfactory. Among these models, the accuracy of GRU and Bi-LSTM is almost same and superior to that of CNN. Nevertheless, we may differentiate between the accuracy of GRU and Bi-LSTM and choose the more accurate of the two. To be more precise, CNN, Bi-LSTM, and GRU achieved 84%, 89%, and 90% accuracy, respectively. As can be seen, the accuracy of GRU is comparable to that of Bi-LSTM, although it is still superior. Therefore, selecting the GRU model for the dataset is preferable. The performance comparison report for CNN, Bi-LSTM, and GRU are shown in Table 2 so that they may be differentiated easily.

Table 2. Overall performance comparison of our used models.

Used Model	Accuracy	Fl-socre	Precision	Recall
Bi-lstm	0.89	0.75	0.86	0.73
CNN	0.84	0.84	0.86	0.84
GRU	**0.90**	**0.88**	**0.88**	**0.88**

Moreover, the accuracy of the GRU model surpasses that of the majority of existing research papers on this topic. On the basis of Bhagat and Mane's [11] study, the majority of models' accuracy for sentiment analysis was between 84% and 87%. However, our model appears to be more accurate than the others.

The confusion matrices of GRU is presented on Fig. 3. In the figure, the rows and columns named from 0 to 5 correspond to the categories of emotions that we defined in our models. They are defined as happy, anger, sadness, surprise, love and fear, respectfully from 0 to 5.

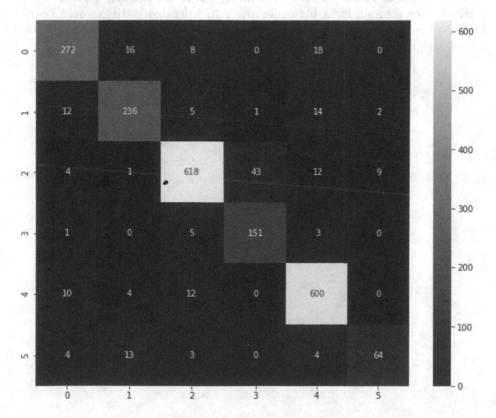

Fig. 3. Confusion Matrix of GRU

Because it is a relatively new concept, only a few frameworks exist to implement it. We utilized Flower for our paper. Flower is a new federated learning framework. Flower is designed to operate with all of them. It focuses on providing tools for effectively implementing federated learning while allowing you to focus on the training itself. It is really simple to set up a basic federated configuration in Flower. In addition, the range of compatible devices is extremely broad, ranging from mobile devices to servers and others. As demonstrated by Beutel et al. [12], the design provides for scalability up to 1000s of clients. We have used 100 clients and 10 federated rounds for our simulation which is shown in Fig. 4. Though we received better accuracy in GRU compared to LSTM for centralized language modeling tasks from our dataset. It showed no difference in performance for federated learning simulation. We only got better accuracy after increasing the federated rounds. The GRU model has less gates compared to LSTM so it is a little speedier in training but it did not help for federated settings. The solution for a better accuracy in federated settings could be to increase the dataset and increasing the federated rounds without changing the model architectures.

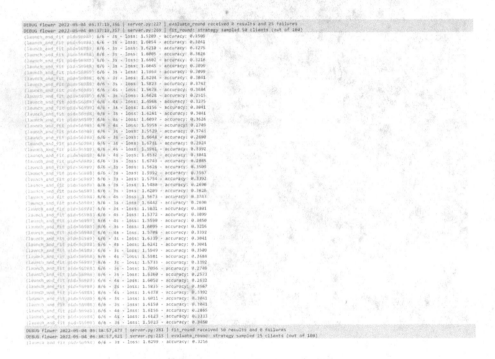

Fig. 4. Accuracy of individual clients for GRU

5   Conclusion

This work discusses detecting emotion using deep learning models and a federated learning architecture. In addition, the top text classification models for usage in the federated learning architecture are displayed. A system like this may be used to assess people's emotions and propose movies and television shows. However, the performance of such a model is dependent on a number of aspects, including the quality of data and parameters. Dataset suppliers should also update their databases as soon as new data becomes available in order to augment models through communication loops. If all of these can be maintained, such an architecture can ensure a very high accuracy, similar to or even better than what we showed.

References

1. Muthukumar, N.: Few-shot learning text classification in federated environments. In: 2021 Smart Technologies, Communication and Robotics (STCR), pp. 1–3 (2021). https://doi.org/10.1109/STCR51658.2021.9588833
2. Liu, D., Miller, T.: Federated pretraining and fine tuning of BERT using clinical notes from multiple silos (2020). https://arxiv.org/abs/2002.08562
3. Leroy, D., Coucke, A., Lavril, T., Gisselbrecht, T., Dureau, J.: Federated learning for keyword spotting (2018). https://arxiv.org/abs/1810.05512
4. Basaldella, M., Antolli, E., Serra, G., Tasso, C.: Bidirectional LSTM recurrent neural network for keyphrase extraction. In: Serra, G., Tasso, C. (eds.) IRCDL 2018. CCIS, vol. 806, pp. 180–187. Springer, Cham (2018). https://doi.org/10.1007/978-3-319-73165-0_18
5. Ge, S., Wu, F., Wu, C., Qi, T., Huang, Y., Xie, X.: FedNER: privacy-preserving medical named entity recognition with federated learning (2020). https://arxiv.org/abs/2003.09288
6. Emotions in text. https://www.kaggle.com/datasets/ishantjuyal/emotions-in-text
7. Zulqarnain, M., Ghazali, R., Ghouse, M.G., Mushtaq, M.F.: Efficient processing of GRU based on word embedding for text classification. JOIV: Int. J. Inform. Vis. **3**(4), 377–383 (2019)
8. Hasib, K.M., Towhid, N.A., Alam, M.G.R.: Online review based sentiment classification on Bangladesh airline service using supervised learning. In: 2021 5th International Conference on Electrical Engineering and Information Communication Technology (ICEEICT) (2021). https://doi.org/10.1109/iceeict53905.2021.9667818
9. Xu, G., Meng, Y., Qiu, X., Yu, Z., Wu, X.: Sentiment analysis of comment texts based on BiLSTM. IEEE Access **7**, 51522–51532 (2019)
10. Adib, Q.A.R., Mehedi, M.H.K., Sakib, M.S., Patwary, K.K., Hossain, M.S., Rasel, A.A.: A deep hybrid learning approach to detect Bangla fake news. In: 2021 5th International Symposium on Multidisciplinary Studies and Innovative Technologies (ISMSIT), pp. 442–447 (2021). https://doi.org/10.1109/ISMSIT52890.2021.9604712
11. Bhagat, C., Mane, D.: Survey on text categorization using sentiment analysis. J. Sci. Technol. Res. **8**, 1189–1195 (2019)
12. Beutel, D.J., et al.: Flower: a friendly federated learning research framework (2020). https://arxiv.org/abs/2007.14390

A Method for Face Image Inpainting Based on Autoencoder and Generative Adversarial Network

Xinyi Gao, Minh Nguyen, and Wei Qi Yan[✉]

Auckland University of Technology, Auckland 1010, New Zealand
weiqi.yan@aut.ac.nz

Abstract. Face image inpainting has great value in the fields of computer vision and digital image processing. In this paper, we propose a face image inpainting method based on autoencoder and Generative Adversarial Network (GAN). The neural network for image inpainting consists of two parts, a generator and a discriminator. The autoencoder is used twice in the discriminator part, after the final inpainted image is generated by local discriminator and global discriminator. The final loss function is obtained by combining Generative Adversarial Loss and Mean Squared Error (MSE) Loss [20]. We improve and implement an image inpainting model with two evaluation metrics, namely, Peak Signal-to-noise Ratio (PSNR) and Structural similarity index measure (SSIM) [27], respectively. The proposed model for image inpainting is much more suitable for face image inpainting.

Keywords: Autoencoder · Generative adversarial network · Face image inpainting · Convolutional neural network

1 Introduction

Image inpainting is a process of inference from existing pixels. The method is applied mainly to fill in missing parts of an image. In 2000, Marcelo's paper [2] firstly proposed image inpainting as a professional technology through computer algorithms, so as to achieve the purpose of image repair. In this algorithm, after a user selects an image region that needs to be repaired, the algorithm will automatically repair the area through pixel information surrounding the missing region.

The purpose of image inpainting [3] is to reconstruct missing areas. Generally speaking, this process is often to repair an image based on existing information. The reconstructed image should be realistic and natural. The indistinguishable image is treated as a high-quality inpainted image [43]. A high-quality face image inpainted can be employed for unlocking mobiles using face recognition.

In recent years, the world has been affected by COVID-19 [28]. To protect us against the virus, we need to wear face masks so as to protect ourselves. While

H. Wang et al. (Eds.): PSIVT 2022, LNCS 13763, pp. 24–36, 2023.
https://doi.org/10.1007/978-3-031-26431-3_3

wearing masks protects our health, it also brings new problems. We need a full face to help us if we want to make quick payments or verify our identity using our faces. However, in this case, we have to take off our masks. Therefore, a fast and accurate face image inpainting method in this epidemic time is very needed.

In this paper, a deep learning method [16] for face image inpainting is proposed. Deep learning is a machine learning method [47] based on data representation learning. Convolutional neural networks (CNN) [14,23], as a kind of method in deep learning, have been utilized to produce reliable results in the field of image inpainting [31]. Autoencoders are deep nets in unsupervised learning [9]. The purpose of an autoencoder is to learn a representation of a set of data. An adversarial generative network (GAN) [35,36] is also an unsupervised learning method whose main structure is constructed by two deep nets which play an adversarial game. The recently proposed model consists of two autoencoders and a GAN net [26].

In the rest of this paper, we will present related work on face image reconstruction in Sect. 2. In the third section, we introduce our method and model. In Sect. 4, we analyze the results of our experiments. Finally, we summarize our work and draw conclusions in Sect. 5.

2 Literature Review

With the development of deep learning, multiple methods for human face [29] image reconstruction are becoming more and more mature. A number of methods and frameworks for face image inpainting are emerging gradually. The typical methods include CNN, GAN, etc., which are available to attain higher-quality inpainting results. In this section, a brief review of the existing face reconstruction methods is depicted and the existing methods are summarized based on advantages and disadvantages.

Convolutional neural network (CNN or ConvNet) is also one of the important methods in deep learning [17,30]. Although CNN can generate a reasonable structure in image restoration, the image generated by CNN [18] has structural inconsistency or fuzzy texture in the relevant regions. A new method [40] was proposed and the reason for this problem is identified, especially, when the deep net borrows textures from the surrounding areas. Therefore, the method was derived from a generative model based on traditional texture and patch synthesis. This model is essentially a feedforward, fully connected network. The net can synthesize new image structures during inpainting, it has been verified to better use surrounding image features as references. The experiments have proved that the proposed model is effective to repair images from multiple datasets including human faces with higher quality than those existing methods. Later on, a new system was proposed to learn from millions of images. The basic principle of this system is based on gated convolution, which eliminates extra marks. In the specific operation of the system, partial convolution is summarized by providing a dynamic feature selection mechanism for each channel of spatial position of all layers.

In addition, the randomness of the mask was considered in the image and a new GAN loss [25] function was proposed, which is called SN-PatchGAN [41]. The experimental results show that the results produced by the system have higher quality and much flexible results. This allows the system to assist users to quickly remove distracting objects, modify image layout, wipe off watermarks [1, 6, 37], etc.

The existing image reconstruction methods are required to pay special attention to the resolution of the target image. In order to solve this problem, Zeng, et al. proposed a different high-quality image reconstruction method [43], which is called Pyramid-context Encoder Network (PEN-Net). In the method, the structure of context encoder is increased, pyramid context encoder, multiscale decoder, and adversarial training loss are established. In this method, U-Net is employed as the backbone, the pyramid context encoder is applied to gradually fill in the missing content and ensure the consistency of the visual effects of image reconstruction. Then, a multiscale decoder with deep supervision function is harnessed to calculate the loss. The use of this method allows the process to converge quickly during training time, and a large number of experiments have proved the reliability and excellent performance of the proposed net.

In order to solve the problem of blurred or missing face images collected due to acquisition method in the process of face recognition, conventional face image restoration models often solve this problem from image viewpoint. The classic structure-based image restoration methods are CNN [32] and generative adversarial network. Wei, et al. put forward a face image reconstruction method based on generative confrontation network from a new perspective [34]. This method locates plane position of a face by determining two parallel lines of a vector. The different planes of the face are determined according to the given parallel lines, edge curve is fitted through straight line segment to make facial contour clearer, and make final facial features quite obvious [5]. Compared with the previous structure-based methods, this method can achieve better visual effects based on edges. The performance of face inpainting is greatly improved. It is worth mentioning that this method is only suitable for small-scale reconstruction processes. If there are too many missing parts in an image, the restoration effect will become vague from the original image.

Image information missing is one of the most popular damages in image damage. The existing image reconstruction algorithms still have shortcomings, such as blurred details and poor visual [39] perception in terms of visual effects and algorithm efficiency after the reconstruction. In order to solve this problem, Heshu et al. [44] proposed a new semantic restoration method for facial images in 2020. On the basis of generating a confrontation network, this method fuses multiscale features of the given face to obtain more details without increasing the parameters. By expanding the receptive field in the deep net [21], the problem of insufficient edge information of the generated image is made up. In addition, the learning ability of the generative network and the discriminative network is justified, which further improved the final performance of the proposed method.

Deep learning is the mainstream method for image restoration. The use of deep learning methods [24,42,45] in image reconstruction can better restore the image texture of human faces and obtain abstract features in the image. Therefore, in the same way, Han et al. [10] also employed generative adversarial network as the basis for image inpainting process. However, they proposed a different method to solve vanishing gradient problem in the training process of GAN model. Evolutionary concepts were adopted to create a Generative Adversarial Network (EG-GAN) with an evolutionary generator for face image restoration. In the training process, EG-GAN updates the parameters of the generative network by combining two cost functions, generates offspring generators through crossover, and adds a matcher-assisted discriminator to criticize the generated images. Through the conception, the generative network continues to be evolved. This not only helps EG-GAN successfully overcome the vanishing gradient problem, but also improves the quality of image reconstruction and generated images that are in line with human vision.

In the following sections, we will briefly describe the method we developed in this paper. The method is slightly different from other work. Our method is use of deep learning [13,33] and adds an autoencoder to enhance our method, so that this method can much effectively resolve the problem of face image inpainting.

3   Methodology

In this research project, we take use of CNN in deep learning [12] as the net base and the GAN model to build a complete network for face image reconstruction, train our image inpainting model through discriminator and generator in the GAN model to achieve higher quality.

As a typical method for face image reconstruction, GAN [4] is also one of the most important methods in this paper, which was firstly proposed in 2014. The basic idea of this method is to deploy two contrastive neural networks against each other. This is a way to get better results by playing against two networks. GAN generally consists of a generative network and a discriminative network. The generator needs to generate more realistic images, the discriminator judges how "real" the input is.

Fig. 1. GAN training process. This network consists of a generator and a discriminator. The discriminator part is composed of a global discriminator and a local discriminator. The discriminator is used to judge whether the image is real or not.

3.1   Generative Network

CNN is the core part of the entire inpainting algorithm, so the convolutional layer becomes the key to our entire CNN algorithm. This is because most of the operations in the entire inpainting process are generated in convolutional layers. The generative network consists of two autoencoders connected. Each autoencoder consists of 12 layers of convolution operations, 4 layers of dilated convolutions, and 2 layers of deconvolutions [7,8] (Table 1). The face image [38] generated by two autoencoders is closer to the "real" image than the image generated by only using one autoencoder (Fig. 2).

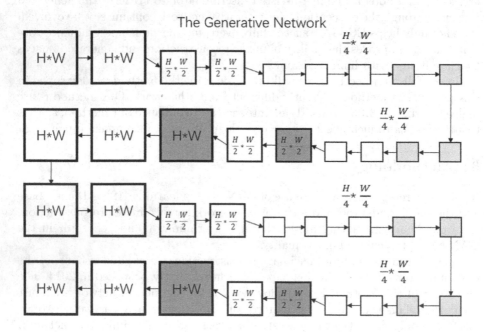

Fig. 2. The generative network consists of a total of 36 layers of convolutional neural networks. There are 24 convolutional layers in the generative network, represented by rectangles with white background color. There are 8 yellow rectangles in total, which are dilated convolution. There are also 4 additional deconvolution layers, represented by blue squares. (Color figure online)

3.2   Discriminator Network

The discriminative network consists of a global discriminator network and a local discriminator network [11]. Its purpose is to judge whether the image generated by the generative network is close to the "real" image and identify whether a part of the image is "real" through a local discriminator. The global discriminator is responsible for the plausibility of overall image inpainting. A more accurate

Table 1. The generative network.

Convolution types	Kernels	Dilations	Outputs
Convolution1	5 × 5	None	64
Convolution2	3 × 3	None	64
Convolution3	3 × 3	None	128
Convolution4	3 × 3	None	128
Convolution5	3 × 3	None	256
Convolution6	3 × 3	None	256
Convolution7	3 × 3	None	256
Dilated Convolution1	3 × 3	2	256
Dilated Convolution2	3 × 3	4	256
Dilated Convolution3	3 × 3	8	256
Dilated Convolution4	3 × 3	16	256
Convolution8	3 × 3	None	256
Convolution9	3 × 3	None	256
Deconvolution1	4×4	None	128
Convolution10	3 × 3	None	128
Deconvolution2	4 × 4	None	64
Convolution11	3 × 3	None	32
Convolution12	3 × 3	None	3
Convolution13	5 × 5	None	64
Convolution14	3 × 3	None	64
Convolution15	3 × 3	None	128
Convolution16	3 × 3	None	128
Convolution17	3 × 3	None	256
Convolution18	3 × 3	None	256
Convolution19	3 × 3	None	256
Dilated Convolution5	3 × 3	2	256
Dilated Convolution6	3 × 3	4	256
Dilated Convolution7	3 × 3	8	256
Dilated Convolution8	3 × 3	16	256
Convolution20	3 × 3	None	256
Convolution21	3 × 3	None	256
Deconvolution3	4 × 4	None	128
Convolution22	3 × 3	None	128
Deconvolution4	4 × 4	None	64
Convolution23	3 × 3	None	32
Convolution24	3 × 3	None	3

and realistic inpainting result is achieved by combining the results of the two discriminators. These two parts of the network are still composed of CNN. The global discriminative network is composed of 5 convolutional layers. The details are demonstrated in Table 2. The local discriminative network consists of 4 convolutional layers. The details are shown in Table 3 (Table 1).

Table 2. The global discriminator network.

Convolution types	Kernels	Dilations	Outputs
Convolution1	5 × 5	None	64
Convolution2	5 × 5	None	128
Convolution3	5 × 5	None	256
Convolution4	5 × 5	None	512

Table 3. The local discriminator network.

Convolution types	Kernels	Dilations	Outputs
Convolution1	5 × 5	None	64
Convolution2	5 × 5	None	128
Convolution3	5 × 5	None	256
Convolution4	5 × 5	None	512
Convolution5	5 × 5	None	512

3.3 Algorithms

Loss function is an important element in deep learning [19,46] . It is generally used to measure the degree of inconsistency between the predicted value of the model and the true value. A loss function can provide a lot of practical flexibility to a neural network, it will define how the output of the network is connected to the rest of the network. Two loss functions are employed in our experiments. One is GAN loss and the other is MSE loss.

Minimax Loss. A GAN can have two loss functions: One for generator training and the other for discriminator training. The generative and discriminative losses look different from one equation [10]. In this experiment, we mainly take use of minimax loss function in GAN model. In the minimax loss function, $D(I, M)$ represents the discriminative network and $G(I, M_i)$ shows the generative network, M is a randomly generated mask, and I is the input image. M_i is the mask image having the exact size of the input image.

$$L_{MinMax} = \min_G \max_D \mathbf{E}[log D(I, M) + log(1 - D(G(I, M_i), M_i))]. \qquad (1)$$

MSE Loss. Mean Squared Error (MSE) is a popular loss function. You need to square the difference between the prediction and the ground truth [48]. Then, it takes average over the entire dataset. Finally, the MSE loss value can be obtained. In the MSE loss function [48], G represents the generative network and I is the input image, $\odot$ is pixel-wise multiplication. The value of MSE loss is always greater than 1.00. The closer this value is to 1.00, the more realistic the training results are

$$L_{MSE} = ||M_i \odot (G(I, M_i) - I)||^2. \tag{2}$$

Joint Loss. The joint loss function is to combine together MSE loss and minimax loss to obtain better training results. In training the network, we firstly employed only the minimax loss. Then we take use of the joint loss for training in later training. Such training methods can effectively improve training results.

$$L_{joint} = \min_{G} \lim \max_{D} \lim \mathbf{E}[L_{MSE} + log(I, M) + log(1 - D(G(I, M_i), M_i))]. \tag{3}$$

In the following sections, we will present our experimental results, which further demonstrate the superiority of our algorithm design.

4 Result Analysis

In this research project, we took use of the CelebA dataset with 202,599 face images for training [15]. CelebA is a large-scale dataset dedicated to face experiments, containing more than 200,000 face images. In addition, the backgrounds of the various face images in this dataset are often complex, which makes this dataset a very suitable training dataset for this study. An example image of the dataset is shown in Fig. 3. There are 2,000 face images which were randomly selected for training and testing.

The images are firstly preprocessed, and the pixels of the images to be used are resized to 128×128. During the model training, we randomly add a mask image whose size ranges from 24×24 to 48×48. The inpainting result is shown in Fig. 4, we see that when we randomly add a mask to the image, the inpainting is accomplished by using the autoencoder. The repaired image is very close to the result of the unbroken image. From a naked eye point of view, this is undoubtedly a very successful restoration. However, we still need data to support the conclusions we see, here we choose PSNR and SSIM as our data support. We took use of PSNR and SSIM as evaluation metrics in the testing phase. PSNR is the most popular objective measure for evaluating image quality. Usually, the larger the PSNR value, the higher the quality of image inpainting. SSIM is a measure of how similar two images are [22]. The result is between 0 and 1.00, and the closer the result is to 1.00, the higher the quality of image inpainting.

Since our generative network is use of two autoencoder networks, it is slower to train than a model with just one autoencoder. But at the same training 1,000

Fig. 3. The example of CelebA dataset.

epochs, the results of our inpainting method are better than that of just using an autoencoder network.

Table 4. Comparison of Image Inpainting Methods.

Model Name	PSNRs	SSIMs
Glcic (One Autoencoder)	31.86	0.89
Our (Two Autoencoder)	36.74	0.91

The test results are shown in Table 4. The average PSNR of the network with only one autoencoder in the generative network is 31.86, and the SSIM is 0.89. Our test result has an average PSNR 36.74, and SSIM is 0.91. We see that our model has higher PSNR compared to the model using one autoencoder, our model is about 5% higher based on this metric. The same is true for another metric, SSIM is 0.02 higher than the model using one autoencoder. By comparison, it is found that our modified model works better. Furthermore, our SSIM is up to 0.91, which is very close to 1.00. The PSNR is also high, which not only proves that our results are very good, but also further shows the reliability of these two indicators. Overall, the deep learning model we used can accurately inpaint missing parts of face images. With a number of iterations, the more

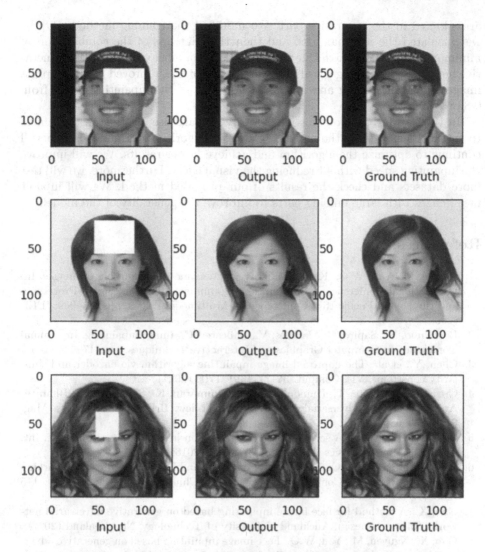

Fig. 4. Three face image inpainting results. The first column is the input image with Mask, the second is the output result, and the third is the ground truth.

iterations, the better the visual effect. Although the model suffers from slow inpainting speed, it is still an efficient model. In addition, the results of SSIM and PSNR are also excellent, the overall reconstruction results are very realistic. These are the great contribution of this paper.

5   Conclusion

This research project investigates face image inpainting based on autoencoder and GAN. We propose a new deep learning model. Two autoencoder networks are adopted in the generative part. We modified the training method. Firstly, we calculated the minimax loss, and then the joint loss of the combination of minimax loss and MSE loss. Due to the increased number of layers of the generative network, the training speed has decreased. But the improved method uplifts image inpainting quality and increases the SSIM of the inpainting result from 0.89 to 0.91.

In the future, based on this result, we will make use of other test methods to further demonstrate the superiority of our algorithm. In addition, we will continue to optimize the algorithm and achieve better results. We will improve the inpainting speed without reducing the visual effect. Furthermore, we will test more datasets and check the results of our proposed method. We will inpaint face images with large missing parts to improve the generality of the model.

References

1. Bansal, M., Yan, W.Q., Kankanhalli, M.S.: Dynamic watermarking of images. In: International Conference on Information, Communications and Signal Processing and the Fourth Pacific Rim Conference on Multimedia, vol. 2, pp. 965–969. IEEE (2003)
2. Bertalmio, M., Sapiro, G., Caselles, V., Ballester, C.: Image inpainting. In: Annual Conference on Computer Graphics and Interactive Techniques, pp. 417–424 (2000)
3. Chen, Y., et al.: The improved image inpainting algorithm via encoder and similarity constraint. Vis. Comput. **37**(7), 1691–1705 (2021)
4. Creswell, A., White, T., Dumoulin, V., Arulkumaran, K., Sengupta, B., Bharath, A.A.: Generative adversarial networks: an overview. IEEE Signal Process. Mag. **35**(1), 53–65 (2018)
5. Cui, W., Yan, W.Q.: A scheme for face recognition in complex environments. Int. J. Digit. Crime Forensics (IJDCF) **8**(1), 26–36 (2016)
6. Ding, W., Yan, W.Q., Qi, D.X.: Digital image scrambling and digital watermarking technology based on Conway's game. J. North China Univ. Technol. **12**(1), 1–5 (2000)
7. Gao, X.: A method for face image inpainting based on generative adversarial networks (Masters thesis). Auckland University of Technology, New Zealand (2022)
8. Gao, X., Nguyen, M., Yan, W.Q.: Face image inpainting based on generative adversarial network. In: International Conference on Image and Vision Computing New Zealand (IVCNZ), pp. 1–6. IEEE (2021)
9. Givkashi, M.H., Hadipour, M., PariZanganeh, A., Nabizadeh, Z., Karimi, N., Samavi, S.: Image inpainting using AutoEncoder and guided selection of predicted pixels. arXiv preprint arXiv:2112.09262 (2021)
10. Han, C., Wang, J.: Face image inpainting with evolutionary generators. IEEE Signal Process. Lett. **28**, 190–193 (2021)
11. Iizuka, S., Simo-Serra, E., Ishikawa, H.: Globally and locally consistent image completion. ACM Trans. Graph. (ToG) **36**(4), 1–14 (2017)
12. Le, H., Nguyen, M., Nguyen, Q., Nguyen, H., Yan, W.Q.: Automatic data generation for deep learning model training of image classification used for augmented reality on pre-school books. In: International Conference on Multimedia Analysis and Pattern Recognition (MAPR), pp. 1–5 (2020)

13. Liang, C., Lu, J., Yan, W.: Human action recognition from digital videos based on deep learning. In: ACM ICCCV 2022 (2022)
14. Liu, Z., Yan, W.Q., Yang, M.L.: Image denoising based on a CNN model. In: International Conference on Control, Automation and Robotics (ICCAR), pp. 389–393. IEEE (2018)
15. Liu, Z., Luo, P., Wang, X., Tang, X.: Large-scale celebfaces attributes (CelebA) dataset. Retrieved August, **15**(2018), 11 (2018)
16. Lu, J., Nguyen, M., Yan, W.Q.: Sign language recognition from digital videos using deep learning methods. In: Nguyen, M., Yan, W.Q., Ho, H. (eds.) ISGV 2021. CCIS, vol. 1386, pp. 108–118. Springer, Cham (2021). https://doi.org/10.1007/978-3-030-72073-5_9
17. Lu, J., Yan, W.Q., Nguyen, M.: Human behaviour recognition using deep learning. In: IEEE International Conference on Advanced Video and Signal Based Surveillance (AVSS), pp. 1–6. IEEE (2018)
18. Mehtab, S., Yan, W.Q.: Flexible neural network for fast and accurate road scene perception. Multimedia Tools Appl. **81**(5), 7169–7181 (2022)
19. Nguyen, M., Yan, W.Q.: Temporal colour-coded facial-expression recognition using convolutional neural network. In: Paiva, S., et al. (eds.) Smart City 360° 2021. LNICST, vol. 442, pp. 41–54. Springer, Cham (2022). https://doi.org/10.1007/978-3-031-06371-8_4
20. Pajot, A., de Bezenac, E., Gallinari, P.: Unsupervised adversarial image inpainting. arXiv preprint arXiv:1912.12164 (2019)
21. Qin, Z., Yan, W.Q.: Traffic-sign recognition using deep learning. In: Nguyen, M., Yan, W.Q., Ho, H. (eds.) ISGV 2021. CCIS, vol. 1386, pp. 13–25. Springer, Cham (2021). https://doi.org/10.1007/978-3-030-72073-5_2
22. Sara, U., Akter, M., Uddin, M.S.: Image quality assessment through FSIM, SSIM, MSE and PSNR- a comparative study. J. Comput. Commun. **7**(3), 8–18 (2019)
23. Shen, D., Nguyen, M., Yan, W.Q.: Flame detection using deep learning. In: International Conference on Control, Automation and Robotics (ICCAR), pp. 389–393. IEEE (2018)
24. Shen, Y., Yan, W.Q.: Blind spot monitoring using deep learning. In: International Conference on Image and Vision Computing New Zealand (IVCNZ), pp. 1–5. IEEE (2018)
25. Siavelis, P.-R., Lamprinou, N., Psarakis, E.Z.: An improved GAN semantic image inpainting. In: Blanc-Talon, J., Delmas, P., Philips, W., Popescu, D., Scheunders, P. (eds.) ACIVS 2020. LNCS, vol. 12002, pp. 443–454. Springer, Cham (2020). https://doi.org/10.1007/978-3-030-40605-9_38
26. Siddavatam, I., Dalvi, A., Pawade, D., Bhatt, A., Vartak, J., Gupta, A.: A novel approach for video inpainting using autoencoders. Int. J. Inf. Eng. Electron. Bus. **13**(6), 48–61 (2021)
27. Tiefenbacher, P., Bogischef, V., Merget, D., Rigoll, G.: Subjective and objective evaluation of image inpainting quality. In: 2015 IEEE International Conference on Image Processing (ICIP), pp. 447–451. IEEE (2015)
28. Velavan, T.P., Meyer, C.G.: The COVID-19 epidemic. Trop. Med. Int. Health **25**(3), 278 (2020)
29. Wang, H., Yan, W.Q.: Face detection and recognition from distance based on deep learning. In: Aiding Forensic Investigation Through Deep Learning and Machine Learning Frameworks, pp. 144–160. IGI Global (2022)
30. Wang, L., Yan, W.Q.: Tree leaves detection based on deep learning. In: Nguyen, M., Yan, W.Q., Ho, H. (eds.) ISGV 2021. CCIS, vol. 1386, pp. 26–38. Springer, Cham (2021). https://doi.org/10.1007/978-3-030-72073-5_3

31. Wang, S.Y., Wang, O., Zhang, R., Owens, A., Efros, A.A.: CNN-generated images are surprisingly easy to spot... for now. In: IEEE/CVF Conference on Computer Vision and Pattern Recognition, pp. 8695–8704 (2020)
32. Wang, X., Zhang, J., Yan, W.Q.: Gait recognition using multichannel convolution neural networks. Neural Comput. Appl. **32**(18), 14275–14285 (2020)
33. Wang, Y., Yan, W.Q.: Colorizing grayscale CT images of human lungs using deep learning methods. Multimedia Tools Appl. **81**, 37805–37819 (2022)
34. Wei, T., Li, Q., Liu, J., Zhang, P., Chen, Z.: 3D face image inpainting with generative adversarial nets. Math. Probl. Eng. **2020**, 1–11 (2020)
35. Yan, W.Q.: Introduction to Intelligent Surveillance. TCS, Springer, Cham (2019). https://doi.org/10.1007/978-3-030-10713-0
36. Yan, W.Q.: Computational Methods for Deep Learning: Theoretic Practice and Applications. Springer, Heidelberg (2021). https://doi.org/10.1007/978-3-030-61081-4
37. Yan, W.Q., Kankanhalli, M.S.: Erasing video logos based on image inpainting. In: IEEE International Conference on Multimedia and Expo, vol. 2, pp. 521–524. IEEE (2002)
38. Yan, W.Q., Kankanhalli, M.S.: Face search in encrypted domain. In: Bräunl, T., McCane, B., Rivera, M., Yu, X. (eds.) PSIVT 2015. LNCS, vol. 9431, pp. 775–790. Springer, Cham (2016). https://doi.org/10.1007/978-3-319-29451-3_61
39. Yan, W., Kieran, D.F., Rafatirad, S., Jain, R.: A comprehensive study of visual event computing. Multimedia Tools Appl. **55**(3), 443–481 (2011)
40. Yu, J., Lin, Z., Yang, J., Shen, X., Lu, X., Huang, T.S.: Generative image inpainting with contextual attention. In: IEEE Conference on Computer Vision and Pattern Recognition, pp. 5505–5514 (2018)
41. Yu, J., Lin, Z., Yang, J., Shen, X., Lu, X., Huang, T.S.: Free-form image inpainting with gated convolution. In: IEEE/CVF International Conference on Computer Vision, pp. 4471–4480 (2019)
42. Yu, Z., Yan, W.Q.: Human action recognition using deep learning methods. In: International Conference on Image and Vision Computing New Zealand (IVCNZ), pp. 1–6. IEEE (2020)
43. Zeng, Y., Fu, J., Chao, H., Guo, B.: Learning pyramid-context encoder network for high-quality image inpainting. In: IEEE/CVF Conference on Computer Vision and Pattern Recognition, pp. 1486–1494 (2019)
44. Zhang, H., Li, T.: Semantic face image inpainting based on generative adversarial network. In: Youth Academic Annual Conference of Chinese Association of Automation (YAC), pp. 530–535. IEEE (2020)
45. Zhang, Q., Yan, W.Q.: Currency detection and recognition based on deep learning. In: IEEE International Conference on Advanced Video and Signal Based Surveillance (AVSS), pp. 1–6. IEEE (2018)
46. Zhang, Q., Yan, W.Q., Kankanhalli, M.: Overview of currency recognition using deep learning. J. Banking Financ. Technol **3**(1), 59–69 (2019)
47. Zhang, Z., Cui, P., Zhu, W.: Deep learning on graphs: a survey. IEEE Trans. Knowl. Data Eng. **34**, 249–270 (2020)
48. Zhao, G., Liu, J., Jiang, J., Wang, W.: A deep cascade of neural networks for image inpainting, deblurring and denoising. Multimedia Tools Appl. **77**(22), 29589–29604 (2018)

Traffic Sign Recognition from Digital Images by Using Deep Learning

Jiawei Xing, Ziyuan Luo, Minh Nguyen, and Wei Qi Yan[✉]

Auckland University of Technology, Auckland 1010, New Zealand
weiqi.yan@aut.ac.nz

Abstract. Traffic signs are essentially needed to obey the traffic rules. Once a driver ignores the signs, especially those critical signs, due to the complexity of actual traffic scenes or the influence of inclement weather conditions, it will lead to violating traffic regulations or traffic accidents, causing casualties and property losses. Therefore, Traffic Sign Recognition (TSR) is an essential part of autonomous vehicles and has important academic significance. The main contributions of this paper are as follows: (1) We apply an algorithm to the dark channel prior, and we also provide a guided image filtering algorithm for image defogging. Our results show that the guided image filtering method is very effective in image defogging. (2) This paper presents a number of deep learning solutions towards the aforementioned problems. Based on the experiments conducted, we discover that YOLOv5 is very suitable for real-time TSR.

Keywords: TSR · Defogging · Faster R-CNN · YOLOv5

1 Introduction

With the continuous growth of populations and the development of our society, cars have become an indispensable means of transportation for people. While people relish the convenience of cars, the new technology also brings a series of inevitable problems to road traffic. The pressure on the urban transportation system is gradually increasing. The most important one is the frequent occurrence of traffic accidents [1]. In order to reduce accidents, advanced accident-avoiding systems have become popular [2]. With the development of traffic sign recognition (TSR), computer-aided systems have undergone a significant leap. Computers have been applied to simulate and process large amounts of visual data. An intelligent driving assistance system simulates the mechanism of the human visual system to complete visual object detection and recognition [3, 4] as well as other applications [5].

In a nutshell, the identification and detection of traffic signs are essential components, especially the research project on the identification of traffic speed limit signs in haze weather, which meets the needs of current automobile development and is conducive to the promotion of scientific and technological knowledge. Therefore, the research work on traffic sign detection under severe weather has important and practical significance. Thus, the goal of this paper is to collect foggy images as our dataset and compare two

H. Wang et al. (Eds.): PSIVT 2022, LNCS 13763, pp. 37–49, 2023.
https://doi.org/10.1007/978-3-031-26431-3_4

different deep learning methods. At the same time, the influence of fogs on visual object recognition is investigated, and finally a TSR method with fast speed and high precision is developed.

The remaining part of this paper is organized as follows: We have our literature review in Sect. 2, and our methods will be addressed in Sect. 3. Our results will be shown in Sect. 4. Our conclusion will be drawn in Sect. 5.

2   Literature Review

2.1   External Factors Affecting Traffic Sign Recognition

With the development of deep learning in artificial intelligence, TSR is being developed rapidly. Many high-end models are now equipped with TSR driver assistance systems to help drivers safely. The current TSR only has a higher accuracy rate when it is sunny and traffic signs are unobstructed, or in severe weather (e.g., foggy, rainy, snowy, etc.), and challenging lighting conditions (e.g., night, direct sunlight, etc.). If a traffic sign is obscured, false recognition or unrecognition may occur. Thus, we describe how these external factors affect TSR and what the differences are; in rainy weather, accurate TSR is also very difficult because fog is static and there is no apparent movement, while raining or snowing has dynamic motion characters [6]. This is very challenging for TSR, because TSR always needs real-time visual object detection. Lighting is also very important for TSR; during the daytime, if sunshine directly lights on a traffic sign or camera, it will cause overexposed. It is often too dark at night, at the same time, the lights will be reflected on traffic signs while driving at night. This may result in incorrect or unrecognizable traffic signs.

In haze weather, due to a number of disordered particles in the air, ambient light will be severely scattered and result in a blurry image; no relevant operations such as feature extraction are used [7]. Throughout the analysis of plenty of haze images and clear images of the same scene, we see that the haze image has specific characteristics. Analyzing these image features helps us identify the haze by using pattern classification [8], the imaging process is conducted on a foggy day by establishing the corresponding atmospheric scattering model and mathematical model [9].

Severe weather, such as haze, directly lead to the decline of image contrast, the reduction of grayscale dynamic range, the reduction of blurring, and the coverage of detailed information. Therefore, it is necessary to study how to restore a clear and fog-free image. At present, the research work on foggy removal is qualitatively grouped into two-fold: One is image restoration, which is based on an established mathematical model and previous knowledge of image degradation and reverses the model to calculate clear and fog-free Images [10]. The other direction is image enhancement which is based on human visual requirements through highlighting image details, filtering noises, and restoring clear images [11]. The difference between them is that image restoration is to improve the understanding of images from the perspective of image essence, image enhancement is based on human visual meaning to improve visual effect of the images to meet the needs of human vision. These algorithms could be applied to traffic sign location detection and traffic sign recognition.

2.2 Related Algorithms

Convolutional neural networks (CNNs) were inspired by cat visual cortex in physiology. There are neuronal cells that are extremely sensitive to external rays of light, which is called receptive field [12]. Since then, visual cortex began to enter our research area and attracted people's attention. Turnaround neural network was firstly applied to hand-written digit recognition. The model [13] cooperated with CNN and achieved excellent results in experiments through setting a precedent for a wide spectrum of applications in the fields of visual object detection, face recognition, speech recognition, and so on. Meanwhile, artificial neural network is improved and promoted. The neural network consists of five parts: Input layer, output layer, convolutional layers and pooling layers, fully connected layer [12]. Based on these neural networks, the workflow of TSR mainly includes three parts. The first is image preprocessing, which usually includes image enhancement, image scaling, and other image processing operations. The second part is traffic sign detection, which includes three important steps: (1) Extract candidate regions, (2) confirm traffic signs, (3) classify traffic signs.

3 Our Method

In this paper, we firstly make use of the guided image filtering algorithm to dehaze images and then compare the images before and after the dehazing process. Then, we introduce how to select the networks, including YOLOv5 and the improved YOLOv5. Finally, we state the evaluation methods of our experiment.

3.1 Dark Channel Prior Defogging Algorithm

The dark channel prior defogging algorithm [14] was firstly proposed in 2009. In the defogging algorithm, a consortium of outdoor sunny images are analysed. In the non-sky part of these images, one or two of the three RGB colour channels of each image have very low intensities [20]. There are four reasons why we take use of this method: The shadow of all kinds of glass, the projection of natural objects, the brightly coloured surface of visual objects, a dull surface of visual objects. As explained, the dark channel is shown as Eq. (1).

$$J^{dark}(x) = \min_{y \in \Omega(x)} (\min_{c \in [r,g,b]} J^c(y)) \tag{1}$$

where a colour channel is presented by r, g, or b as the components of c, J^{dark} is the image dark channel. At the same time, from the prior knowledge, we know that the grayscale intensity of a pixel in the dark channel is very low, namely, J^{dark} tends to 0.

In Eq. (1), atmospheric light is assumed to be the known variable. In fact, for any input image, 0.10% of the maximum grayscale intensity of pixels in the dark channel image corresponds to the average grayscale of pixels in the corresponding position of each channel of the original image, so as to obtain the atmospheric light of each channel.

On the premise that atmospheric light is assumed to be known, the atmospheric scattering model is transformed into

$$\frac{I^c(x)}{A^c} = t(x)\frac{J^c(x)}{A^c} + 1 - t(x) \tag{2}$$

where c means that each channel needs to be tackled separately. At the same time, we consider the light transmission $t(x)$ as a constant, both sides of Eq. (2) are filtered twice to give the minima,

$$\min_{y\in\Omega(x)}(\min_c(\frac{I^c(x)}{A^c})) = \tilde{t}(x)\min_{y\in\Omega(x)}(\min_c(\frac{J^c(x)}{A^c})) + 1 - \tilde{t}(x) \tag{3}$$

where $\tilde{t}(x)$ is a constant, the minimum value $\tilde{t}(x)$ is calculated, J represents the original image, from the previous dark channel prior, we see that J^{dark} is close to 0. Combined with Eq. (1), we have

$$\min_{y\in\Omega(x)}(\min_c\left(\frac{J^c(y)}{A^c}\right)) = 0. \tag{4}$$

By substituting Eq. (4) to Eq. (3), the estimated value of transmittance $\tilde{t}(x)$ is obtained. The calculation is conducted as follows,

$$\tilde{t}(x) = 1 - \min_{y\in\Omega(x)}(\min_c\frac{I^c(y)}{A^c}) \tag{5}$$

In real cases, even in sunny days with good line of sight, there will still be tiny droplets and aerosol particles in the atmosphere. If all the fog is removed, it will have an impact on the realism of images. Therefore, a factor ω is introduced into Eq. (5), whose value is between [0, 1.00], Eq. (5) thus becomes:

$$\tilde{t}(x) = 1 - \omega\min_{y\in\Omega(x)}(\min_c\frac{I^c(y)}{A^c}) \tag{6}$$

where ω is generally set as 0.95. If $I(x)$ is very small, the value of J will be too large, resulting in a lot of noises in the whole image. Therefore, a threshold t_0 should be set, if $t(x)$ is less than t_0, let $t(x) = t_0$, the final one is shown as Eq. (7),

$$\tilde{t}(x) = 1 - \min_{y\in\Omega(x)}(\min_c\frac{I^c(y)}{A^c}) \tag{7}$$

3.2 Guided Image Filtering

Image defogging is an important pre-processing for the haze removal, which enhances visual effects such as edges and contours. Figure 1 is a pipeline of the haze removal process by using the dark channel prior algorithm.

Image filtering algorithm adopts an image to guide and filter the target image so that the final output image roughly resembles to the target image, the texture is akin

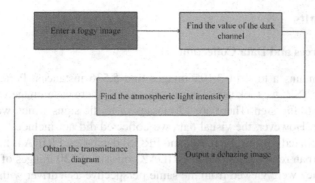

Fig. 1. The workflow of fog removal algorithm

to the guiding image. The guiding or reference image is either a different one or the same one as the input image itself. If the guiding image is equivalent to the input image, the filtering becomes an edge-preserving operation, which is able to be used for image reconstruction. By using visual features from the guided image filtering, haze image processing for traffic signs achieved the ideal results after image denoising [19], image smoothing, and fog removal.

3.3 YOLOv5 Model for Traffic Signs Recognition

In haze weather, the problem of traffic sign images will lead to a decline in the recognition accuracy of deep learning models, which poses a threat to traffic safety requirements. At the same time, the angle and size of the traffic sign will lead to a decrease in recognition accuracy. The rapidity of real-time TSR also has high requirements on computational speed of the model. Thus, we improve YOLOv5 model, which has great advantage in small object detection, while taking into account of TSR accuracy rate and speed, so as to better complete TSR in haze weather. At the same time, we have also improved the YOLOv5 model for TSR by using satellite images, another auxiliary landmark detection is proposed so as to achieve better results.

YOLO is a fast and compact open-source object detection model [15–17]. Compared with other nets, it has strong performance with very good stability. YOLO framework treats visual object detection as a regression problem, which is the first one that harnesses deep neural network in the end-to-end way that predicts the class and bounding box of visual objects. At present, YOLOv5 has faster recognition speed and smaller network size than YOLOv4 [18]. While model training by using different datasets, YOLOv3 and YOLOv4 need a program to calculate the initial anchor box, YOLOv5 automatically calculate the best anchor box for multiple datasets. In YOLOv5, we have fine-tuned the parameters, set the learning rate as 1.20×10^{-3}, the momentum as 0.95, the batch size as 16, and the epoch is assigned to 200.00 according to the batch size.

4 Our Results

4.1 Data Sources and Data Collection

Our dataset contains a total of 3,105 images and 5,536 instances. Pertaining to the experiments for TSR, we took use of our own dataset, where each image was manually labelled with a traffic sign. There are 12 classes of traffic signs which were included in this database. However, the visual data we collected did not include foggy images. Thus, we also utilized FRIDA, FRIDA2, and FROSI databases. FRIDA is made up of 90 images of 18 urban road scenes, while FRIDA2 consists of 330 images of 66 different road scenes. They were viewed from the same perspective as a driver with a variety of fogs in original images: Homogeneous fog, heterogeneous fog, cloudy fog, and cloudy heterogeneous fog, as well as the traffic signs like give-way, watch-out for pedestrians, etc. The FROSI dataset contains fog visibility from 50 m to 400 m with 1,620 traffic signs at various locations. By using these datasets, we are able to train our YOLOv5 model and Faster R-CNN model much comprehensively. Amongst them, 60% images were used for training, 20% for validation, and 20% for testing.

4.2 Comparison and Analysis of Two Defogging Model

In this section, we analyse and compare the defogging results by using the dark channel algorithm and the guided image filtering method. Figure 2 shows the output of each defogging algorithm.

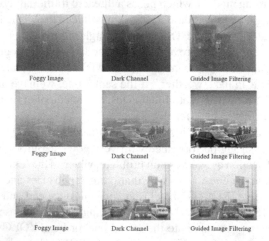

Fig. 2. The results of defogging methods for various scenes.

We see from the results that the dehazing algorithm based on guided image filtering is robust, the dehazing outcome is stable for multiple scenes, it obtains a better defogging result with less colour distortion or darkening of the image. On the contrary, it plays a key role in enhancing the colour images.

4.3 TSR Experiments

In our experiments, we optimized our parameters of Faster R-CNN, we set momentum as 0.90, learning rate as 0.01, maximum epochs as 200, batch size as 24, and weight attenuation as 3.00×10^{-4}. At the same time, we took use of the fully connected layer and ReLU activation function to extract visual features of objects from given images.

Table 1. Experimental results of Faster R-CNN in various whether conditions

Weather	Precision	Recall	mAP@0.5
Sunny	0.97	0.97	0.97
Foggy	0.89	0.90	0.90
Weather	Precision	Recall	mAP@0.5

Table 2. Experimental results of Faster R-CNN with guided image filtering

Weather	Precision	Recall	mAP@0.5
Sunny	0.96	0.96	0.96
Foggy	0.93	0.93	0.93
Weather	Precision	Recall	mAP@0.5

In our experiment, we grouped our data into sunny days and foggy days, and derived the difference between recall, precision, and mAP with and without guided image filtering, as shown in Table 1 and Table 2. These two tables compare the accuracy and recall rates before and after using guided image filtering on sunny and foggy days. Faster R-CNN has higher accuracy and recall rates.

In Table 1 and Table 2, we compare the accuracy and recall rates before and after using guided image filtering on sunny and foggy images. The Faster R-CNN has a higher precision and recall rates. We took use of a guided image filtering method to defog the foggy day images. By using guided image filtering, the TSR accuracy based on sunny images is much higher than that on foggy images. Throughout using guided image filtering method to defog the given images, the accuracy rate by using the images with sunny days is 0.70% lower, the accuracy on foggy days is 3.00% higher, because the guided image filtering method not only removes the fog from the foggy images, but also adds a small number of noises to the sunny images.

Table 3 shows the TSR results using YOLOv5 without guided image filtering. We see from Table 3 that YOLOv5 has higher recognition accuracy and recall rate by using the images shot on sunny days, but the accuracy decreases by using the images on foggy days. At the same time, the recall rate dropped by 6.50%, which is significantly lower than the accuracy and recall rates of images on sunny days. In order to improve the TSR accuracy of images on foggy days, the experimental results of YOLOv5 after using guided image filtering are shown in Table 4. The TSR accuracy rate of images on sunny days has dropped by 0.30%. The reason is that we added a plethora of noises to the traffic signs whilst removing the fogs, but the accuracy of images on foggy days has increased 3.90% compared with previous results, which effectively improve the accuracy of the visual object recognition with the images taken on foggy days.

YOLOv5 model, which is good at small targets and multi-target detection, conducts multitarget detection in complex scenes such as landmark images by improving the optimization ability of loss function in the adaptive balance of foreground and background loss. In other words, the improved loss function makes the model paying much attention on the image with small-size objects after defogging, which focuses on a variety of traffic signs, and accurately recognizes visual objects from complicated road conditions.

Table 3. Experimental result of Faster R-CNN with guided image filtering.

Weather	Precision	Recall	mAP@0.5
Sunny	0.96	0.96	0.96
Foggy	0.88	0.89	0.89
Weather	Precision	Recall	mAP@0.5

Table 4. Experimental result of Faster R-CNN with guided image filtering.

Weather	Precision	Recall	mAP@0.5
Sunny	0.95	0.96	0.96
Foggy	0.92	0.93	0.93
Weather	Precision	Recall	mAP@0.5

4.4 Result Comparisons

In this section, we compare the experimental results of YOLOv5 and other models. Figure 3 shows our TSR in sunny weather conditions, Fig. 4 and Fig. 5 indicate the results from videos with fogs. Figure 6 shows the results with different datasets.

In Fig. 3, we see that the TSR results reveal that Faster R-CNN often misses or fails to detect if the signs are far away from our camera. In contrast, YOLOv5 has a much higher recognition accuracy and computing speed while recognizing small objects or objects that are moving faster. Figure 4 and Fig. 5 show the recognition results on a foggy day, the results are roughly similar to those on a sunny day.

The video we tested is composed of 2,590 frames after processing. YOLOv5 takes 9.00×10^{-3} s to cope with each frame. Under the same accuracy rate, YOLOv5 has a faster recognition speed. Because TSR is often used for real-time object detection and recognition with high requirements of computing speed, YOLOv5 is more suitable for TSR. Figure 8 shows the recognition results of the two methods in the FRIDA dataset.

From Fig. 4 and Fig. 5, we see that both methods achieve accurate detection of traffic signs against a complex fog background. YOLOv5 method did so perfectly. It also benefits from a lighter model size and computing speed. Overall, YOLOv5 performs better if recognizing small objects (Fig. 7).

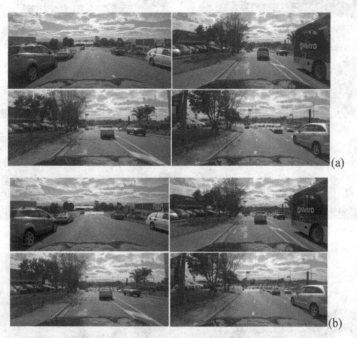

Fig. 3. The TSR results on sunny days (a) Faster R-CNN (b) YOLOv5.

(a)   (b)

Fig. 4. The TSR results by using Faster R-CNN (a) and YOLOv5 (b) on the same scene.

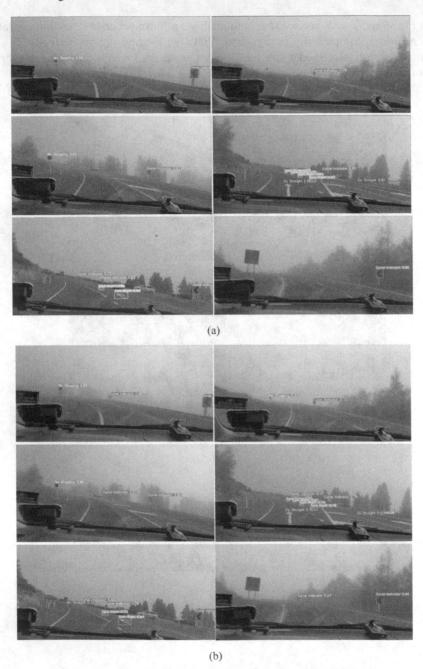

(a)

(b)

Fig. 5. The TSR results on foggy days (a) R-CNN (b) YOLOv5.

(a)

(b)

Fig. 6. The TSR results based on FRIDA dataset (a) Faster R-CNN (b) YOLOv5.

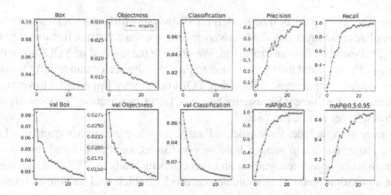

Fig. 7. TSR results by using YOLOv5

4.5 Analysis and Discussions

In the experiments, Fig. 8 shows how each metric changes as the number of iterations increases. In the case where the prediction of bounding boxes decreases with the increase of iterations currently, mAP increases with the growth of iterations at this time. It shows

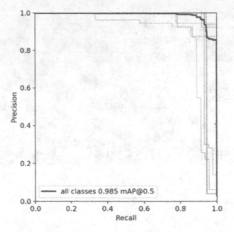

Fig. 8. The PR curve of YOLOv5.

that as the number of iterations rises, the proposed net in this paper is getting better and better. The accuracy and recall will increase with the iterations of the network training. This indicates that the number of true positive samples in the detection also grows as the number of iterations boosts up. Figure 8 is the PR curve of the test results of our experiment, y-axis is the accuracy rate, x-axis is the recall rate. The PR curve is very close to the top-right corner, which indicates that the model is effective. Therefore, the TSR based on YOLOv5 is better which has been well developed.

5   Conclusion

In this paper, we choose the best network for TSR by using different backbone networks. Then we utilize cross-layer links and activation functions to construct feature maps more efficiently, followed by feature extraction. We provide the method of YOLOv5 to detect traffic signs. We improved the loss function to improve the performance of YOLOv5. In our experimental comparisons, we see that YOLOv5 is very important. However, with similar accuracy, real-time TSR usually requires faster recognition. This confirms that YOLOv5 is a better choice for TSR.

Our future work includes three aspects. Firstly, we will continue to expand our dataset by adding more samples in various lighting conditions, such as fog and rain. Second, we compare more object recognition and detection methods in TSR. Finally, we will use more evaluation methods to evaluate our model, which will be able to intuitively discover the shortcomings of our model and make our model more robust and powerful.

References

1. Litman, T., Burwell, D.: Issues in sustainable transportation. Int. J. Global Environ. Issues **6**(4), 331–347 (2010)
2. Berkaya, S.K., Gunduz, H., Ozsen, O., Akinlar, C., Gunal, S.: On circular traffic sign detection and recognition. Expert Syst. Appl. **48**, 67–75 (2016)

3. Shi, X., Fang, X., Zhang, D., Guo, Z.: Image classification based on mixed deep learning model transfer learning. J. Syst. Simul. **28**, 167 (2016)
4. Ma, X., Fu, A., Wang, H., Yin, B.: Hyperspectral image classification based on deep deconvolution network with skip architecture. IEEE Trans. Geosci. Remote Sens. **56**, 4781–4791 (2018)
5. Pan, C., Sun, M., Yan, Z., Shao, J., Wu, D., Xu, X.: Vehicle logo recognition based on deep learning architecture in video surveillance for intelligent traffic system. In: International Conference on Smart and Sustainable City (2013)
6. Garg, K., Nayar, S.K.: Detection and removal of rain from videos. In: IEEE CVPR (2004)
7. Li, B., Wang, S., Zheng, J., Zheng, L.: Single image haze removal using content-adaptive dark channel and post enhancement. IET Comput. Vis. **8**(2), 131–140 (2014)
8. Peng, J., Liu, B., Dong, W., Wang, J., Wang, Y.: Method of image enhancement based on multi-scale retinex. Laser Infrared **38**(11), 1160–1163 (2008)
9. Nayar, S.K., Narasimhan, S.G.: Vision in bad weather. In: IEEE International Conference on Computer Vision (1999)
10. Huang, D., Huang, W., Gu, P., Liu, P., Luo, Y.: Image super-resolution reconstruction based on regularization technique and guided filter. Infrared Phys. Technol. **83**, 103–113 (2017)
11. Feng, X., Li, J., Hua, Z.: Low-light image enhancement algorithm based on an atmospheric physical model. Multimed. Tools Appl. **79**(43–44), 32973–32997 (2020). https://doi.org/10.1007/s11042-020-09562-6
12. Hubel, D.H., Weisel, T.N.: Receptive fields and functional architecture of monkey striate cortex. J. Physiol. **195**(1), 215–243 (1968)
13. Ripley, B.D.: Pattern Recognition and Neural Networks. Cambridge University Press, Cambridge (1996)
14. He, K., Sun, J., Tang, X.: Single image haze removal using dark channel prior. IEEE Trans. Pattern Anal. Mach. Intell. **33**(12), 2341–2353 (2011)
15. Redmon, J., Divvala, S., Girshick, R., Farhadi, A.: You only look once: unified, real-time object detection. In: IEEE Conference on Computer Vision and Pattern Recognition (CVPR), pp. 779–788 (2016)
16. Simonyan, K., Zisserman, A.: Very deep convolutional networks for large-scale image recognition. In: International Conference on Learning Representations (2015)
17. Rezatofighi, H., Tsoi, N., Gwak, J., Sadeghian, A., Reid, I., Savarese, S.: Generalized intersection over union: a metric and a loss for bounding box regression. In: IEEE/CVF CVPR, pp. 658–666 (2019)
18. Luo, Z., Nguyen, M., Yan, W.Q.: Sailboat detection based on automated search attention mechanism and deep learning models. In: International Conference on Image and Vision Computing New Zealand (IVCNZ), pp. 1–6 (2021)
19. Liu, Z., Yan, W.Q., Yang, M.L.: Image denoising based on a CNN model. In: International Conference on Control, Automation and Robotics (ICCAR), pp. 389–393 (2018)
20. Wang, X., Zhang, J., Yan, W.Q.: Gait recognition using multichannel convolution neural networks. Neural Comput. Appl. **32**(18), 14275–14285 (2019). https://doi.org/10.1007/s00521-019-04524-y

Youtube Engagement Analytics via Deep Multimodal Fusion Model

Minh-Vuong Nguyen-Thi[1,2], Huy Le[1,2], Truong Le[1,2], Tung Le[1,2], and Huy Tien Nguyen[1,2(✉)]

[1] Faculty of Information Technology, University of Science, Ho Chi Minh, Vietnam
{18120265,18120182,21c11038}@student.hcmus.edu.vn,
{lttung,ntienhuy}@fit.hcmus.edu.vn
[2] Vietnam National University, Ho Chi Minh City, Vietnam

Abstract. As popularity of video-sharing platforms, content creators have a high demand to produce content which attracts the large amount of viewers. There are many factors related to engagement: visual, sound, transcript, title etc. To take into account of these factors, we propose a deep multi-modal hybrid fusion for YouTube video engagement. Our architecture allows us to be easy to adapt state-of-the-art models for a particular task or variety of modalities, then fuse them to obtain more information aim to classify better. A proposed residual block as a simple neuron architecture search is used to get better features extracted. Our work is at the forefront of classifying YouTube video engagement and promises to broaden the research community's reach. Through detailed experiments, we proved that the model is the state-of-the-art in problem YouTube video engagement analytics.

Keywords: YouTube · Video Engagement · Multi-modal · Data Fusion · Architectural Search · Big Data · Data Mining · Social Media

1 Introduction

With the development of the Internet and social network, online communication through famous platforms such as Facebook, Twitter, Quora, TikTok, or YouTube become popular. These platforms provide clients with abilities to create and share information, news, and personal experiences with others every time, everywhere, even to become an official job. Brand owners choose them as a core place to build marketing campaigns for their products.

Established in 2005, YouTube [1] is a content-sharing platform made by users, and currently the biggest one in the world. Persons making shared clips are content creators, or also known as YouTubers. Viewers and YouTubers connect each other based on subscriber models. In particular, subscribers receive notifications of new content and updates from Youtubers. To earn more money, spread the videos to more people, and increase the number of subscribers, Youtubers need to maximize popularization of their videos' content and constantly improve the

H. Wang et al. (Eds.): PSIVT 2022, LNCS 13763, pp. 50–60, 2023.
https://doi.org/10.1007/978-3-031-26431-3_5

quality of the videos. Therefore, Youtubers have demand to know whether their video attracts a lot of engagements or not as well as the underlying reason for this engagement. From that, they can identify which parts need to be improved. With this idea, we propose a model predicting the engagement level of a video prior to publication.

There is a difference between video engagement and video popularity. Video popularity shows parameters related to interactions with users such as the number of views, comments, or trending topics. However, video engagement focuses on the video content. In this work, we evaluate the engagement aspect of video. Therefore, we employ EnTube [2], a dataset including content features such as video, audio, title, thumbnail, and tags as well as labels of engagement level.

Recent research in this topic focuses on proposing metrics to evaluate engagement of a video, regards to [2–5], for online lecture videos [6], for advertisement [7], for Youtube video [5,8]. The authors apply machine learning methods such as Random Forest, KNN on social features. On the other hand, we analyze engagement via video content itself without the social features. [2] propose a baseline for YouTube video engagement task. They use a multimodal technique working effectively in the case of having various components (e.g., visual, textual, acoustic features etc). To enhance this baseline, we propose a novel architecture to effectively fuse these components.

Our main contributions are as follows:

(i) We propose a deep multimodal fusion architecture for Youtube video engagement;
(ii) A proposed residual block as a simple neuron architecture search extracts robust features.
(iii) Our proposed model achieves state-of-the-art video engagement classification task for Youtube videos.

2 Related Works

Heretofore, few researches related to building models predicting engagement of videos. There are a lot of types of videos such as lectures, advertisements, videos game, or youtube videos that we are working on.

For lectures, Bulathwela et al. [6] performed feature extraction manually to get features such as word count, video duration, speaker speed, etc., then made experiments to analyze engagement using lots of different models. Bulathwela et al. used MNET metric [6] and classical machine learning models such as linear regression, support vector regression (SVR), and ridge regression (RR). Moreover, Bulathwela used SHapley Additive exPlanations (SHAP) [9] which is a deep learning model-agnostic framework that quantifies the impact of features on the model predictions, then visualized features important from input features to select or prune after using machine learning models mentioned below. The disadvantage of the model is defining features themselves which takes much time.

Besides, lectures videos usually bring characteristics about academics and education, sometimes appear in YouTube videos which are usually colorful, emotional, and diverse content.

In 2015, Aguiar et al. provided a dataset including interactions between clients and video advertisements on websites [8]. Data input consists of the website's information such as user's IP address, URL redirect, or interactions such as video-watching time, click time, etc. The dataset was used as the input to classify that a user would be exit the video, and when: the beginning, middle (25%, or 50%, 75%) or the end of the video (5 classes). Aguiar used traditional machine learning models such as Naive Bayes, Decision Tree, Random Forests, and Stacking. This work helps to solve the recommendation problem, and the features extracted must be tracked and collected manually. Besides, the input is interactions between clients, not be a video content and be collected in context of a unpublished video.

Videos about advertisements have been demanded to predict engagement. Chaturvedi et al. [7] proposed Heterogeneous Engagement Auxiliary DeepWalk (HEAD) algorithm, a similarity network and graph-embedding model DeepWalk. That aims to fusion heterogeneous data such as view count and view duration, then classify video engagement and detect fraud of advertisements videos on YouTube. Input data is simple numerical data such as view count, and view duration; then embed them. However, for unpublished videos, this features are not available.

For videos on YouTube, few researchers research to propose metrics and engagement classifiers, so far. Wu et al. [5] proposed a formula to measure video engagement, and models to predict engagement as well. This work performed two regression tasks: relative engagement and watch percentage from video context, topics, and channel reputation. Predicting was performed before publishing, Wu et al. extracted features include: video duration, context information such as resolution quality, language, category, and engagement history of the channel own the video from uploaded video rating, view rating. To predict, Wu et al. used basic machine learning such as linear regression and KNN. Using the input data made predicting to be highly biased. Parameters related to channel reputation have a high impact in predicting, leaded to a video having good content but being published by a new channel has low engagement, and vice versa.

In 2021, research by Yu et al. [10] proposed the model can generate thumbnail selection for videos on YouTube which makes engagement as well as possible. They used the context gating layer aim to further extract context from each of the modules before and after fusing. We use their architecture as the comparison in the experiment step due to the similarity of the idea of using video content and evaluating video engagement.

[2] with the main contribution is data EnTube with more than 20000 videos and Q-score metric, then built a baseline model using deep learning for extracting feature, multi-modal technique to classify engagement level as well. In their model, multimodal architecture is a fully connected layer before fusing, then

there is a fully connected layer again. It can make the loss of much information in each component, besides can not get information across modalities.

A multimodal fusion survey in [11] shows that hybrid fusion is a better technique in multimodal by when combined to get inter and intra of modalities, overcome the worse in two remaining approaches is early fusion and late fusion.

With the works mentioned below, almost related works had to define and extract features manually, besides, used the traditional machine learning models. Features from input data were impacted by social such as users, providers, etc. With our work, we propose a new deep multi-modal hybrid fusion aim to have a joint presentation of all components.

3 Our Model

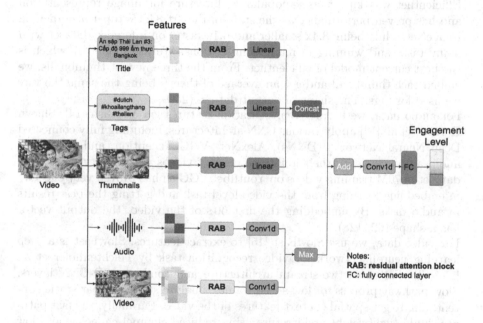

Fig. 1. The full architecture of our models

Using Q-score metric from [2] to label, we build a model using multi-modal fusion to classify the engagement level (engage/neutral/not engage) of a YouTube video that has not yet been released, base on its components including title, all tags, three newest updated thumbnails, video (in the first 60 s) and audio which are extracted from the video had just mentioned. The components are extracted from dataset Entube [2].

We design our model architecture including two stages showed in Fig. 1: Sect. 3.1 Feature Extraction and Sect. 3.2 Deep multimodal hybrid fusion

3.1   Feature Extraction

For each modal, we use pretrained model to extract features. In particular:

- For text data (i.e., title and tags), we employ PhoBERT-base [12] to represent these Vietnamese text inputs. PhoBERT is a transformer model pre-trained on Vietnamese corpus and achieves strong results in four natural language processing tasks, include: POS tagging, Dependency parsing, NER vá NLI. The output is a vector that has a shape (768,).
  With tags, because of having more than one in a video, we get a vector in each tag, then calculate the mean of them. The output is a vector that has a shape (768,).
- For thumbnail data, Efficientnet model [13] is used to extract features. Efficientnet provides a hybrid scaling method that systematically studies the balance of scaling of network depth, width, and resolution for good results. Efficientnet was known as a popular architecture for image representation and has proven performance as the state-of-the-art 84.3% top-1 accuracy on ImageNet, while being 8.4x smaller and 6.1x faster on inference dataset with many tasks and winning in many competitions. We use model b7 which is the best current model of efficientnet. From the three newest thumbnails, we embed each thumbnail and get an average of them - being the same the way we used for tags. The shape of output data is (2560,).
- For audio data, we extract representation features via VGGish [14]. Shawn Hershey et al. [14] apply various CNN architectures, including fully connected Deep Neural Networks (DNNs), AlexNet, VGG, Inception, and ResNet to audio and investigate their ability to classify videos with a very large scale dataset of 70M training videos on Youtube. VGGish has proven very effective in embedding learning from the video-level task and getting the best results in audio tasks. By embedding the first 60 s of the video, the output vector has a shape (62, 128).
- For video data, we use SlowFast [15] to extract features. SlowFast is a deep learning neuron network for video recognition task by Feichtenhofer et al. [15]. SlowFast uses two-stream architecture and combines 3D-CNN layers. Slow pathway process for low-speed frames, analyze static or near static content, aim to get spatial context features of the video. Parallelly, the fast pathway builds lightweight architecture using reduced channel capacity, and low resolution but the high frequency and near-continuous frames to get useful temporal information. Besides, SlowFast builds the lateral connections from the fast to the slow pathway to add features for the slow pathway through each layer. SlowFast is known as the state of the art for tasks based on the video. With the good idea using a slow path and fast path, SlowFast outperformed too many current architectures and become a pre-trained model used popularly. (2304,1,2,2) is the outputs' shape.

3.2   Multi-modal

After handling raw inputs into vectors, we perform to fusion and classify. A video has many components, so we choose a multi-modal approach, especially it is data

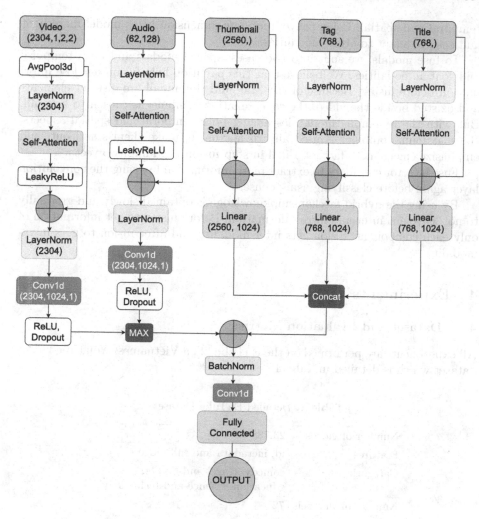

Fig. 2. The detailed architecture of stage 2 - Multimodal Fusion

fusion technique aim to leverage all of them and learn both inter-modality and intra-modality. Each component is seen as a modal. We use a hybrid mechanism to learn flexibly and information across modalities. In particular, each component extract features map first to can get important information. With popular and proven architecture for efficiency, self-attention [16] layer is used in each modal then. It is a layer in the residual block as a part of a neural architecture search [17] for each modality aim to search latent features better after many epochs as well keep information in the original modality (Fig. 2).

After that, a fully connected layer is used for temporal modals: title, tag and thumbnail, and convolution one dimension layer for modals having both temporal and spatial. Using convolution one dimension helps model more light and easy to adapt to other modalities.

To fuse modals, we split into two cases: spatial modals and both temporal and spatial modalities. We believe that this partition help fusion not lose information before fusing. Because of title, tag and thumbnail are distinct elements and existed beside the video, the concatenation combiner is chosen to keep all. But with the remaining modalities having both temporal and spatial aspects, the maximum combiner is used aim to maximize, make them stand out, and emphasize engagement factors. Final in step fusion is adding two vectors.

Fused Vector continues to extract more information by using the convolution layer again before classifying using dense.

By using the hybrid mechanism, knowledge is obtained slowly and gradually to not leave out inter and intra information. Before fusion to get information of only each component, fusion gets inter-modality and after fusion to gets intra-modality.

4   Experiments

4.1   Dataset and Evaluation Metrics

All experiments are performed on the EnTube [2], a Vietnamese YouTube videos dataset which is detailed in Table 1.

Table 1. Detailed EnTube Dataset

Number of videos	23,738
Features	id, metadata and full video
Categories	comedy, travel-and-events, education, science-and-technology
Number of channels	72
Period time	12 years
Train dataset	videos are published from 2010–2019
Validation dataset	videos are published in 2020
Test dataset	videos are published in 2021

Title, tags, and thumbnails are extracted from the metadata of the video. EnTube is a variety dataset with many types of data and gets almost components in a video which related to video content. It also provides labels based on Q-score [2]. Q-score is a metric that is proven is less biased to view, and the number of subscribers.

Train dataset, validation dataset and test dataset are splitted by years in Table 1.

4.2 Experimental Settings

In our model, we take advantage of pre-trained models for extracting features from components. The name of the pre-trained models' version is presented in Table 2. Besides, we also provide the range of our tuning process of components including optimizer, combiners, batch size data, learning rate or hyperparameters in the optimizer, and the number of the dense layer as well nodes in it. These choices come from the results and the infrastructures in the experimental environment.

Table 2. Detailed of Components Setting

Component	Value
PhoBert	vinai/phobert-base
Efficientnet	b7
VGGish	harritaylor/torchvggish
SlowFast	r50
Combiners	max, add, concat, mul
Optimizer	SGD, Adam
Loss Function	CrossEntropyLoss
Batch-size	$i \in \{16, 32, 64, 128\}$
Learning-rate	$i \in \{ae - b\}$ with $a \in \{1, 3, 6, 9\}, b = \overline{1, 5}$
Fully-connected layers	1024 - 512 - 128 - 3

Beside our model, we try to implement [10] to experiment with many approaches and demonstrate the efficiency of our architecture.

4.3 Results

Youtube video engagement analytics is a quite new topic in the research market. So there are fewer papers about both dataset and model. We use [2] as a baseline to compare. Besides, we use the architecture in [10] as another approach to building model on our dataset. Furthermore, we perform two our architecture which are using and no using residual attention blocks to check their impact. All experiments of four models are conducted in 5 running times. Then, the best and average results are also presented in Table 3.

Table 3. The details of the comparison between models

Model	The best F1_score	The average F1_score	Support
Baseline [2]	0.6174	0.6097 ± 0.0066	2805
Architecture in [10]	0.6271	0.6203 ± 0.0058	2805
Our model (no RAB)	0.6250	0.6190 ± 0.0060	2805
Our model (using RAB)	**0.6401**	**0.6329 ± 0.0062**	2805

From Table 3, F1_score in our work rises by **2.3%** and **1.3%** respectively when comparing with baseline model and related architecture. The average F1_score reflects complete superiority in both mean and standard deviation. The result shows that context-gating gives improvement to the model. However, by using residual attention block and combiners selectively, the F1 score goes up considerably, to 64.01%. Another one Table 3 shown that the architecture using context-gating is more stable than our model, with standard deviations are 0.58% and 0.62%, although not a lot.

We also try to change how to fusion by using different combiners such as maximum(max), addition(add), concatenation(concat) and multiplication(mul). In the architecture, there are three places to fusion data. We conduct experiments to replace each combiner. After experiments, the configuration of our model is the best, proving that the chosen component we mentioned in model Sect. 3.2 is reasonable and efficient. Table 4 is a case of choosing addition combiner to fuse all components. It is evident that there is a significant difference if changing the combiner.

Table 4. The details of the comparison between combiner if final combiner is add

	ADD	MUL	MAX	CONCAT
ADD	62.90	63.04	62.90	63.22
MUL	63.51	60.88	61.21	62.82
MAX	62.36	60.99	62.18	**64.01**
CONCAT	60.55	61.83	61.78	-

Using different combiners impacts highly to model's score, especially the minimum value shown in Table 4 is 60.88% while the maximum one is 64.01%. It can evident that using addition or concatenation for the first combiner and addition or maximum for the second combiner, with the final fusion being addition get better results.

5   Discussion

For the above results, we can solve the problem of predicting video engagement, and help YouTubers or content-creators can have a view of their videos related to engagement.

However, with only predicting, it is not optimized for YouTubers to know that we evaluate which component(s) make the video engage or not, help them can be easy to find reasons and improve the video quickly. From the thinking, in the feature, building a model can point out the components where and why they are good or bad makes sense, and is essential. To solve that, we plan to use explained artificial intelligence (XAI). With this idea, we hope that researchers can work together to solve the problem, make it sense, and support the creation of excellent content videos.

6   Conclusion

In this work, we presented a deep multimodal hybrid fusion to classify the engagement of a Youtube video. Our model is easy to adapt components of a video and focus on the video's contents. With our architecture, information is extracted in each modality as well across modalities. A proposed residual block as a simple neuron architecture search is used to get better features extracted. Our experiment proved our model outperformed the baseline model and another architecture which is the most relevant as the idea under varying evaluations to become the state of the art in problem YouTube video engagement analytic. Moving forward, we promise to implement explained artificial intelligence to explain our model's output and help YouTubers or content creators to clear problem in their videos.

Acknowledgment. This research is supported by research funding from Faculty of Information Technology, University of Science, Vietnam National University - Ho Chi Minh City, and Gender & Diversity Project - APNIC Foundation.

References

1. Wattenhofer, M., Wattenhofer, R., Zhu, Z. (eds.): The YouTube Social Network (2012)
2. EnTube: A Dataset for YouTube Video Engagement Analytics (2022)
3. Wiebe, E.N., et al.: Measuring engagement in video game-based environments: investigation of the user engagement scale. Comput. Hum. Behav. **32**, 123–132 (2014)
4. Fox, C.M., Brockmyer, J.H.: The development of the game engagement questionnaire: a measure of engagement in video game playing: response to reviews. Interact. Comput. **25**(4), 290–293 (2013)
5. Wu, S., Rizoiu, M.-A., Xie, L.: Beyond views: measuring and predicting engagement in online videos. In: Twelfth International AAAI Conference on Web and Social Media (2018)
6. Bulathwela, S., et al.: Predicting engagement in video lectures. arXiv preprint. arXiv:2006.00592 (2020)
7. Chaturvedi, I., et al.: Predicting video engagement using heterogeneous DeepWalk. Neurocomputing **465**, 228–237 (2021)
8. Aguiar, E., Nagrecha, S., Chawla, N.V.: Predicting online video engagement using clickstreams. In: IEEE International Conference on Data Science and Advanced Analytics (DSAA), pp. 1–10. IEEE (2015)
9. Lundberg, S.M., Lee, S.-I.: A unified approach to interpreting model predictions. In: Advances in Neural Information Processing Systems, vol. 30 (2017)
10. Yu, Z., Shi, N.: A multi-modal deep learning model for video thumbnail selection. arXiv preprint. arXiv.2101.00073 (2020)
11. Joshi, G., Walambe, R., Kotecha, K.: A review on explainability in multimodal deep neural nets. IEEE Access **9**, 59800–59821 (2021)
12. Nguyen, D.Q., Nguyen, A.T.: PhoBERT: pre-trained language models for Vietnamese. arXiv preprint. arXiv:2003.00744 (2020)

13. Tan, M., Le, Q.: EfficientNet: rethinking model scaling for convolutional neural networks. In: International Conference on Machine Learning. PMLR, pp. 6105–6114 (2019)
14. Hershey, S.: CNN architectures for large-scale audio classification. In: IEEE International Conference on Acoustics, Speech and Signal Processing (ICASSP), pp. 131–135. IEEE (2017)
15. Feichtenhofer, C., et al.: Slowfast networks for video recognition. In: Proceedings of the IEEE/CVF International Conference on Computer Vision, pp. 6202–6211 (2019)
16. Vaswani, A., et al.: Attention is all you need. In: Advances in Neural Information Processing Systems, vol. 30 (2017)
17. Elsken, T., Metzen, J.H., Hutter, F.: Neural architecture search: a survey. J. Mach. Learn. Res. **20**(1), 1997–2017 (2019)

Dynamic Point Cloud Compression with Cross-Sectional Approach

Faranak Tohidi[1]($\boxtimes$), Paul Manoranjan[1], and Anwaar Ulhaq[2]

[1] Charles Sturt University, Bathurst, Australia
{ftohidi,mpaul}@csu.edu.au
[2] Charles Sturt University, Port Macquarie, Australia
aulhaq@csu.edu.au

Abstract. A dynamic point cloud (DPC) is a set of points irregularly sampled from the continuous surfaces of objects or scenes, comprising texture (i.e., colour) and geometry (i.e., coordinate data). The DPC has made it possible to closely mimic the real world's natural reality and significantly improve training, safety, entertainment, and quality of life. However, to be even more effective, more realistic, and broadcast successfully, the dynamic point clouds require higher compression due to their massive volume of data compared to the traditional video. Recently, MPEG finalized a Video-based Point Cloud Compression (V-PCC) standard as the latest method of compressing both geometric and texture dynamic point clouds, which has achieved the best rate-distortion performance for DPC so far. However, V-PCC requires huge computational time due to expensive normal calculation and segmentation, sacrifices some points to limit the number of 2D patches, and cannot occupy all spaces in the 2D frame, resulting in the inefficiency of video compression. The proposed method addresses these limitations using a novel cross-sectional approach to cut the whole DPC frame into different sections considering the main view, shape, and size. This approach reduces expensive normal estimation and segmentation, retains more points, and utilizes more space for 2D frame generation, leading to more compression compared to the VPCC. The experimental results using standard video sequences show that the proposed technique can achieve better compression in both geometric and texture data compared to the latest V-PCC standard.

Keywords: Point cloud compression · cross-section · 3D compression

1 Introduction

Currently, there is fast growth in immersive augmented reality because of advances in 3D rendering. Emerging technologies enable real-world objects, persons, and scenes to convincingly move dynamically across our view using a 3D point cloud [1, 2]. Dynamic 3D point cloud has found significant applications in recent evolutions in technological developments, including autonomous driving, virtual reality (VR), augmented reality (AR), robotics, telehealth, telecommunication [3, 4], and, most recently, Metaverse. However, DPCs, in their raw format, occupy an enormous amount of memory for storage

© Springer Nature Switzerland AG 2023
H. Wang et al. (Eds.): PSIVT 2022, LNCS 13763, pp. 61–74, 2023.
https://doi.org/10.1007/978-3-031-26431-3_6

and also bandwidth for transmission. For example, if a typical DPC currently used in entertainment is considered, it includes around 1 million points per frame and a frame rate of 30 Hz. Consequently, a total bandwidth of more than 3 Gbps would be required without any compression [3, 4]. Therefore, an efficient compression method is needed due to using the existing available bandwidth.

Several compression methods have been tried in the recent past, and none of them have been found to be the complete solution. There are three different categories of point clouds, each of which has its own standard and benchmark dataset to make research comparisons. Category 1 is Static point clouds (e.g., statues), Category 2 is dynamic point clouds (e.g., human video sequences), and Category 3 is dynamically acquired point clouds (e.g., LiDAR point clouds) [5–8]. There are two different leading compression technologies currently used for point cloud compression (PCC) standardization which are called video-based point cloud compression (V-PCC) and geometry-based point cloud compression (G-PCC). The reference software available for V-PCC is TMC2 which is more suitable for Category 2, and TMC13, the reference software for G-PCC, is more suitable for Categories 1 and 3 [3, 9]. G-PCC encodes the content directly in the 3D space, while the V-PCC coding is based on converting 3D to 2D data for compression. G-PCC utilizes data structures and their proximity, such as an octree and k-d tree that describe the locations of the points in the 3D space, whereas the other main compression technology V-PCC takes advantage of existing 2D video compression and converts the 3D point cloud data to the collection of multiple 2D images [3].

1.1 Introducing V-PCC Method

We have chosen to focus on improving DPCs (Category 2); therefore, we need to begin by explaining the most current standardized method for V-PCC (2020–21):

Taking advantage of 2D video compression involves two main steps: firstly, converting from 3D to multiple 2D data; then, in the second step, an existing video compression technique such as High-Efficiency Video Coding (HEVC) is applied to the 2D frames.

As it can be seen from Fig. 1, an input point cloud is converted to multiple 2D data called Atlas (multiple projected maps), then it is compressed by the 2D video encoder to produce a bitstream. For each Atlas, there are three associated images: a binary image named occupancy map, which shows whether a pixel corresponds to a valid 3D projected point, at least two layers of geometry map that contain the depth information, and at least two layers of attribute map that contains the texture information [10, 11].

In converting 3D to 2D, a point cloud is divided into patches based on an estimation of a normal vector at each point of a point cloud input and by grouping adjacent points with a similar directional plane. The 3D patches are orthogonally projected onto a 2D domain. The projected patches are packed into 2D packing images (Fig. 1). This last process involves packing the extracted patches into a 2D map of either texture or geometry as well as all layers represented while minimizing the space in between which is unused [12, 13].

The limitation of the 2D packing is that a pixel of the 2D packed image can correspond to one or more 3D points because several 3D points may be placed on the same projection plane, and some of the points may be lost due to self-occlusion. To solve this issue, TMC2 (V-PCC) uses several layers for all the points of a point cloud along each projection plane.

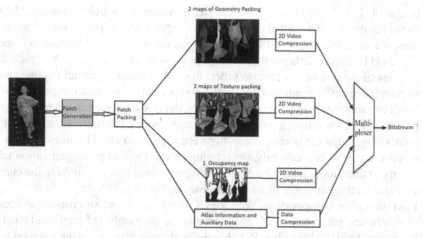

Fig. 1. V-PCC method overview showing patch generation, patch packing, and the three types of maps before 2D video compression to create a compressed bitstream.

The standard recommends requiring at least two layers (or up to sixteen) for geometry and attribute. Extra layers of projection may reduce missing points through the 3D to 2D projection step; however, it increases overall bitrates.

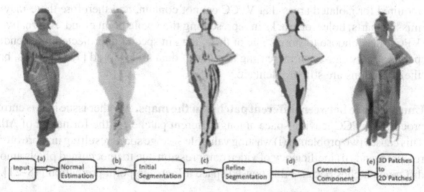

Fig. 2. The involved process of patch generation using the V-PCC method including normal estimation, initial segmentation, refining segmentation, and connected component [11].

1.2 Limitations of the Current Standard Dynamic Point Cloud Compression Technology

We wanted to focus on improving the following limitations of V-PCC for dynamic point cloud compression:

A. **Extensive time.** The first issue is the huge computational time requirement, primarily because of the first step in V-PCC, which is dividing a point cloud into patches [11, 14]. The time involved in patch generation is quite considerable due to the involvement of normal estimation and segmentation. This is one of the most complex processes in the V-PCC method (shaded in Fig. 1 and explained more in Fig. 2) [11]. Figure 2 shows the involved process of generating patches, including a series of procedures in precise order: normal estimation, initial segmentation, segmentation refinement, and connected component or segmenting patches. As a result of using estimation for normal vectors, the initial projection plane index may be inaccurate. Therefore, a refining procedure is required in the next step for all 3D points using adjacent points. These steps are applied to all 3D points in the point cloud iteratively; consequently, the refining process within patch generation takes extensive time, more than 50% of the patch generation process, making the current standard method unviable in most real-time applications [11, 15].

B.   **Lost data after compression.** With V-PCC, some points are still missed as a result of two issues: projecting to 2D and limitation of the number of generated patches:

(i)   Projecting to 2D: Although V-PCC has defined more than one layer, even up to 16 layers for each geometry and texture map, the problem of lost points has not been solved, as there remain some points that even sixteen layers cannot cover because of self-occlusion (self-occluded points cannot be captured) [7, 16].

(ii) Limitation of the number of generated patches: The number of patches depends on the complexity of the point cloud. Although V-PCC uses as many patches as they can, they are not enough to capture the whole point cloud in detail. V-PCC may decide to ignore isolated points because of the need for many more patches required for isolated areas that VPCC cannot contain, and therefore there may be missing parts, holes, or cracks in representing the whole point cloud. Alternatively, VPCC may choose to store some of those data in special unprojected independent patches. This causes an increasing amount of data to be stored [7, 17]. Thus, both their solutions are still problematic.

C.   **Unused space between different patches in the maps.** Another issue in this current process is VPCC leaving space among different patches in the formation of Atlas. This causes two problems: (i) wasting valuable storage space resulting in more bitrate required, and (ii) inefficiency of video compression due to unoccupied pixels among different patches because this unused space affects temporal prediction [18–21].

To address the above limitations, we propose a cross-sectional-based approach as an alternative to the time-consuming patch generation approach. In the proposed method, the efficiency of 2D video compression is improved due to two factors: Firstly, retaining the similarity of neighboring points within each cross-section results in more coherence after projection. Secondly, most 2D cross-sections are rectangular in shape, which can be interlocked with each other more neatly than irregular shapes of patches in V-PCC. This reduces bitrate due to fewer unoccupied pixels between 2D projected images and improves temporal prediction in the 2D video for better compression.

1.3 Contributions and Benefits of the Proposed Cross-Sectional Approach

There are four main research contributions of the proposed cross-sectional segmentation method compared to the existing V-PCC standard:

- Introducing a cross-section-based patch generation technique to minimize the data loss in the existing patch generation step.
- Arranging the patches in the 2D Atlas more compactly during the compression step to achieve better compression.
- Introducing simplified steps for segmentation focusing on the shape of the object so that the object area is divided into similar parts or sections, achieving better temporal correlation and reduction in computational complexity.
- Providing more emphasis on selecting the main view during the segmentations process in the proposed cross-section approach to improve the viewer's experience.

2 Proposed Method

To increase the efficiency of the V-PCC standard, we introduce a novel cross-sectional approach as a solution that does not require so much patch generation or loss of data due to that step. We crosscut similar shapes in the point cloud and separate them. The reason for cross-sectioning the point cloud is that it is a simple way of separating different sections and reducing data loss of the point cloud before converting them to 2D. Then we treat each cross-section as an individual discrete point cloud, allowing us to evaluate all points on each axis. The other advantage is that most 2D cross-sections projected are rectangular in shape and, therefore, can better fit into the Atlas. This results in allowing more compression due to less unused space between cross-sections. Whereas the V-PCC method produces irregular shapes which are harder to combine into one rectangular Atlas and causes more unused space among them.

2.1 Five Key Priorities for Cross-Sectional Segmentation

As we know, a DPC is a 3D object which is represented by only its surfaces. Therefore, we collect data from only its surfaces when cross-sectioning a DPC. In doing this, there are five priorities to consider: The first priority is to consider the main view perspective because we want to improve the viewer's experience most of all. Next, we consider that the initial cutting should be from the direction with the longest axis because it gives us more opportunity to divide the point cloud into selected and similar sections. The third priority is that we also need to consider the number of data layers to find the best direction of cross-sectioning because there are always at least two layers of data in each direction (except at the end of each axis, where there is just one layer of data). This will enable us to separate those layers into different cross-sections and project each section individually to avoid self-occlusion. These first three priorities will help us select which direction to cross-section the point cloud first. Then along that selected direction, we consider our fourth priority: as long as there are not more than two layers in that direction, there is no need for more cross-sections since all points can be projected onto two planes. Therefore, the proposed cross-sectional method can increase the amount of compression, especially in less complex parts of the point cloud. Lastly, we aim to have each selected cross-section as wide as possible while trying similar cross-section shapes. This helps us to minimize the unused space between patches, which results in increasing the efficiency of 2D video compression.

2.2 Detailed Cross-Sectional Process

As we mentioned earlier, in a point cloud, the objects are represented by their surface, not by their volume. Therefore cross-sectioning aims to find rings or broad elliptical cylinders of points in one focus area of the 3D object, e.g., head, leg, et cetera. Then, we take each broadly cylindrical cross-section as an individual point cloud. We aim to cut the point cloud so that there is only one broadly elliptical cylinder of points in each segment, and all the points are part of one similar-sized cylindrical shape. To find the number of cylindrical shape segments, we need to calculate the distance between the points on the rings (x_i, z_i, y) and their center (x_c, z_c, y). This distance (d) can be calculated using the following two formulas:

$$d^2 = (x_i - x_c)^2 + (z_i - z_c)^2 \tag{1}$$

where:

$$(x_c, z_c, y) = ((x_{max} - x_{min})/2, (z_{max} - z_{min})/2, y) \tag{2}$$

Once we know the distances of points situated on the surface of the point cloud, we try to find all similar-sized cylindrical shapes. To do this we use the following equation: (e.g., cylinders along the y axis)

$$\frac{x^2}{a^2} + \frac{z^2}{b^2} = 1 \tag{3}$$

where a and b are the semi-major axis and semi-minor axis of the elliptic cylinder. For points to be on a similar-sized cylindrical shape, the distance of those points located on each segment with their center should be approximately between "a" and "b" of an elliptic cylinder ($a \leq d \leq b$).

Since there may be some distortion around each cross-section after compressing, we propose to consider overlapping the edge areas of the adjacent cross-sections to avoid losing data points.

Figure 3 (left) shows how *Longdress* (as a standard test point cloud sequence) is cross-sectioned into five key segments which are similar (in shape and size) to demonstrate that the allocated segments are made as big as possible in the direction of the chosen axis. In Fig. 3 (right), these *Longdress* segments are shown from the other axis to demonstrate that the divided sections can be projected on 2D rectangles and still cover a large area of the original object. Of course, the advantage is that within each of these sections, the point cloud data retain their connections to one another, which allows more efficient video compression and reconstruction.

The next example (Fig. 4) shows the other standard test point cloud sequences, including Loot, Red and black, and Soldier. The video sequences are divided into two

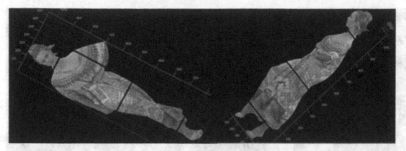

Fig. 3. The proposed cross-sections of the Longdress point cloud into five sections shown two different views where black lines indicate the cross-section locations.

segments (because their shapes are not as complex as Longdress), since there are two similar cylinders in their legs, and their body can be considered as another elliptical cylinder segment. Here we could make more segments to achieve greater detail. Although there will be a slight increase in the bitrate, the proposed method has achieved a much better quality when the number of sections is denser. Please note that the number of cross-sectional segments depends on the shape and complexity of the point cloud.

Therefore, the proposed method has greater flexibility to both save bitrate in the less detailed areas or increase segments for detailed viewing. Some cross-sections may not need more than one layer of the map for projecting because those sections are sparse in points and include only one layer of data. Therefore, we can have more compression for that segment and also for reserving space for those segments which need more layers for more detail.

2.3 Possibility for Further Segmentation to Achieve Even Greater Quality

To achieve more quality in critical areas of the DPC, we can again cut each segment into further sections as needed. For example, to preserve realistic detail in the more complex areas of Longdress, e.g., her face, we suggest making vertical sections to the head section, as Fig. 5 shows.

We aim to cross-section the individual segments so that we minimize the data changes as a result of 3D-2D-3D conversions. Figure 5 illustrates how much data can be kept unchanged after 3D-2D-3D conversion if projected only in one plane. In fact, the green areas in Fig. 5 are points that remain the same after projecting on the front plane. Therefore, we try to keep greener (unchanged) points in one cross-section. As an example, in this picture (Fig. 5 (right)), the center of the face is contained in one cross-section, and the other two sides of the face are segmented into two other cross-sections. The aim for the whole head is to choose key areas for segmenting so that each chosen cross-section includes as many green (unchanged after projection) points as possible while making the cross-sectioned area as large as possible.

Since any cylinder can be further cross-sectioned into additional parts to combat data occlusion, the way of cross-sectioning is critical. Each cylinder is cross-sectioned so that the width of each cross-section is decided according to the minimal occlusion of the data on that elliptical cylinder. This is particularly important for points on the

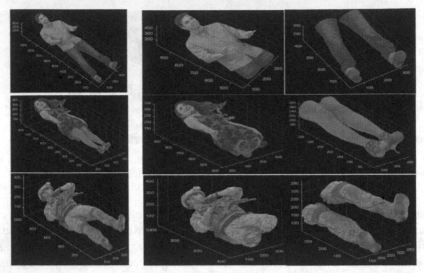

Fig. 4. The proposed cross-sections for three standard point cloud video sequences, including Loot, Red and black, and Soldier, show that only two cross-sections are needed.

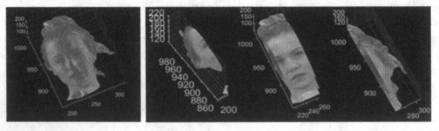

Fig. 5. *Longdress* face in the process of further segmentation to achieve better quality. The green points are the points that remain unchanged after projection on the front plane.

edges of the cylinders. By cross-sectioning this way, it is possible to project two edges cross-sections of the cylinder on fewer planes and cover most of the head and neck data, minimizing data loss in projecting to 2D images. As it is evident in Fig. 5, the center cross-section of her face can be fitted better into the 2D map after projection because it has a rectangular shape reducing the amount of space that is required for compression, thus solving the third issue of unused space between different patches in V-PCC.

3 Experimental Results

The performance of the cross-sectional approach proposed in this paper was determined using V-PCC reference software TMC2 to compare the performance of both methods. We chose Longdress, Loot, Soldier, and Red and black as standard test point cloud sequences. To compare the proposed method with V-PCC, we have segmented Longdress into five and the rest into two cross-sections. There are two visual comparisons to observe in addition to several objective quality evaluations.

|First frame | Second frame | Differences between the 1st and 2nd frames|

a. Comparing two consecutive frames of *Loot*, using the proposed cross-sectional method.

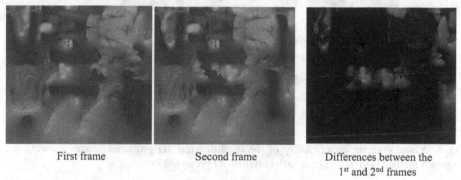

|First frame | Second frame | Differences between the 1st and 2nd frames|

b. Comparing two consecutive frames of *Loot*, using the V-PCC method.

Fig. 6. The difference between the two frames is shown as coloured in the right picture, while black areas show the similarities of those frames. This figure shows that the difference between two consecutive frames using the proposed method is less, which means having a greater temporal correlation compared with V-PCC.

3.1 Visual Comparisons of the Methods

Visual comparisons are illustrated in Fig. 6 and 7 to show the efficiency of the proposed cross-sectional method:

Figure 6a (top) shows the proposed method's results, demonstrating that the similarity between two successive frames is greater than the same frames using V-PCC, as shown in Fig. 6b (bottom). Figure 6 illustrates two improvements using the proposed method which shows two consecutive frames and their differences: Firstly, the average absolute difference between two frames produced by the proposed cross-sectional method is 6.48, whereas the V-PCC method is 10.44, which means the proposed method has greater temporal correlation (around 62% better). Secondly, as seen from the Figs, 2D cross-sections projected are fitted into the map better; therefore, the unoccupied pixels between 2D shapes inside the frames have been decreased using the proposed method. Therefore, these two improvements achieved by the proposed method increased the efficiency of the existing 2D video compression.

Figure 7 shows a close-up of Longdress arm and dress, comparing the quality of the original 2D projected image and the two reconstructed images after compression. The reconstructed image is visibly closer to the original image using the proposed method, while in V-PCC reconstructed image, there is more blurring of arm edges and the dress pattern as denoted by red arrows on the image.

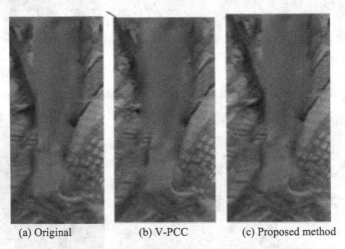

(a) Original   (b) V-PCC   (c) Proposed method

Fig. 7. Visual comparison of quality of the reconstructed 2D projected images showing the proposed method is visually closer to the original 2D projected image.

3.2 Objective Evaluations Comparing Both Methods

Objective quality evaluations and comparisons are demonstrated in Fig. 8 and Tables 1, 2, and 3. In this comparison, we focused on quality measured by PSNR (Peak Signal to Noise Ratio) and bitrate of 2D video compression for geometry and texture. The rate-distortion curves by the proposed (red) and the V-PCC methods (blue-dotted) using Soldier, Red and black, Loot, and Longdress video sequences are illustrated in Fig. 8. The quality of geometry and texture are shown to be at least 1.85 dB higher using the proposed method compared to the V-PCC for the same bit rate, for all four datasets. The quality of reconstructed Longdress for both geometry and texture has improved more than the others. This is because we have used five cross-sections for Longdress while Loot, Red and black, and Soldier had only two cross-sections. BD-Rate is provided to compare the rate-distortion performance of the proposed method and the V-PCC method. The BD Rate is obtained as the average or integral of the bitrate difference between two codecs at the same quality. The results under common test conditions are shown in Tables 1 and 2 for geometry and texture quality respectively, which show BD-Bit rate and BD-PSNR. As seen, there is a great improvement in the proposed method for both BD-PSNR and BD-Bit rate means the proposed method can reconstruct frames with higher quality using a lower bit rate. Table 3 shows data loss using the proposed and V-PCC methods for four datasets. It can be seen from this table that data loss using the proposed method is less. The pre-processing for generating patches is one of the most time-consuming steps in V-PCC because it needs to estimate the normal for each point in the whole point cloud, and segment and refine the many patches. Fortunately, the proposed method's need for patch generation and refining has decreased by utilizing the proposed novel cross-sectional approach.

Table 1. BD-Bit rate and BD-PSNR of four different types of video sequences of Geometry performance.

Sequence	BD-Bit rate	BD-PSNR
Red and black	−23%	1.95
Loot	−19%	1.85
Soldier	−21%	2.05
Longdress	−38%	3.69

Table 2. BD-Bit rate and BD-PSNR of four different types of video sequences of Texture performance.

Sequence	BD-Bit rate	BD-PSNR
Red and black	−38%	2.1
Loot	−49%	3.02
Soldier	−46%	2.52
Longdress	−69%	5.1

Table 3. Comparison of data loss between the proposed and V-PCC methods for four different types of datasets.

Sequence	Data loss by V-PCC	Data loss by the proposed method
Red and black	9.4%	8%
Loot	12%	11%
Soldier	11%	10.1%
Longdress	9.8%	8.9%

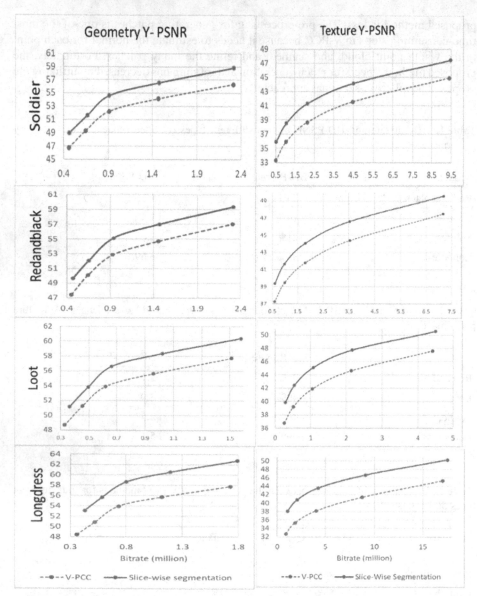

Fig. 8. The rate-distortion curves by the proposed (red) and the V-PCC methods (blue-dotted) using four standard video sequences. The quality of geometry and texture are shown to be higher using the proposed method compared to the V-PCC for the same bit rate, for all four datasets.

4   Conclusion

The focus of this research was to address three critical issues which existing standard dynamic point cloud compression (V-PCC) is still facing: Firstly, improving the quality of compressed point cloud to enhance the realistic experience for the viewer. Secondly, to assist the development of real-time processing by eliminating the need for most patch generation. Thirdly, minimizing data loss during patch generation by considering all available points on each axis while cross-sectioning. We have achieved these goals by proposing a new method of cross-sectional segmentation of point clouds.

The proposed method has been shown to be able to retain more of the original data points and their proximity to each other. Therefore, the proposed method is able to increase the efficiency of 2D video compression while preserving bitrate, resulting in improved 3D dynamic point cloud quality and an enhanced viewer experience.

We have used cross-sectional cylindrical segmentation to produce more rectangular and similar 2D projected images. These are able to reduce unoccupied pixels in the 2D Atlas while maintaining similarity between adjacent projected images, thereby keeping neighbouring points connected to improve the efficacy of video compression and reconstruction. By sacrificing a very small amount of bitrate, we were able to achieve a much higher quality after compression than the current standard. The proposed method has been shown to have great potential for improvement of dynamic point cloud compression and it is expected that further research on the cross-sectional approach will result in even greater progress in real-time applications.

References

1. Yu, S., Sun, S., Yan, W., Liu, G., Li, X.: A method based on curvature and hierarchical strategy for dynamic point cloud compression in augmented and virtual reality system. Sensors (Basel) **22**(3), 1262 (2022)
2. Wang, D., Zhu, W., Xu, Y., Xu, Y., Yang, L.: Visual quality optimization for view-dependent point cloud compression. In: 2021 IEEE International Symposium on Circuits and Systems (ISCAS) (2021)
3. Graziosi, D., Nakagami, O., Kuma, S., Zaghetto, A., Suzuki, T., Tabatabai, A.: An overview of ongoing point cloud compression standardization activities: video-based (V-PCC) and geometry-based (G-PCC). APSIPA Trans. Sign. Inf. Proc. **9**, E13 (2020)
4. Fan, H., Yang, Y., Kankanhalli, M.: Point 4D transformer networks for spatio-temporal modeling in point cloud videos. In: 2021 IEEE/CVF Conference on Computer Vision and Pattern Recognition (CVPR), pp. 14199–14208 (2021)
5. Fan, H., Yu, X., Yang, Y., Kankanhalli, M.: Deep hierarchical representation of point cloud videos via spatio-temporal decomposition. IEEE Trans. Pattern. Anal. Mach. Intell. **44**, 9918–9930 (2021)
6. Wang, G., Chen, M., Liu, H., Yang, Y., Liu, Z., Wang, H.: Anchor-based spatio-temporal attention 3-D convolutional networks for dynamic 3-D point cloud sequences. IEEE Trans. Instrum. Meas. **70**, 1–11 (2021)
7. Cao, C., Preda, M., Zakharchenko, V., Jang, E.S., Zaharia, T.: Compression of sparse and dense dynamic point clouds—methods and standards. Proc. IEEE **109**(9), 1537–1558 (2021)
8. Ahmmed, A., Paul, M., Murshed, M., Taubman, D.: Dynamic point cloud compression using a cuboid oriented discrete cosine based motion model. In: ICASSP IEEE International Conference on Acoustics, Speech and Signal Processing (ICASSP), pp. 1935–1939 (2021)
9. Liu, H., Yuan, H., Liu, Q., Hou, J., Liu, J.: A comprehensive study and comparison of core technologies for MPEG 3-D point cloud compression. IEEE Trans. Broadcast. **66**(3), 701–717 (2020)

10. Ahmmed, A., Paul, M., Murshed, M., Taubman, D.: Dynamic point cloud geometry compression using cuboid based commonality modeling framework. In: IEEE International Conference on Image Processing (ICIP), pp. 2159–2163 (2021)
11. Kim, J., Kim, Y.H.: Fast grid-based refining segmentation method in video-based point cloud compression. IEEE Access **9**, 80088–80099 (2021)
12. Ahmmed, A., Paul, M., Pickering, M.: Dynamic point cloud texture video compression using the edge position difference oriented motion model. In: Data Compression Conference (DCC), p. 335 (2021)
13. Rhyu, S., Kim, J., Im, J., Kim, K.: Contextual homogeneity-based patch decomposition method for higher point cloud compression. IEEE Access **8**, 207805–207812 (2020)
14. Xiong, J., Gao, H., Wang, M., Li, H., Lin, W.: Occupancy map guided fast video-based dynamic point cloud coding. IEEE Trans. Circuits Syst. Video Technol. **32**(2), 813–825 (2022)
15. Seidel, I., et al.: Memory-friendly segmentation refinement for video-based point cloud compression. In: IEEE International Conference on Image Processing (ICIP), pp. 3383–3387 (2021)
16. Zhu, W., Ma, Z., Xu, Y., Li, L., Li, Z.: View-dependent dynamic point cloud compression. IEEE Trans. Circuits Syst Video Technol. **31**(2), 765–781 (2021)
17. Li, L., Li, Z., Liu, S., Li, H.: Efficient projected frame padding for video-based point cloud compression. IEEE Trans. Multimed. **23**, 2806–2819 (2021)
18. Li, L., Li, Z., Liu, S., Li, H.: Occupancy-map-based rate distortion optimization and partition for video-based point cloud compression. IEEE Trans. Circuits Syst. Video Technol. **31**(1), 326–338 (2021)
19. Li, L., Li, Z., Zakharchenko, V., Chen, J., Li, H.: Advanced 3D motion prediction for video-based dynamic point cloud compression. IEEE Trans. Image Process. **29**, 289–302 (2020)
20. Kim, J., Im, J., Rhyu, S., Kim, K.: 3D motion estimation and compensation method for video-based point cloud compression. IEEE Access **8**, 83538–83547 (2020)
21. Li, L., Li, Z., Liu, S., Li, H.: Rate control for video-based point cloud compression. IEEE Trans. Image Process. **29**, 6237–6250 (2020)

Event-Based Visual Sensing for Human Motion Detection and Classification at Various Distances

Fabien Colonnier(✉)(iD), Aravind Seeralan(iD), and Longwei Zhu(iD)

Institute for Infocomm Research, A*STAR, Singapore 138632, Singapore
`fabien_colonnier@i2r.a-star.edu.sg`

Abstract. In Human Research and Rescue scenarios, it is useful to be able to distinguish persons in distress from rescuers. Assuming people requiring help would wave to attract attention, human motion is thus a significant cue to identify person in needs. Therefore, in this paper, we aim at detecting and classifying human motion at different depths with low resolution. The task is fulfilled thanks to an event-based sensor and a Spiking Neural Network (SNN). The event-based sensor has been chosen as a suitable device to register motion specifically. While SNN is appropriate to process the event-based data, it is also a suitable algorithm to be implemented in low-power neuromorphic device, allowing for a longer operating time. In this study, we gather new data with similar classes to the IBM DVS Gesture dataset at various distances. We show we can achieve an accuracy up to 91.5% on a validation set obtained at different depths and lighting conditions from the training set. We also show that having an Region of Interest detection leads to better accuracy compare to a full frame model on untrained distances.

Keywords: Spiking Neural Network · Gesture Classification · Human Detection · Event-based vision

1   Introduction

Human detection is a first required effort in many cases, such as crowd counting [33], social robot interaction [28,32] and also research and rescue scenario [21]. In this last case, adding gesture recognition could help to discriminate person in needs to the rescue teams. In a Human interaction case, it could also be useful for the robot to understand human gesture to respond appropriately, a road officer might indicate to change course or an elderly person might do a gesture to make the robot move out of the path. In all these examples, being able to distinguish motion patterns at various distances would be helpful.

Human detection and tracking with RGB camera is a well known problem [9], with several detection solutions from template matching [19] to deep learning

This research was supported by Programmatic grant no. A1687b0033 from the Singapore governments Research, Innovation and Enterprise 2020 plan (Advanced Manufacturing and Engineering domain).

© Springer Nature Switzerland AG 2023
H. Wang et al. (Eds.): PSIVT 2022, LNCS 13763, pp. 75–88, 2023.
https://doi.org/10.1007/978-3-031-26431-3_7

method with YOLO architecture [17,24]. Human pose detection and tracking could be a first step to understand the meaning of the sequential poses made. Deep learning methods manage to identify body poses reliably even from a 2D image [36]. But action recognition has also been attempted with some successes. [28] *et al.* exploited the joint localization from the kinect sensor (which provides RGBD images [35]) to classify gesture with an Hidden Markov Model. Controlling gestures have been well classified using a 3D-Convolutional Neural Net and LSTM (Long Short-Term Memory) for data recording in front of a laptop [20,31]. Pigou *et al.* used a Residual Network (ResNet) architecture to tackle Gesture and Sign Language recognition from RGB images [26]. It is interesting to notice that the approach chosen computed the image difference as input of the classifier.

Indeed, event-based visual sensors or Neuromorphic Visual Sensors (NVS) provides direct information about the variation in light intensity at the pixel level [13]. Each pixel is endowed with its own circuit and triggers events when the change in light intensity crosses a threshold, ON or OFF when it increases or decreases, respectively. As these sensors respond to a variation of light or motion in their Field Of View (FOV), they are very well suited to provide motion information. Thus, several datasets for gesture recognition have already been created. One can mention the DVS Gesture dataset [4], the ASL-DVS for sign language recognition [5] or even DHP19 dataset for 3D human pose estimation [7].

In all these works, the distance to the subject is always relatively short to the sensor, either frame-based or event-based sensors. Thus, in this study, we investigate the robustness of gesture classification at different ranges.

Even if more and more sensors with higher resolutions are available commercially and should be preferred to help in increasing the range of detection, it should be noticed that the low resolution problem would still remain as farther the distance, fewer pixels are producing events. Thus, having a system robust to the distance to the subject would still be beneficial in the future.

1.1 Contribution

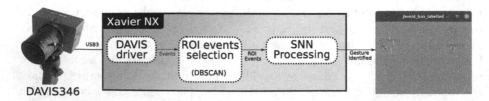

Fig. 1. Event-based visual processing with event clustering and gesture classification thanks to a Spiking Neural Network

As a proof of concept, we investigate the use of neuromorphic sensing and processing to solve this problem. Indeed, it seems appropriate to use Spiking Neural

Network (SNN) which are working well with time related features and could be made energy efficient with the use of appropriate hardware [3,4,10]. Event-based sensing is also indicated as input for SNN as the events are a kind of spike, which avoid a signal to spike conversion. It is also very suitable for unattended sensor as it is energy efficient.

Our main contributions can be summed up as follows:

- A dataset creation for Gesture recognition at different depths.
- A study of the most reliable CNN architecture for gesture classification.
- A gesture classification framework 1 for multiple human subjects for application with low-power consumption with a 3D DBSCAN as an attention mechanism [12].

1.2 Related Work

Hand pose estimation from event-based sensor has also been addressed [27]. In this study, a simulator and a dataset of hand moving close to the sensor are created. A standard ResNet-18 architecture is trained on synthetic data to regress the hand pose. Bi *et al.* used also a conventional CNN architecture to perform sign language recognition from event-based sensor [5].

Other datasets have been created to tackle the gesture recognition problem using only visual inputs [4]. Recently, mixing visual input with EMG data has been shown to improve the classification accuracy [8]. These previous studies developed SNN solutions to classify the gestures with even hardware implementation on either IBM TrueNorth [3] or Intel Loihi [10]. Indeed, even if some specific computing device enhanced Neural network computation like the Movidius Myriad products [2] and could already reduce the energy consumption, it is still believed that neuromorphic solutions could achieve even lower power consumption [6]. The DVS Gesture dataset was also used to perform transfer learning efficiently [30]. Unsupervised learning have also shown good results in Gesture classification but not equivalent to state-of-the art yet [34]. So far in these studies, the distance to the subject has not being addressed. Only Kaiser *et al.* used a detection mechanism with an constant size ROI to improve robustness of fully connected model toward translation [16].

Detection and tracking with NVS sensors has been an fruitful area of study. In the early works, human tracking is performed with some robustness toward occlusion thanks to a Gaussian Mixture Models [25]. Hinz *et al.* used a DBSCAN (Density-Based Spatial Clustering of Applications with Noise) method and Mean-shift to perform multi-object tracking, applied to cars in their work [15], whereas Mondal *et al.* showed that a k-means clustering with an optimization on the k value could achieve better accuracy [23]. Motion segmentation could also help in identifying moving objects [22,37], but more efforts needs to be done to adapt these algorithm into a gesture recognition framework. Indeed, some limitation might arise targeting deformable objects.

2   Methods

2.1   Dataset

Acquisition. The dataset presented here can be considered as an extension of the IBM DVS Gesture [4] as the same classes have been recorded. This choice was made to evaluate if by adding multiple depth, similar accuracy could be reached to the initial dataset. Moreover, it could later be used in transfer learning applications. As a reminder, Table 1 displays the 11 classes that can be found in the initial DVS Gesture and this dataset.

The dataset records the 11 gestures from 4 subjects at 7 different locations (see Fig. 2). Each gesture is recorded during around 24 s and split into 4 samples of 6 s, 3 for training and 1 for testing. Later, a validation set is recorded in a similar fashion with 4 subjects, but with different locations and background.

As the resolution is a determining factor for recognition, given a focal length, the DAVIS346 was preferred to record the data compared to the DVS128 [18] used in the IBM DVS Gesture dataset. Thus increasing the possible range of the recordings. In this experiment, a lens of 4 mm focal length and the distance of the subjects from the sensor ranged from 2.40 m up to 8.20 m, under lighting from 110 to 250lux.

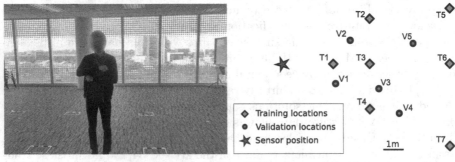

(a) Dataset acquisition environment   (b) Locations of the dataset recordings

Fig. 2. Description of the dataset environment and locations. The training and testing are marked as T_i whereas validation samples V_i.

Table 1 shows that the event rate is relatively well correlated with the distance. It is not surprising as the subject covers a larger FOV (Field Of View) at short distance which leads to more pixels triggering events. It can also be noticed that at farther distance the contrast needs to be slightly higher to trigger an event as the background lighting will reduce the perceived contrast.

Training Samples. As only one subject is present in front of a static background in each recording, the samples were cropped and resized to a 32×32 window. The cropping was performed after a noise filtering with a Near-Neighbor

Table 1. Event rate in $kevts/s$ for the various depths and classes (StD stands for standard deviation)

Classes	Depth			average	StD
	248 cm	425 cm	820 cm		
clap	12.9	9.2	5.8	9.3	3.6
right wave	20.5	11.1	5.8	12.5	7.5
left wave	20.3	10.9	5.7	12.3	7.4
right cw	28.3	14.7	6.5	16.5	11.1
right ccw	32.2	15.2	6.3	17.9	13.1
left cw	33.9	13.8	6.2	17.9	14.3
left ccw	33.6	14.1	6.3	18.0	14.1
arm roll	13.9	9.1	5.7	9.6	4.2
air drum	15.3	9.1	5.6	10.0	4.9
air guitar	13.8	9.2	5.6	9.5	4.1
random	50.3	16.9	7.2	24.8	22.6
average	25.0	12.1	6.0		
StD	11.8	2.9	0.5		

filter, which means that all the events with no events triggered in a one pixel neighborhood during a short period of times are removed. Then, an histogram is computed by summing the number of events per row and per column over the full sample time. A threshold is applied to select the most active part of the frame. The events are then projected on a 32×32 input size frame and used as input for the SNN. This detection method is used as a baseline as it yields good results on the one-subject samples. However, it cannot be used in the case of multiple subjects or moving sensors.

2.2 Network Architecture and Training Method

The SNN was trained using SLAYER [29]. The architecture used was kept simple to allow a potential implementation on an embedded neuromorphic chip. The selected architecture is composed of 2 Convolution layers and 2 fully connected layers followed by a 2-layer classifier.

A model with full frame with similar architecture was also trained as reference. Neuron model is the basic unit which accumulates and transmits the information by its membrane potential voltage and spikes. Over the time, the neuron itself maintains an internal voltage and will emit a spike when the threshold is reached. Two different type of neuron model were utilized in this paper. The first one followed the Spike Response Model (SRM), which is one of the most versatile and simplest neuron model and can be described as follows:

$$u_i^l(t) = \sum_j (W_{ij}^{l-1}(\epsilon * s_j^{l-1})(t) + (\nu * s_j^l)(t)) \tag{1}$$

where the membrane potential $u_i^l(t)$ in neuron i within layer l at time t, updating by the incoming spikes s_j^{l-1}. The SRM kernel and refractory kernel described by $\epsilon(t)$ and $\nu(t)$ are both an alpha potential function α [14] as below:

$$\alpha(t) = \frac{t}{\tau} e^{-\tau t} \tag{2}$$

Considering the computational limitation of the edge computing devices, an even simpler Leaky Integrate and Fire (LIF) neuron model is introduced. The ϵ kernel is replaced by an exponential decay, whereas the refractory one is removed and the membrane potential is put to zero after each spike. The exponential decay function used here is more computationally friendly as it can be computed using a bit shift of the membrane potential.

The parameters used during the training are shown in Table 2.

Table 2. The parameters for both neuron models

Neuron model	τ_ϵ	τ_ν	threshold
SRM	10	5	5
LIF	17.2	$\emptyset$	10

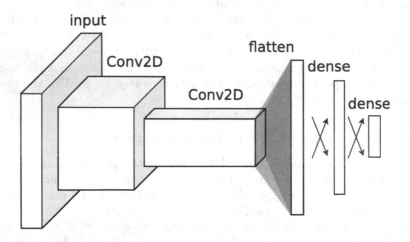

Fig. 3. Architecture of the Spiking Neural Network

In this paper, we investigate 4 slightly different models with various complexity. The common architecture is displayed in Fig. 3 which shows the input layer followed by two 2D convolution layers and two dense layers.

Table 3 reports the details of each architectures. The first model takes the full frame as input and reduced the input size thanks to a max pooling layer before applying the sets of 2D convolution and max pooling and dense layers. The second model is using an attention mechanism to get an input frame size of 32×32 which reduced the number of parameters overall while focusing on the Region-of-Interest. The third model is identical with the previous one but uses the simplified LIF neuron model. Finally, the fourth one is using a stride 2 for each convolution layer removing the max pooling layer.

All the models were trained with the NADAM optimizer [11] with a learning rate of 0.002 for the models using the SRM neuron model and 0.001 using the LIF one.

Table 3. Model descriptions and parameters count. The architecture is described using Xp for an XxX max pooling layer, YcZ for a convolution layer with Y kernels and ZxZ kernel size and then the number of neurons is indicated for the fully connected layers

Models	neuron type	input size	architecture	Number of parameters
1	SRM	$346 \times 260 \times 2$	4p-16c5s1-2p-32c3s1-2p-flat-512-11	5516635
2	SRM	$32 \times 32 \times 2$	16c5s1-2p-32c3s1-2p-flat-512-11	1060187
3	LIF	$32 \times 32 \times 2$	16c5s1-2p-32c3s1-2p-flat-512-11	1060187
4	LIF	$32 \times 32 \times 2$	16c5s2-32c3s2-flat-512-11	1060187

2.3 Detection Algorithm Using a Density-Based Algorithm

A standard solution to get the position of an object over time in the FOV is to perform detection and tracking. It is the way to achieve efficient tracking of an identified object. However, in the case of gesture classification, the goal is to get the relative position of the hand and arm over time. In order to replicate training situation, the ROI size and position would ideally not move during the time of the sample.

In this work, a static sensor is used thus only moving objects are triggering events in the Field Of View (FOV). In the case of non-overlapping objects, the detection could be easily done by clustering the events. The strategy used is to accumulate events in a constant time-window and perform a Density based clustering with the DBSCAN algorithm [12]. The events are converted in a 3D point cloud with x-pixel, y-pixel and event time as the dimension. The time is scaled to provide a relative distance relevant to the spatial dimensions. Figure 4 displays the clustering results and the box extraction performed on events input. The boxes are obtained by overlapping the clusters on a 2D frame. The advantage of performing the clustering on 3D data is the integrated noise filtering in the process; no special care is required except correct parameter selection.

This simple clustering method is used as a computationally lightweight with its $\mathcal{O}(n \log n)$ complexity. Thus, using the SNN doing the recognition task taking advantage of an energy efficient hardware.

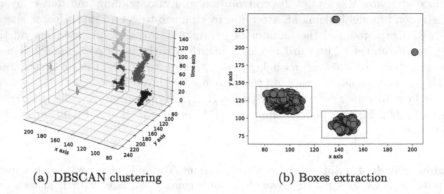

(a) DBSCAN clustering   (b) Boxes extraction

Fig. 4. Detection processing with events. Figure (a) shows the output of the clustering on an example with 2 subjects performing arm roll and right hand counter clockwise motions. The time axis is scaled up 50 times. Figure (b) reports the projected clusters on a 2D frame with the box extraction for each motion.

However, this solution introduced some forms of latency as the events need to be accumulated over a period of time before being processed. Another obvious drawback is the ROI detection will not be able to differentiate overlapping subjects over time. A proper tracking algorithm could help with this issue, as it has been shown in [1], but might fail due to the large shape variations over time, especially for the rotating arm classes.

3 Experimental Results

3.1 Classification Accuracy

Figure 5 reports the loss and the accuracy evolution during the training. It shows that the full frame model is actually overfitting as the maximum training accuracy reaches close to 100% but only 93.2% accuracy was achieved on the testing set. The attention here proved to be useful to reduce the number of parameters and the overall size of the network in order to be more hardware friendly. Compared to full frame input, the accuracy on the testing set is slightly lower with the same SRM neuron model, but is higher with the LIF one. Training with an attention mechanism using a constant ROI size has already been attempted to introduce robustness in translation without using convolution layer [16]. As here, we are resizing the input, it might help keep a similar scale relative to the distance, even if the event rate is significantly different (see Table 1).

The final training and testing accuracies are reported in Table 4, alongside with the validation one. The full frame model does not generalize well to the new locations recording whereas the other ones do. It should be also noticed that the accuracy is on par with the 91.77% in [4] and close to the 93.64% reported for the initial DVS Gesture in [29] while using an 8-layer fully connected architecture.

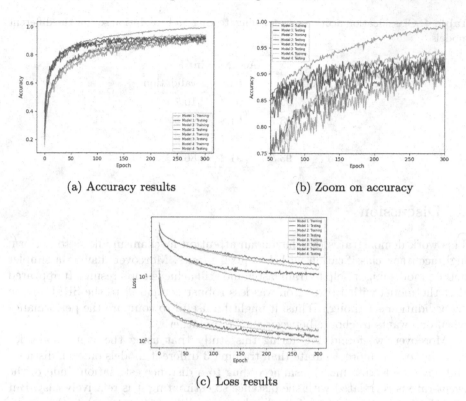

(a) Accuracy results (b) Zoom on accuracy

(c) Loss results

Fig. 5. Training and testing results for the 4 models presented in Table 3, according to the training epochs

It shows it is possible to train a network and achieve similar accuracy to close distance recordings.

3.2 Detection on Multiple Targets

In order to test the detection as well as the classification, another set of data with different light conditions and multiple targets was recorded. Figure 6 displays some examples and more recordings are provided in the video as supplementary data. The lighting environment was between 190 and 370Lux. It can be seen that the bounding box is not always covering all the events triggered by the human subject (see Fig. 6a in particular). However, the SNN is still able to classify the gesture correctly. An attempt was made with moving subject still performing the motion. It still can recognize the gesture but the misclassification occurrences are non-negligible (see video as supplementary data).

For this test, the SNN used was the model 2 as it showed the most robustness on the validation set. The algorithm was implemented on a Jetson Xavier NX. The computation time of the SNN was about $0.58s \pm 0.11StD$ per inference, which is around 2.56 times faster than real-time.

Table 4. Classification accuracy on training, testing and validation set for the different models

| | Accuracy in % | | |
Model	training	testing	validation
1	99.4	93.2	10.7
2	93.7	91.8	91.5
3	94.8	93.7	89.8
4	93.5	91.2	86.4

4   Discussion

This work demonstrates that having an attention mechanism allows to perform high accuracy classification with less pixel inputs. Moreover, having a simpler neuron model might help to train faster and still achieve good results. It appeared that the model with LIF neuron was less robust compared to the SRM one on the validation set though. Thus, it might be useful to compare the performance when one wants to choose between one or the other.

Moreover, we found out during this study that using the same model for each distance is more accurate than training 3 different models on each distance and have a selection mechanism according to a distance estimation. Indeed, the event-rate is correlated with the distance so estimating it is relatively easy. But as each models are more specialised, it becomes difficult to interpolate the results in between trained distances which leads to inaccurate classification.

To perform gesture classification, it is assumed that the ROI size and position need to be constant throughout the gesture acquisition. The solution found here is to accumulate events and provide them at regular intervals. These intervals should be large enough to enable a correct classification (1.5 s in this study). This induces a large latency as the SNN cannot process the data before the accumulation is completed in order to have this constant ROI.

A constant window could be the solution assuming the subject does not move too much. The classifier needs to be robust to cropping in case the subject moves out of the predefined area. It can be argued that providing a relative point of reference during the acquisition of the sample could help the SNN to relatively assess the position of the new events. But adding this information in a spike form is not trivial and might lead to a larger Network and more events to be generated, potentially increasing the power consumption.

It could be interesting to resize the input of the DVS Gesture dataset and see if the same accuracy is achieved. This investigation could lead the way to perform data augmentation and achieve similar results while avoiding data recordings.

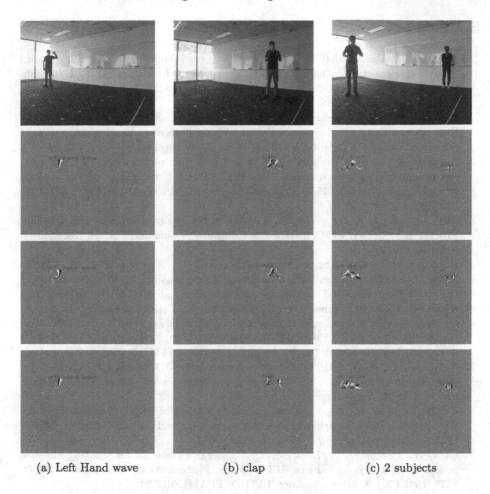

(a) Left Hand wave   (b) clap   (c) 2 subjects

Fig. 6. Target detection with DBSCAN method and classification

5   Conclusion

In this study, we show that detecting a specific gesture could be done efficiently with a neuromorphic solution and full event-based processing. Having an attention mechanism helps to cope with the various distance of the subject.

In a later work, we aim to achieve similar gesture classification on a mobile platform with a lower latency. The objective would be to use a neuromorphic hardware to achieve low-power consumption on such a task. It would demonstrate the possibility of robot-human interaction such as gesture control with neuromorphic solution.

Acknowledgment. The authors would like to thank Austin Lai Weng Mun for his help in the dataset collection.

References

1. Acharya, J., et al.: EBBIOT: a low-complexity tracking algorithm for surveillance in IoVT using stationary neuromorphic vision sensors. In: 2019 32nd IEEE International System-on-Chip Conference (SOCC), pp. 318–323 (2019). https://doi.org/10.1109/SOCC46988.2019.1570553690

2. Agarwal, S., Hervas-Martin, E., Byrne, J., Dunne, A., Luis Espinosa-Aranda, J., Rijlaarsdam, D.: An evaluation of low-cost vision processors for efficient star identification. Sensors **20**(21), 6250 (2020). https://doi.org/10.3390/s20216250

3. Akopyan, F., et al.: TrueNorth: design and tool flow of a 65 mw 1 million neuron programmable neurosynaptic chip. IEEE Trans. Comput. Aided Des. Integr. Circuits Syst. **34**(10), 1537–1557 (2015). https://doi.org/10.1109/TCAD.2015.2474396

4. Amir, A., et al.: A low power, fully event-based gesture recognition system. In: Proceedings of the IEEE Conference on Computer Vision and Pattern Recognition (CVPR) (2017)

5. Bi, Y., Chadha, A., Abbas, A., Bourtsoulatze, E., Andreopoulos, Y.: Graph-based object classification for neuromorphic vision sensing. In: Proceedings of the IEEE/CVF International Conference on Computer Vision (ICCV) (2019)

6. Blouw, P., Choo, X., Hunsberger, E., Eliasmith, C.: Benchmarking keyword spotting efficiency on neuromorphic hardware. In: Proceedings of the 7th Annual Neuro-Inspired Computational Elements Workshop. NICE 2019, Association for Computing Machinery, New York (2019). https://doi.org/10.1145/3320288.3320304

7. Calabrese, E., et al.: DHP19: dynamic vision sensor 3D human pose dataset. In: Proceedings of the IEEE/CVF Conference on Computer Vision and Pattern Recognition (CVPR) Workshops (2019)

8. Ceolini, E., et al.: Hand-gesture recognition based on EMG and event-based camera sensor fusion: a benchmark in neuromorphic computing. Frontiers Neurosci. **14**, 637 (2020). https://doi.org/10.3389/fnins.2020.00637

9. Choi, W., Pantofaru, C., Savarese, S.: A general framework for tracking multiple people from a moving camera. IEEE Trans. Pattern Anal. Mach. Intell. **35**(7), 1577–1591 (2013). https://doi.org/10.1109/TPAMI.2012.248

10. Davies, M., et al.: Loihi: a neuromorphic manycore processor with on-chip learning. IEEE Micro **38**(1), 82–99 (2018). https://doi.org/10.1109/MM.2018.112130359

11. Dozat, T.: Incorporating Nesterov momentum into Adam. In: ICLR Workshop (2016)

12. Ester, M., Kriegel, H.P., Sander, J., Xu, X.: A density-based algorithm for discovering clusters in large spatial databases with noise. In: Proceedings of the Second International Conference on Knowledge Discovery and Data Mining, pp. 226–231. KDD 1996, AAAI Press (1996)

13. Gallego, G., et al.: Event-based vision: a survey. IEEE Trans. Pattern Anal. Mach. Intell. **44**(1), 154–180 (2022). https://doi.org/10.1109/TPAMI.2020.3008413

14. Gerstner, W.: Chapter 12 a framework for spiking neuron models: the spike response model. In: Moss, F., Gielen, S. (eds.) Neuro-Informatics and Neural Modelling, Handbook of Biological Physics, vol. 4, pp. 469–516. North-Holland (2001). https://doi.org/10.1016/S1383-8121(01)80015-4

15. Hinz, G., et al.: Online multi-object tracking-by-clustering for intelligent transportation system with neuromorphic vision sensor. In: Kern-Isberner, G., Fürnkranz, J., Thimm, M. (eds.) KI 2017. LNCS (LNAI), vol. 10505, pp. 142–154. Springer, Cham (2017). https://doi.org/10.1007/978-3-319-67190-1_11

16. Kaiser, J., et al.: Embodied neuromorphic vision with continuous random back-propagation. In: 2020 8th IEEE RAS/EMBS International Conference for Biomedical Robotics and Biomechatronics (BioRob), pp. 1202–1209 (2020). https://doi.org/10.1109/BioRob49111.2020.9224330
17. Lan, W., Dang, J., Wang, Y., Wang, S.: Pedestrian detection based on yolo network model. In: 2018 IEEE International Conference on Mechatronics and Automation (ICMA), pp. 1547–1551 (2018). https://doi.org/10.1109/ICMA.2018.8484698
18. Lichtsteiner, P., Posch, C., Delbruck, T.: A 128×128 120 db 15 μs latency asynchronous temporal contrast vision sensor. IEEE J. Solid-State Circ. **43**(2), 566–576 (2008). https://doi.org/10.1109/JSSC.2007.914337
19. Lin, Z., Davis, L.S.: Shape-based human detection and segmentation via hierarchical part-template matching. IEEE Trans. Pattern Anal. Mach. Intell. **32**(4), 604–618 (2010). https://doi.org/10.1109/TPAMI.2009.204
20. Liu, Y., et al.: Dynamic gesture recognition algorithm based on 3D convolutional neural network. Computational Intelligence and Neuroscience 2021(4828102) (2021). https://doi.org/10.1155/2021/4828102
21. Lygouras, E., Santavas, N., Taitzoglou, A., Tarchanidis, K., Mitropoulos, A., Gasteratos, A.: Unsupervised human detection with an embedded vision system on a fully autonomous UAV for search and rescue operations. Sensors **19**(16), 3542 (2019). https://doi.org/10.3390/s19163542
22. Mitrokhin, A., Fermüller, C., Parameshwara, C., Aloimonos, Y.: Event-based moving object detection and tracking. In: 2018 IEEE/RSJ International Conference on Intelligent Robots and Systems (IROS), pp. 1–9 (2018). https://doi.org/10.1109/IROS.2018.8593805
23. Mondal, A., Das, M.: Moving object detection for event-based vision using k-means clustering. In: 2021 IEEE 8th Uttar Pradesh Section International Conference on Electrical, Electronics and Computer Engineering (UPCON), pp. 1–6 (2021). https://doi.org/10.1109/UPCON52273.2021.9667636
24. Nguyen, H.H., Ta, T.N., Nguyen, N.C., Bui, V.T., Pham, H.M., Nguyen, D.M.: Yolo based real-time human detection for smart video surveillance at the edge. In: 2020 IEEE Eighth International Conference on Communications and Electronics (ICCE), pp. 439–444 (2021). https://doi.org/10.1109/ICCE48956.2021.9352144
25. Piatkowska, E., Belbachir, A.N., Schraml, S., Gelautz, M.: Spatiotemporal multiple persons tracking using dynamic vision sensor. In: 2012 IEEE Computer Society Conference on Computer Vision and Pattern Recognition Workshops, pp. 35–40 (2012). https://doi.org/10.1109/CVPRW.2012.6238892
26. Pigou, L., Van Herreweghe, M., Dambre, J.: Gesture and sign language recognition with temporal residual networks. In: Proceedings of the IEEE International Conference on Computer Vision (ICCV) Workshops (2017)
27. Rudnev, V., et al.: Eventhands: Real-time neural 3d hand pose estimation from an event stream. In: Proceedings of the IEEE/CVF International Conference on Computer Vision (ICCV). pp. 12385–12395 (October 2021)
28. Saha, S., Lahiri, R., Konar, A., Banerjee, B., Nagar, A.K.: HMM-based gesture recognition system using kinect sensor for improvised human-computer interaction. In: 2017 International Joint Conference on Neural Networks (IJCNN), pp. 2776–2783 (2017). https://doi.org/10.1109/IJCNN.2017.7966198
29. Shrestha, S.B., Orchard, G.: SLAYER: spike layer error reassignment in time. In: Bengio, S., Wallach, H., Larochelle, H., Grauman, K., Cesa-Bianchi, N., Garnett, R. (eds.) Advances in Neural Information Processing Systems, vol. 31, pp. 1419–1428. Curran Associates, Inc. (2018). https://papers.nips.cc/paper/7415-slayer-spike-layer-error-reassignment-in-time.pdf

30. Stewart, K., Orchard, G., Shrestha, S.B., Neftci, E.: Online few-shot gesture learning on a neuromorphic processor. IEEE J. Emerg. Sel. Top. Circ. Syst. **10**(4), 512–521 (2020). https://doi.org/10.1109/JETCAS.2020.3032058
31. Ur Rehman, M., et al.: Dynamic hand gesture recognition using 3D-CNN and LSTM networks. Comput. Mater. Continua, **70**, 4675–4690 (2021). https://doi.org/10.32604/cmc.2022.019586
32. Xu, D., Wu, X., Chen, Y.L., Xu, Y.: Online dynamic gesture recognition for human robot interaction. J. Intell. Robot. Syst. **77**(4), 604–618 (2010). https://doi.org/10.1109/TPAMI.2009.204
33. Zhang, C., Li, H., Wang, X., Yang, X.: Cross-scene crowd counting via deep convolutional neural networks. In: Proceedings of the IEEE Conference on Computer Vision and Pattern Recognition (CVPR) (2015)
34. Zhang, Y., et al.: An event-driven spatiotemporal domain adaptation method for DVS gesture recognition. IEEE Trans. Circuits Syst. II Express Briefs **69**(3), 1332–1336 (2022). https://doi.org/10.1109/TCSII.2021.3108798
35. Zhang, Z.: Microsoft kinect sensor and its effect. IEEE Multimedia **19**(2), 4–10 (2012). https://doi.org/10.1109/MMUL.2012.24
36. Zheng, C., et al.: Deep learning-based human pose estimation: a survey. CoRR abs/2012.13392 (2020). https://arxiv.org/abs/2012.13392
37. Zhou, Y., Gallego, G., Lu, X., Liu, S., Shen, S.: Event-based motion segmentation with spatio-temporal graph cuts. IEEE Trans. Neural Netw. Learn. Syst. 1–13 (2021)

On Low-Resolution Face Re-identification with High-Resolution-Mapping

Loreto Prieto[1], Sebastian Pulgar[1], Patrick Flynn[2], and Domingo Mery[1(✉)]

[1] Department of Computer Science, Pontificia Universidad Catolica de Chile, Santiago, Chile
domingo.mery@uc.cl
[2] Department of Computer Science and Engineering, University of Notre Dame, Notre Dame, IN, USA

Abstract. Low-resolution face re-identification refers to the problem of identifying if the same person's face appears in two images: one image is low resolution (LR), *e.g.*, from a surveillance camera, and the another one is high resolution (HR), *e.g.*, from a government-issued identification. Research in low-resolution face re-identification has been increasing in the past few years. It can be divided into three categories: *i)* methods upscaling the LR image to the HR space (HR-mapping), *ii)* methods employing LR and HR robust features, and *iii)* methods learning a unified space representation. In this work, we focus on face re-identification using HR-mapping because it yields better results. Our main contribution is an experimental protocol that can be used as guideline in this task. In research, protocols are often neglected and researchers that utilize previous work on their projects have to allocate a significant amount of time to replicating inadequately described methods. We use our experimental protocol as a guideline to create a set of training and testing pairs for face re-identification using dataset VGG-Face-2. In addition, we conducted 18 experiments to validate the experimental protocol. In our experiments, we measured "d-prime" (d') and the area under the ROC curve (A_z). We obtained: $d' = 1.236$ and $A_z = 0.81$ for a 14×14 LR pixel size set, $d' = 1.900$ and $A_z = 0.91$ for a 28×28 LR pixel size set and $d' = 2.787$ and $A_z = 0.97$ for a 56×56 LR pixel size set. We believe that our protocol can be very helpful for researchers in the field because it can be used as a set of guidelines for building comparable and replicable work of their own.

Keywords: Face re-identification · Face recognition · Low-resolution images

1 Introduction

Face re-identification refers to the problem of when given two face photos captured at different times and with different cameras, how to determine if they are of the same person [21]. With the current face recognition methods the task for high-resolution images scenarios can be solve with relative ease [6]. Yet within this task, there are certain scenarios in which one face is high resolution (HR) but the second face is low resolution (LR), as shown in Fig. 1. These scenarios have proven quite challenging [5,29,38] and have been referred to as Low-Resolution Person Re-Identification. One of the most common cases in LR person re-identification is a suspect lookout in security cameras.

© Springer Nature Switzerland AG 2023
H. Wang et al. (Eds.): PSIVT 2022, LNCS 13763, pp. 89–102, 2023.
https://doi.org/10.1007/978-3-031-26431-3_8

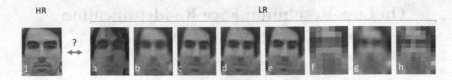

Fig. 1. Low resolution face re-identification task: Is person 1, at the left, present in the right array a–h, or he is missing?. In this example, all pictures belong to the same person.

Both private and public sectors have a big interest in this topic, especially when there are not enough security personnel. Surveillance cameras constantly capture face images of subjects which tend to be low resolution, as the cameras cover a wide area rather than a specific point, and present changes in pose and light.

This work defines a protocol for the methods and for the datasets preparation for person re-identification in low-resolution settings. An experimental protocol consists of agreed-upon guidelines for a type of experiment. Protocols are enablers to building the necessary collaborative work. In complex experiments, such as low-resolution face recognition, collaboration and comparison are mandatory for proving a hypothesis. Protocols are often relegated as they are partly not considered important enough [32]. This negligence then falls on the researchers themselves who tried to utilize previous works for their projects only to find methods are inadequately described, or worse, don't work at all. Protocols seek to address this shortcoming. Thus, our contributions are fourfold: *i)* We defined a realistic dataset with low-resolution images using training, validation, and testing sets. *ii)* We tested several open-source computer vision algorithms for this task. *iii)* We designed and trained new computer vision models for this task. *iv)* We defined an evaluation protocol to compare these algorithms.

In our work, 18 experiments have been conducted to validate the proposed protocol. In several of these experiments, we have used two novel methods as components, build with GAN and Siamese networks techniques. In particular, we trained a set of GANs networks to up-scale the images from 14×14, 28×28, and 56×56 pixels to 112×112 pixels and a Siamese network for the face matching. For each experiment, we evaluated their performance as specified by the protocols and compared and discussed their results.

2 Related Works

It is well known, that the accuracy of face recognition algorithms decreases when low resolution is present in at least one of the images. In the last decade, many research teams have dedicated their efforts to solving this problem (for further details see [20]). In the literature review, we observe that LR face re-identification can be divided into three main categories (see Fig. 2):

i) **HR-mapping:** It refers to methods that up-scales the low-resolution (LR) image to the high-resolution (HR) space before any comparison is done. Recent works combine several novel techniques to achieve this task [5,18,21,22,34].
ii) **LR & HR robust features:** Several robust face feature can be obtained for a high resolution face [6,30]. Recent works have focused in calculating LR robust face fea-

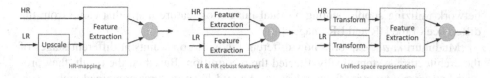

Fig. 2. Low resolution face re-identification approaches.

tures, these are generally handcrafted and based in texture or color. Some examples are [24,38].

iii) **Unified space representation:** Methods in this category focused on learning from both the HR and LR images. Afterwards, the images are projected into the learned space and similarity is measure with the projections. Both linear and non-linear spaces can be used. Some examples are [1, 10, 44, 48].

Up-scaling LR images introduces more data on the pixel level which should aid the recognition rate. However, it risks adding artifacts to the image which can affect recognition rate. For recognition purposes, using up-scaling usually return better results than comparing the LR and HR images directly.

For face super-resolution, several models using deep learning methods have surpassed works with handcrafted solutions. Wang *et al.*, question whether large-capacity and data-driven methods have outperformed handcrafted work by proposing an end-to-end CNN based sparse modeling method that achieved better performance by employing a cascade of super-resolution convolutional nets (CSCN) trained for small scaling factors [43].

In other works, Jiang *et al.*, were able to alleviate the noise effect during up-scaling by proposing a CNN to learn the denoiser prior, which is then plugged into a model-based optimization to jointly benefit the merits of model-based optimization and discriminative inference, as well as proposing an improved patch-based method which leverages contextual information to develop a more robust and efficient context-patch face hallucination algorithm [13–15].

Traditional image up-scaling methods treat image noise on a pixel level without considering the whole image structure. Lu *et al.*, propose a unified framework for representation-based face super-resolution by introducing a locality-constrained low-rank representation scheme [23].

Jia *et al.*, propose a recognition oriented feature hallucination method to map the features of a LR facial image to its High Resolution (HR) version [12]. They extract PCA features from both images and then applied CCA to establish the coherent subspaces between both PCA features. Then employ a recognition rate guided prediction model with adaptative Piecewise Kernel Partial Least Squares to map the LR feature to the HR version. Finally, a weighted combination of the hallucinated PCA features and the Local Binary Pattern Histogram (LBPH) features are adopted for face recognition.

Conventional super-resolution methods rely heavily on alignment of the face and in low-resolution unconstrained environments have a diverse range of poses and expressions. Yu *et al.*, proposed an end-to-end transformative discriminative neural network, employing the spatial transformation layers to devise super-resolving for unaligned and very small face images [47]. Later, they developed an attribute-embedded up-sampling network utilizing supplementing residual images or feature maps that came from the difference of the HR and LR images [46].

Mudunuri *et al.*, explored how different kinds of constraints at different stages of the architecture systematically affected the recognition. Based on the result, they proposed an inter-intra classification loss for the mid-level features combined with super-resolution loss at the low-level feature in the training procedure [26].

Cheng *et al.*, recognize super-resolution as an effective approach for low resolution person re-identification [5]. However, they note that it is limited due to dramatically more difficult gradients back-propagation during training. He proposes a model training regularisation method, called Inter-Task Association Critic, which discovers an association between image super-resolution and person re-identification adding it as an extra learning constrain.

In the last decade we have observed tremendous improvements in face re-identification. However, it is clear that face re-identification is far from perfect and still an open problem when tackling low-resolution face images. To our knowledge no protocols for low-resolution face re-identification have been published to this day. It is essential for agile research that this protocol is created and adopted so further research can encourage innovation through collaboration.

3   Proposed Protocol for HR-Mapping

We observe that HR-mapping can easily be divided into four key-components for two input images LR and HR (see Fig. 3):

① **Up-scaling:** The main goal of this component is to up-scale the image to the same resolution as the HR. This can be achieved by different methods: learning-based methods such as super-resolution [17, 19, 35, 41, 42, 49] or handcrafted algorithms (*e.g.*, bicubic interpolation, Lanczos interpolation over 8×8 neighborhood, re-sampling using pixel area relation, nearest neighbor interpolation) [3, 16].

② **Feature extraction:** Comparing pixel by pixel would be a terrible idea in many cases, especially if any pose, light or expression variation is present. There are abundant methods to extract a feature or embedding from an image. In this component the goal is to use one of these methods to get the feature vectors $\mathbf{p}$ (for the HR image) and $\mathbf{q}$ (for the up-scaled LR image). It is recommended to use a method specific for faces [6, 28, 30, 39] but it is not a restriction [9, 33, 37].

③ **Feature comparison:** Once we have two features, vectors $\mathbf{p}$ and $\mathbf{q}$, one for each image, we need a method to compare them. Calculating the distance between them is the best way to get a score, *e.g.*, Euclidean distance: $\|\mathbf{p} - \mathbf{q}\|$), or cosine distance:

Fig. 3. Proposed HR-Mapping protocol.

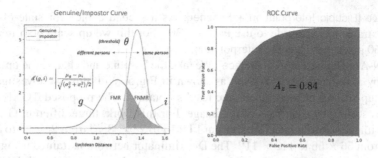

Fig. 4. Example of a genuine/impostor curve.

$\langle \mathbf{p}, \mathbf{q} \rangle / (\|\mathbf{p}\| \|\mathbf{q}\|)$ (the dot product of uninorm vectors). Now, we can setup a scoring system where a smaller value (for Euclidean distance) or larger value (for cosine distance) means a higher probability both images belong to the same person.

④ **Matching:** Once we have all the scores, we need to determine a threshold to establish when a pair of images is considered the same person. In our experiments, we use the above mentioned Euclidean distance. Thus, if the images score is lower than the threshold then we consider them of the same person. Otherwise the pair of images belongs to different people. *Genuine* and *Impostor* distributions can be used to visualize the results, an example can be observed in Fig. 4. For this, we separate the testing results into a set with all the scores belonging to genuine pairs (both faces belong to the same person, see curve g in Fig. 4) and impostors pairs (the faces belong to different people, see curve i in Fig. 4). Then we assume a normal distribution for each set and plot them. The more separate the curves are the best the algorithm. From this data we can calculate the d' value, as define in equation of Fig. 4, the large d' value, the better the performance of the biometric system. In addition, the Receiver Operation Curve (ROC) with the area under the curve (A_z) are computed. The ROC curve plots the False Match Rate (FMR, the rate at which the experiments miscategorizes a impostor pair as genuine) and False Non-Match Rate (FNMR, the rate at which the experiments miscategorizes a genuine pair as impostor) as illustrated in Fig. 4 (see more details of this metrics in [31]).

4   Methods for HR-Mapping

In this subsection, we will explain the 18 methods that we evaluated in our experiments to depict the use of the protocol. For each method we have clearly stated the algorithm used for up-scaling and feature extraction following Fig. 3. In all of them, we used the Euclidean distance. In this explanation, we use the following nomenclature: "**Method Name** [up-scaling method ① + feature extraction method ②]"

1. Bi-Arc (Baseline) [Bicubic + ArcFace]: A baseline is a minimum start-point used for comparisons. For this purposes we decide to use bicubic interpolation as an up-scaling method, as it is widely used. For feature extraction we use Arcface [6] a state-of-the-art deep network for face recognition.

2. Bi-Face [Bicubic Interpolation + Facenet]: As a second choice for state-of-the-art feature extraction, we decide to use Facenet [30]. For this we up-scale both images to 160×160 pixels with bicubic interpolation.

3. TGAN-Arc [Trained GAN + Arcface]: We take the baseline and change the up-scaling method by a Trained GAN (TGAN) as shown in Fig. 5. With this, we investigate if a different up-scaling method affects the results obtained. The proposed TGAN does a two times scaling by each pass of the image. For this work, three different GANs are trained with the same architecture: *i)* from 14×14 to 28×28, *ii)* from 28×28 to 56×56 and *iii)* from 56×56 to 112×112. The Discriminator network is trained using binary cross-entropy as a loss function. The Generator Network was trained with VGG Loss function as describe in [19].

4. TGAN-GSia [Trained GAN + GAN Trained Siamese]: In this experiment, we use the above-mentioned TGAN to upscale all the images in the three lower resolutions. Then we use this up-scaled images as test subjects for a GAN Trained Siamese. For feature extraction we build a Siamese network where the columns are based on the VGG-face Architecture [28] (see Fig. 6). The objective of this experiment is to see how neuronal networks trained specific for the task would behave. A visual representation of this method for a $(28 \times 28, 112 \times 112)$ images pair can be seen in Fig. 7.

$\rightarrow$ For the next four experiments, called 'Interpol + GTS', we designed a neuronal network for the up-scaling method with known interpolations. For each interpolation we obtained the up-scaled images for the three lower resolutions. Then we use this up-scaled images and the GAN Trained Siamese as explained above to get the features.

5. Area-GTS [Area Interpolation + GAN Trained Siamese]: It interpolates using pixel area relation is calculated as implemented by OpenCV [3].

6. Bi-GTS [Bicubic Interpolation + GAN Trained Siamese]: It interpolates on an interval using a polynomial [16] as implemented by OpenCV [3].

7. Lanc-GTS [Lanczos Interpolation + GAN Trained Siamese]: It uses Lanczos interpolation over 8×8 neighborhood as implemented by OpenCV [3].

8. NN-GTS [Nearest Neighbor Interpolation + GAN Trained Siamese]: It selects the value of the neighboring point as implemented by OpenCV [3].

$\rightarrow$ For the next four experiments, called 'Interpol + TS', we train the same Siamese architecture using the interpolation up-scaled pairs as input. This training is done separately for each of the interpolations.

9. Area-TS [Area Interpolations + Area Interpolation in Trained Siamese]: We use Area interpolation as explained in experiment 5.

10. Bi-TS [Bicubic Interpolations + Bicubic Interpolation in Trained Siamese]: We use Bicubic interpolation as explained in experiment 6.

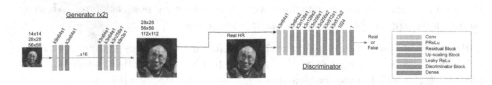

Fig. 5. Proposed GAN network (TGAN).

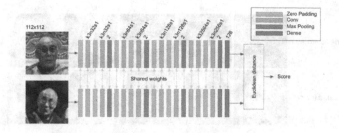

Fig. 6. Proposed Siamese network.

Fig. 7. Trained GAN + GAN Trained Siamese method for 28×28 to 112×112.

11. Lanc-TS [Lanczos Interpolations + Lanczos Interpolation in Trained Siamese]: We use Lanczos interpolation as explained in experiment 7.

12. NN-TS [Nearest Neighbor Interpolations + Nearest Neighbor Interpolation in Trained Siamese]: We use nearest neighbor interpolation as explained in experiment 8.

→ For the next six experiments, called 'GAN's', we use a known Generative Adversarial Network to upscale LR image.

13. ESRGAN-TSia [ESRGAN + Trained Siamese]: ESRGAN [41] is a neuronal network based in SRGAN with improvements in three aspects: *i)* adopting a deeper model using Residual-in-Residual Dense Block without batch normalization layers, *ii)* employing a Relativistic average GAN instead of the vanilla GAN and *iii)* modifying the perceptual loss by using the features before activation.

14. GPEN256-Arc [GPEN256 + ArcFace]: Similar to precious method, we use another GAN. GPEN [45] architecture is based on an encoder and a decodertrained with images of 256×256 pixels. We use ArcFace as feature extractor.

15. GPEN256-Arc [GPEN512 + ArcFace]: We repeat experiment 14 using GPEN trained with images of 512×512 pixels.

16. GFPGAN1-Arc [GFPGAN-v1 + ArcFace]: In this method we use another GAN. GFPGAN [40] architecture is based on an U-Net model for spacial features and a GAN. We use ArcFace as feature extractor.

17. GFPGAN2-Arc [GFPGAN-v2 + ArcFace]: We repeat experiment 16 using the improved version of GFPGAN (v2) that has been trained with more images than previous version (v1) using a pre-processing technique.

18. EGFPGAN2-Arc [ESRGAN/GFPGAN-v2 + ArcFace]: We combine both GAN's ESRGAN [41] and GFPGAN [40] for upscaling. We use ArcFace as feature extractor.

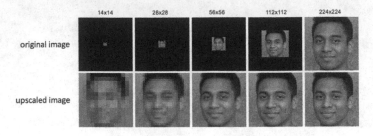

Fig. 8. Examples of face images with different sizes. It is clear how difficult is to recognize a face of 14 × 14 pixels.

5 Proposed Dataset Protocol

It is important when choosing a dataset to keep in mind: *i)* Are there enough images and subjects to train heavy models? *ii)* Are the images of reasonable quality and sharp enough? *iii)* Do the images represent the problem we are looking to solve? (*i.e.*, if we are training an algorithm to recognize people outdoors, are the images in our dataset outdoors or indoors?). *iv)* Are the images real low/high resolution or a big down-scale/upscale needed?

The first step in creating the protocol is to choose the resolutions for the dataset. For high resolution images, previous works have proposed to use for example 224 × 224 [30,36] or 112 × 112 pixels [6]. We decide to use the latter to reduce the gap between the number of pixels in the high and low resolutions.

As for low resolutions, several articles have recognized that a face with a tight bounding box smaller than 32 × 32 pixels begins to present a significant accuracy challenge to face recognition systems [2]. According to [8], 16 × 16 is very close to the minimum resolution that allows for facial recognition. For our protocol, a 14 × 14 pixels resolution is a good fit, this way the up-scaling algorithms can be set to do × 8 augmentation instead of a decimal one. We created a second low-resolution group of 28 × 28 pixels, in some datasets, it is fair to consider it a low resolution if the images have a reasonable amount of background to account for. Finally, for a third group, faces of 56 × 56 pixels are recommended since some up-scaling algorithm would do a × 2 three times instead of one augmentation of × 8. Images depicting faces in the different resolutions can be seen in Fig. 8.

If any interpolation is needed, bicubic interpolation should be used. Since inorganic information is created when up-scaling an image special care needs to be dedicated so never to do a bicubic interpolation from a lower resolution to a higher one. Also, big down-scales are not recommended since real low-resolution images have more types of challenges than just low resolution (*i.e.*, blurriness, artifact due to low-rate compression, acquisition conditions that add noise to the image) [20].

For the pair of high resolution and low-resolution images, two algorithms were done: one to create pairs between two different resolutions and a second one within the same resolution in case it is needed for experiments. The algorithms ensure that there is an equal amount of positive and negative pairs for training and that each image from the lower resolution is at least on one pair (see more details in [25]).

For pair creation between two different resolutions, we start by creating a dictionary where each key is a subject ID from the upper-resolution set and the values are the names for the images each subject has. Then, we start going over every subject in the lower resolution set and check if the subject exists in the upper-resolution set. If so, we pick a random image from this subject and save it as a positive pair. Afterward, we compute the negative pair or pairs depending if it is a training set or testing set respectively. For training, we proceed to choose a subject from the upper resolution and image of that subject randomly (the subject needs to be different from the lower resolution) and save it as a negative pair. For testing, for each subject in the upper resolution, a random image is picked and saved as a negative pair.

For pair creation within the same resolution, we also start by creating a dictionary with all the subjects and images per subject of the resolution set. Then for each subject in the dictionary, if the subject has at least two images, we iterate through all the subject images picking another random image from the subject and saving it as a positive pair. Then we compute the negative pair or pairs depending if it is training (positive and negative should have the same amount) or testing respectively. For training, a random subject and an image from that subject are picked randomly and saved as a negative pair. For testing, we iterate for each different subject in the dictionary picking a random image and saving it as a negative pair.

It should be noted that this protocol was thought for datasets with a significant amount of subjects and images per subject. So the pair lists are constructed with the use of randomly picking images and subject to avoid having an unmanageable amount of pairs. On the other hand, for big dataset computing, all the possible subjects for negative pair combinations can cause an unmanageable amount of pairs for testing. In cases like this, we recommend obtaining one negative pair for each positive pair (same as training). Afterward, we need to prove the pair set obtained is representative of the testing set, several pair sets should be obtained and observe how much the results vary with different pair sets. If the variance of the result is little to none then we can consider the pair sets representative.

New datasets are constantly being created for specific needs. We believe each dataset owner should use this protocol as a guideline for creating their pairs for training, validation and testing sets and publish them together with the dataset itself.

6 Experiments

It is very important for evaluation that we use a testing set to match the characteristics of the real world problem we are aiming to solve. In Table 1, we have made a comparison of the most common dataset that can be used for LR Face Re-identification: VGG-Face-2 [4], SCFace [7], ICB-RW [27] and LFW [11]. We can see that both ICB-RW and VGG Face have more real world characteristics. Also, VGG-Face-2 has significantly more identities but lacks an existing protocol making it harder for researchers to compare their results.

Table 1. Comparison of commonly used datasets in LR Face Re-identification.

	VGG-Face-2	SCFace	ICB-RW	LFW
Number of identities in testing set	500	130	90	697
Captured in the wild or closed set	Wild	Closed	Wild	Wild
Some low resolution	Yes	Yes	Yes	No
Within subject variance in pose	Yes	Yes	Yes	Yes
Within subject variance in age	Yes	No	No	No
Variance in lightning	Yes	No	Yes	Yes
Surveillance Quality	No	Yes	Yes	No
Publishing year	2018	2011	2015	2007
Existing protocol	No	Yes	Yes	Yes

In this section, we will explain how we applied the dataset protocol to VGG-Face-2 dataset [4]. It contains more than 9,000 identities with an average of 362 images per identity and a total of more than 3.3 million faces. VGG-face-2 images are centered on the face allowing some background to be present. It is important to know that more than half of this images have a resolution lower than 100 pixels with a significant amount under 50 pixels. All the faces are captured in the wild with variations in pose, emotions, lighting and occlusion situation.

First we noticed most of the images were not square but had enough background to crop. To keep as much of the image as possible we grabbed the difference between height and width and cropped the largest one. The difference was divided into two and then the image cropped in both sides, keeping the face centered and the image squared in the final result.

To correctly divide the images in the four resolutions ($14 \times 14, 28 \times 28, 56 \times 56$ and 112×112 pixels), we first ordered them by height and counted the amount of images under 112 pixels (a total of 490,692 for the training set and 26,371 images for the testing set). Then we divided the total number of images by three (163,564 images for training, 8.791 images for testing) and started down-scaling to the lower resolution by order ($14 \times 14, 28 \times 28, 56 \times 56$) until each set had as many as 163,564 images for training and 8,791 images for testing. Such that the smallest 163,564 images where down-scaled to 14×14 for the training set and so on. This way the minimum incorrectness in real low resolution was added as possible. Afterwards, the same number of images was picked by resolution order of a resolution higher than 112 so that this set was also composed of 163.564 images for training and 8,791 images in testing.

Pairs for the following sets matches were created ($14 \times 14, 112 \times 112$), ($28 \times 28, 112 \times 112$), ($56 \times 56, 112 \times 112$) and ($112 \times 112, 112 \times 112$). The testings pairs were created with the same method as training pairs, a random subject id different to the current one with a random image was picked for the negative pair giving the same amount of positive and negative pairs. Since this is a smaller subset of the testing pairs the pair creation was repeated several times checking for variations in results, there where only variation on the second decimal number not making any change in which

Table 2. Experiments results (three best results by resolution in bold).

Type	Exp	Name	14 × 14		28 × 28		56 × 56		Average	
			d'	A_z	d'	A_z	d'	A_z	d'	A_z
Baseline	1	Bi-Arc	0.411	0.61	0.933	0.74	1.523	0.86	0.956	0.74
Simple	2	Bi-Face	0.462	0.63	**1.900**	**0.91**	**2.787**	**0.97**	**1.716**	**0.84**
TGAN	3	TGAN-Arc	0.253	0.57	0.959	0.75	1.547	**0.87**	0.920	0.73
	4	TGAN-GSia	**1.156**	**0.79**	**1.421**	**0.84**	1.388	0.83	1.322	0.82
Interpol + GTS	5	Area-GTS	0.448	0.62	0.582	0.66	0.653	0.67	0.561	0.65
	6	Bi-GTS	0.619	0.67	0.724	0.69	0.720	0.69	0.688	0.68
	7	Lanc-GTS	0.613	0.67	0.704	0.69	0.708	0.69	0.675	0.68
	8	NN-GTS	0.448	0.62	0.582	0.66	0.653	0.67	0.561	0.65
Interpol + TS	9	Area-TS	**1.202**	**0.80**	1.400	0.84	1.420	0.84	**1.341**	**0.83**
	10	Bi-TS	1.041	0.76	1.373	0.83	1.424	0.84	1.279	0.81
	11	Lanc-TS	1.007	0.76	1.371	0.83	1.426	0.84	1.268	0.81
	12	NN-TS	**1.236**	**0.81**	1.416	**0.84**	1.449	0.84	**1.367**	**0.83**
GAN's	13	ESRGAN-TSia	0.514	0.64	0.894	0.73	1.106	0.78	0.838	0.72
	14	GPEN256-Arc	0.310	0.57	0.973	0.76	1.460	0.76	0.914	0.70
	15	GPEN512-Arc	0.261	0.54	1.121	0.74	1.632	0.79	1.005	0.69
	16	GFPGAN1-Arc	0.232	0.54	0.945	0.71	1.553	0.84	0.910	0.70
	17	GFPGAN2-Arc	0.203	0.53	0.951	0.72	**1.603**	0.85	0.919	0.70
	18	EGFPGAN2-Arc	0.213	0.53	**1.453**	**0.84**	**1.763**	**0.88**	1.143	0.75

experiment was better or worse. We call the created dataset VGG-Face-2LR, and it can be downloaded from our website.[1]

We conducted the 18 experiments explained in Sect. 4. The results are summarized in Table 2. Some conclusions can extracted from this results: *i)* As seen from experiments with interpolations (Experiments Interpol + GTS and Interpol + TS) it is best for the Siamese network (second group) to be trained by the same up-scaling algorithms. *ii)* It is a known fact that training neuronal networks can be quiet time and resources consuming. Adding to this the performance the experiments Interpol + TS had, it is possible to say that interpolations offer a good solution when resources are scarce. *iii)* For the 56 × 56 pixels we can see that feature extraction models trained for higher resolution tend to work better than those train with lower resolutions. *iv)* As future work, a pre-trained GAN network could be added to the feature extraction network and trained as one whole model. It is our intuition that this will create images that do not visually correct but maximize the classification, hence removing a limitation that the current TGAN-GSia model has. It should be noted that such model would not belong to the HR-mapping category but the unified space representation, since we are not trying to up-scale the image but to obtain a feature for each image in a unified space.

---

[1] See https://domingomery.ing.puc.cl/material/.

7 Conclusions

Over the past years we have witnessed remarkable advancement in face recognition. With some applications that were once considered science-fiction. It is clear that there is still more work to be done with low resolution images, especially in low resolution face re-identification whether it is done by humans or machines. In this work, the attempt was to establish a useful protocol that could aid the advancement in this field. Protocols do not place a burden on research, but rather are a agreed set of guidelines for writing understandable work that can be used by other researchers. Protocols are the stepping stone for reproducibility, the difference between science and a simple opinion.

We have detailed the first protocol for HR-mapping and a dataset protocol for face re-identification. To validate these protocols we have used them as a guideline to create a set of training and testing pairs for face re-identification using VGG-face-2 dataset. We have also put together 18 experiments to validate the experimental protocol. Obtaining a $d' = 1.236$ and $A_z = 0.81$ for a 14×14 LR pixel size set, $d' = 1.900$ and $A_z = 0.91$ for a 28×28 LR pixel size set and $d' = 2.787$ and $A_z = 0.97$ for a 56×56 LR pixel size set, surpassing the baseline.

We hope that these protocols serve a basis for future researchers as they build their own research, making it comparable and replicable. As future work, protocols for the other categories (LR and HR robust features and Unified space representation) can be created, further standardizing the research in this field. It should be noted that the same dataset protocol could be used, making the comparison between categories seamless and consistent.

Acknowledgments. This work was supported by National Center for Artificial Intelligence CENIA FB210017, Basal ANID.

References

1. Al-Maadeed, S., Bourif, M., Bouridane, A., Jiang, R.: Low-quality facial biometric verification via dictionary-based random pooling. Pattern Recogn. **52**, 238–248 (2016)
2. Boom, B., Beumer, G., Spreeuwers, L.J., Veldhuis, R.N.: The effect of image resolution on the performance of a face recognition system. In: 2006 9th International Conference on Control, Automation, Robotics and Vision, pp. 1–6. IEEE (2006)
3. Bradski, G.: The OpenCV library. Dr. Dobb's J. Softw. Tools (2000)
4. Cao, Q., Shen, L., Xie, W., Parkhi, O.M., Zisserman, A.: VGGFace2: a dataset for recognising faces across pose and age. In: International Conference on Automatic Face and Gesture Recognition (2018)
5. Cheng, Z., Dong, Q., Gong, S., Zhu, X.: Inter-task association critic for cross-resolution person re-identification. In: Proceedings of the IEEE/CVF Conference on Computer Vision and Pattern Recognition, pp. 2605–2615 (2020)
6. Deng, J., Guo, J., Niannan, X., Zafeiriou, S.: ArcFace: additive angular margin loss for deep face recognition. In: CVPR (2019)
7. Grgic, M., Delac, K., Grgic, S.: SCface-surveillance cameras face database. Multimed. Tools Appl. **51**(3), 863–879 (2011)
8. Harmon, L.D.: The recognition of faces. Sci. Am. **229**(5), 70–83 (1973)
9. He, K., Zhang, X., Ren, S., Sun, J.: Deep residual learning for image recognition. In: Proceedings of the IEEE Conference on Computer Vision and Pattern Recognition, pp. 770–778 (2016)

10. Heinsohn, D., Villalobos, E., Prieto, L., Mery, D.: Face recognition in low-quality images using adaptive sparse representations. Image Vis. Comput. **85**, 46–58 (2019)
11. Huang, G.B., Mattar, M., Berg, T., Learned-Miller, E.: Labeled faces in the wild: a database for studying face recognition in unconstrained environments. In: Workshop on Faces in 'Real-Life' Images: Detection, Alignment, and Recognition (2008)
12. Jia, G., Li, X., Zhuo, L., Liu, L.: Recognition oriented feature hallucination for low resolution face images. In: Chen, E., Gong, Y., Tie, Y. (eds.) PCM 2016. LNCS, vol. 9917, pp. 275–284. Springer, Cham (2016). https://doi.org/10.1007/978-3-319-48896-7_27
13. Jiang, J., Ma, J., Chen, C., Wang, Z.: Noise robust face image super-resolution through smooth sparse representation. IEEE Trans. Cybern. **47**(11), 3991–4002 (2016)
14. Jiang, J., Yu, Y., Hu, J., Tang, S., Ma, J.: Deep CNN denoiser and multi-layer neighbor component embedding for face hallucination. arXiv preprint arXiv:1806.10726 (2018)
15. Jiang, J., Yu, Y., Tang, S., Ma, J., Qi, G.J., Aizawa, A.: Context-patch based face hallucination via thresholding locality-constrained representation and reproducing learning. In: 2017 IEEE International Conference on Multimedia and Expo (ICME), pp. 469–474. IEEE (2017)
16. Keys, R.: Cubic convolution interpolation for digital image processing. IEEE Trans. Acoust. Speech Signal Process. **29**(6), 1153–1160 (1981)
17. Kim, D., Kim, M., Kwon, G., Kim, D.S.: Progressive face super-resolution via attention to facial landmark. arXiv preprint arXiv:1908.08239 (2019)
18. Kim, M., Jain, A.K., Liu, X.: AdaFace: quality adaptive margin for face recognition. In: Proceedings of the IEEE/CVF Conference on Computer Vision and Pattern Recognition (CVPR), pp. 18750–18759 (2022)
19. Ledig, C., et al.: Photo-realistic single image super-resolution using a generative adversarial network. In: Proceedings of the IEEE Conference on Computer vision and Pattern Recognition, pp. 4681–4690 (2017)
20. Li, P., Prieto, L., Mery, D., Flynn, P.: Face recognition in low quality images: a survey. arXiv preprint arXiv:1805.11519 (2018)
21. Li, P., Prieto, L., Mery, D., Flynn, P.J.: On low-resolution face recognition in the wild: comparisons and new techniques. IEEE Trans. Inf. Forensics Secur. **14**(8), 2000–2012 (2019)
22. Li, P., Prieto, M.L., Flynn, P.J., Mery, D.: Learning face similarity for re-identification from real surveillance video: a deep metric solution. In: 2017 IEEE International Joint Conference on Biometrics (IJCB), pp. 243–252. IEEE (2017)
23. Lu, T., Xiong, Z., Zhang, Y., Wang, B., Lu, T.: Robust face super-resolution via locality-constrained low-rank representation. IEEE Access **5**, 13103–13117 (2017)
24. Lu, Z., Jiang, X., Kot, A.: Deep coupled resnet for low-resolution face recognition. IEEE Signal Process. Lett. **25**(4), 526–530 (2018)
25. Main-Author, A.: Title similar to the title of this paper. Master's thesis, Department of Computer Science, Some University, Some Country (2020)
26. Mudunuri, S.P., Sanyal, S., Biswas, S.: GenLR-Net: deep framework for very low resolution face and object recognition with generalization to unseen categories. In: 2018 IEEE/CVF Conference on Computer Vision and Pattern Recognition Workshops (CVPRW), pp. 602–60209. IEEE (2018)
27. Neves, J., Proença, H.: ICB-RW 2016: international challenge on biometric recognition in the wild. In: 2016 International Conference on Biometrics (ICB), pp. 1–6. IEEE (2016)
28. Parkhi, O.M., Vedaldi, A., Zisserman, A.: Deep face recognition. In: Proceedings of the British Machine Vision Conference 2015 (BMVC 2015), pp. 1–12 (2015)
29. Saha, P., Das, A.: NFGS enabled face re-identification for efficient surveillance in low quality video. In: 2019 Fifth International Conference on Image Information Processing (ICIIP), pp. 114–118. IEEE (2019)

30. Schroff, F., Kalenichenko, D., Philbin, J.: FaceNet: a unified embedding for face recognition and clustering. In: Proceedings of the IEEE Conference on Computer Vision and Pattern Recognition, pp. 815–823 (2015)
31. Schuckers, M.E.: Computational Methods in Biometric Authentication: Statistical Methods for Performance Evaluation. Springer, Heidelberg (2010)
32. Selwood, D.L.: Commentary: reproducible science, why protocols matter. Chem. Biol. Drug Des. **93**(6), 975–978 (2019)
33. Simonyan, K., Zisserman, A.: Very deep convolutional networks for large-scale image recognition. arXiv preprint arXiv:1409.1556 (2014)
34. Singh, N., Rathore, S.S., Kumar, S.: Towards a super-resolution based approach for improved face recognition in LR environment. Multimed. Tools Appl. **81**, 38887–38919 (2022)
35. Sønderby, C.K., Caballero, J., Theis, L., Shi, W., Huszár, F.: Amortised map inference for image super-resolution. arXiv preprint arXiv:1610.04490 (2016)
36. Szegedy, C., et al.: Going deeper with convolutions. In: Proceedings of the IEEE Conference on Computer Vision and Pattern Recognition, pp. 1–9 (2015)
37. Szegedy, C., Vanhoucke, V., Ioffe, S., Shlens, J., Wojna, Z.: Rethinking the inception architecture for computer vision. In: Proceedings of the IEEE Conference on Computer Vision and Pattern Recognition, pp. 2818–2826 (2016)
38. Tang, Y., Yang, X., Wang, N., Song, B., Gao, X.: Person re-identification with feature pyramid optimization and gradual background suppression. Neural Netw. **124**, 223–232 (2020)
39. Viola, P., Jones, M.J.: Robust real-time face detection. Int. J. Comput. Vis. **57**(2), 137–154 (2004)
40. Wang, X., Li, Y., Zhang, H., Shan, Y.: Towards real-world blind face restoration with generative facial prior (2021). https://arxiv.org/abs/2101.04061
41. Wang, X., et al.: ESRGAN: enhanced super-resolution generative adversarial networks. In: Proceedings of the European Conference on Computer Vision (ECCV) (2018)
42. Wang, Y., Perazzi, F., McWilliams, B., Sorkine-Hornung, A., Sorkine-Hornung, O., Schroers, C.: A fully progressive approach to single-image super-resolution. In: Proceedings of the IEEE Conference on Computer Vision and Pattern Recognition Workshops, pp. 864–873 (2018)
43. Wang, Z., Liu, D., Yang, J., Han, W., Huang, T.: Deep networks for image super-resolution with sparse prior. In: Proceedings of the IEEE International Conference on Computer Vision, pp. 370–378 (2015)
44. Wang, Z., Yang, W., Ben, X.: Low-resolution degradation face recognition over long distance based on CCA. Neural Comput. Appl. **26**(7), 1645–1652 (2015). https://doi.org/10.1007/s00521-015-1834-y
45. Yang, T., Ren, P., Xie, X., Zhang, L.: GAN prior embedded network for blind face restoration in the wild (2021). https://arxiv.org/abs/2105.06070
46. Yu, X., Fernando, B., Hartley, R., Porikli, F.: Super-resolving very low-resolution face images with supplementary attributes. In: Proceedings of the IEEE Conference on Computer Vision and Pattern Recognition, pp. 908–917 (2018)
47. Yu, X., Porikli, F.: Face hallucination with tiny unaligned images by transformative discriminative neural networks. In: Thirty-First AAAI Conference on Artificial Intelligence (2017)
48. Zhao, K., Xu, J., Cheng, M.M.: RegularFace: deep face recognition via exclusive regularization. In: Proceedings of the IEEE Conference on Computer Vision and Pattern Recognition, pp. 1136–1144 (2019)
49. Zhao, L., Bai, H., Liang, J., Zeng, B., Wang, A., Zhao, Y.: Simultaneous color-depth super-resolution with conditional generative adversarial networks. Pattern Recogn. **88**, 356–369 (2019)

On Skin Lesion Recognition Using Deep Learning: 50 Ways to Choose Your Model

Domingo Mery[1(✉)], Pamela Romero[1], Gabriel Garib[1], Alma Pedro[1],
Maria Paz Salinas[2], Javiera Sepulveda[2], Leonel Hidalgo[2], Claudia Prieto[3],
and Cristian Navarrete-Dechent[2]

[1] Departments of Computer Science, Pontificia Universidad Catolica de Chile,
Santiago, Chile
domingo.mery@uc.cl
[2] Departments of Dermatology, Pontificia Universidad Catolica de Chile,
Santiago, Chile
[3] Departments of Electrical Engineering, Pontificia Universidad Catolica de Chile,
Santiago, Chile

Abstract. Skin cancer is a highly relevant health problem around the world. The World Health Organization (WHO) reports that one-third of the diagnosed cancers are skin cancer. It is well known that early detection of skin cancer significantly increases the prognosis of patients. In many cases, however, the absence of clinical devices and qualified experts makes this task very difficult. To overcome this problem, in the last years advanced deep learning techniques have been proposed to recognize skin cancer automatically showing promising results. In this work, we evaluate 50 deep learning approaches on the well-known HAM10000 dataset of dermatoscopic images from seven different skin lesion categories. The approaches have been evaluated using the same experimental protocol. In our experiments, the performance of each approach in terms of accuracy and computational time are measured. In addition, the number of trainable parameters and the number of features of the last layer of the deep learning architecture are given. Thus, comparison between the approaches can be easily established. The results showed that the best performance has been achieved by a deep learning approach based on visual transformers with 84.29% of accuracy on the testing subset. We know that these results may vary significantly on other datasets. For this reason, rather than establish which method is the best, the main contribution of this work is to make the 50 deep learning approaches available in a simple way for future research in the area. We believe that this methodology, *i.e.*, training, testing and evaluating many deep learning methods, can be very helpful to establish which is the best architecture and what is the highest performance that can be achieved on new datasets.

Keywords: Deep learning · Image classification · Medical imaging · Skin lesion recognition

1 Introduction

Skin cancer is a relevant worldwide problem in public health. The World Health Organization (WHO) reports that one-third of the diagnosed cancers are skin cancer [38]. Its

© Springer Nature Switzerland AG 2023
H. Wang et al. (Eds.): PSIVT 2022, LNCS 13763, pp. 103–116, 2023.
https://doi.org/10.1007/978-3-031-26431-3_9

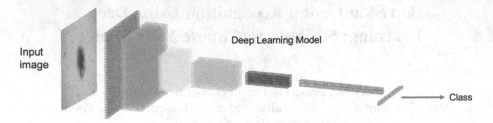

Fig. 1. Block-diagram for skin lesion recognition using a deep learning model: the input is a dermatoscopic image, and the output is the number class (in our experiments, a number between 0 and 6 as shown in Fig. 2).

early detection significantly increases the chances for successful treatment and survival. Nevertheless, early detection can be difficult in many places where qualified experts or adequate medical tools are scarce.

Research on automatic skin lesion diagnosis has been developing for almost 30 years. After our literature review, we can observe that research in the dermatology area is currently an evolving field with Artificial Intelligence (AI) to establish automatic and accurate diagnoses (Fig. 1). For example, it has been reported that, in distinguishing melanoma and nevi on dermatoscopic images, some deep learning models systematically outperformed dermatologists (see [11]). Although AI cannot replace the expertise and knowledge of highly-trained professionals (dermatologists), it is a great contribution and support for them ('augmented intelligence') or for general physicians (non-dermatologists), especially for the early detection of disease [21,36].

Nevertheless, we observe a *generalization problem* in the dermatological tools based on AI, because models trained on a dataset cannot generalize well to other datasets [40]. This is a very known problem in AI in dermatology, see for example [12,37]. To tackle this problem, probably we will need new experimental protocols, new standards and new datasets from multi-sources that include different skin types and demographic groups. This means that in the future a wide variety of new experiments will have to be conducted to validate the models correctly in new scenarios. This would ensure the clinical use of these tools in a safe and reliable manner.

In this paper we want to contribute with a simple and effective experimental evaluation. We evaluated 50 deep learning approaches on the well-known HAM10000 dataset of dermatoscopic images from seven different skin lesion categories. The approaches have been evaluated using the same experimental protocol and performance metrics are given for each one. After some analysis we conclude which approach is the best one... on *this* dataset. We acknowledge that these results may vary significantly on other datasets.

For these reasons, rather than establish which method is the best, the main contribution of this work is to make the 50 deep learning approaches publicly-available for future research in the area. We believe that this methodology, *i.e.*, training, testing and evaluating a myriad of deep learning methods, can be very helpful to establish which is the best architecture and what is the highest performance that can be achieved on new datasets.

2   Related Works

In this Section, we give some advances in image acquisition, image processing and machine learning in the recognition of skin lesions. Finally, we present some concluding remarks in this field.

Image Acquisition: In image acquisition we distinguish several sensors that can be used to acquire dermatological images. Many times, more than one technique is used on a single patient. The following are the more relevant:

i) Clinical photography: Clinical imaging in dermatology corresponds to those images acquired by digital cameras [45]. In the last years, images acquired by smartphones [2] have been used to expand access to specialists or teledermatology [32,36].

ii) Dermoscopy: Dermoscopy, called dermatoscopy, epiluminescence microscopy or skin surface microscopy, examines the skin in-vivo using a hand-held device called a *dermatoscope*, a tool that has become an essential part of the clinical examination of dermatologists [13,32]. It consists of a polarized and non-polarized light source and a magnifier (typically 10× [28]). It is used to evaluate skin structures within the epidermis and dermis by reducing surface reflectance [20]. Dermatoscopic images can be acquired by a smartphone [35]. It is a high-resolution skin imaging technique that allows visualization of deeper skin structures. Dermoscopy in comparison with naked eye examination has improved the diagnosis performance [51].

iii) Other non-invasive techniques: Other techniques in for skin cancer detection in dermatology have been developed like electrical impedance spectroscopy (EIS), multispectral imaging, high-frequency ultrasonography (HFUS), optical coherence tomography (OCT), and reflectance confocal microscopy (RCM) in the detection of skin cancer [16,20,23]. Confocal microscopy, for example, allows for more detailed visualization of skin lesions in vivo [19].

Image Processing: Image Processing has been used to transform the input image into a new output image. The idea here is to improve the classification task using a new version of the input image. We distinguish four main groups of methods:

i) Color processing: Different color spaces, *e.g.*, RGB, HSV, L*a*b, HSI, L*u*v, have been evaluated [7], and color transformations like color constancy has been proposed [6], in order to obtain a new color image that appears similar to an image acquired under a canonical light source. The idea here is to extract new robust and invariant features that can improve the performance of the classification.

ii) Segmentation: The region of the lesion is isolated from the background of the image [41,53]. Thus, both images (original and segmented) are available for the machine learning step. This is done in order to provide the machine learning algorithms with the information of where the lesion is. In the last years, segmentation of skin lesion has been done by complex deep learning architectures like fully convolutional networks (FCN) [44], full resolution convolutional networks (FrCN) [1], U-Net [42] and SegNet [5] (see more details in [18]).

iii) Filtering: The input image is filtered in order to enhance the details of the image. Since hair occlusion can significantly decrease the performance of the recognition model, image processing methods like skin lesion restoration for hair removal have been developed in the last years. See for example an automatic hair segmentation method using adaptive threshold from edge and branch length measures [31], and a method based on hybrid convolutional and recurrent neural networks [3].

iv) Simulation: A realistic hair simulator is proposed in [4] that can be used to test the image processing methods and evaluate how the hair affect the skin lesions diagnosis.

Machine Learning: Three eras have been recognized in the develop of automatic skin lesion recognition [55]:

i) Classical Machine Learning (1994–2011): classical classifiers like Bayesian classifiers, logistic regressions, nearest neighbors (kNN) and simple neural networks with some handcrafted features like asymmetry, border, color and diameter and evolving (ABCDE) [9], Menzie's method and 7-point checklist [27], and some image processing techniques – see for example [17].

ii) Support Vector Machines (2011–2016): more sophisticated classifiers with nonlinear kernels and engineering features like local binary patterns (LBP) – see for example [7].

iii) Deep Learning (2017–today): convolutional neural networks (CNN) and other architectures with thousands of images for training [15]. Deep learning has significantly increased classification performance [40,41,56]. Deep learning models can learn from training data a robust feature representation avoiding the extraction and setup of handcrafted or engineering features. In addition, they are able to solve the recognition problem (classification) directly from training data with minimal user guidance. In dermatology for instance, some studies have reported that approaches based on CNN have achieved human-level (or even better) in the recognition performance of skin lesions in diagnosing close-up and dermatoscopic images of skin lesions in a simulated static environment [40]. In [56], an attention residual learning convolutional neural network (ARL-CNN) model is proposed to improve its ability for discriminative representation by generating attention maps for low layers of the CNN architecture that uses the feature maps learned by high layers.

Conclusions: After our literature review, we distinguish some problems that are present when designing a method of an automated skin lesion recognition are:

i) Datasets: Training and testing data is not enough [56]. We need large datasets (with ground truth diagnoses) with balanced classes, that fully represent all demographic groups [40]. In addition, we have to deal with many images with 'artifacts' (*e.g.*, ruler markers, hair), and images with quality problems (*e.g.*, poor contrast, blurred) [41].

ii) Metadata: The question of whether addition of metadata can improve the performance of the models is not well understood [39,56] (for example, can we use the age and sex of the patient, and location of the lesion in our model?).

iii) Intra-class and inter-class: the images of the same class can be very different (high intra-class variation), the images of different classes can be very similar (high inter-class similarity) [56].

iv) Explainability: There is a lack of explainable models that can show the semantically meaning full of the parts of the skin lesions [56].

v) Generalization: Results presented in many papers that work well on a specific dataset can vary significantly on other datasets, or on the same dataset but with different configurations (when splitting training/testing subsets in a different way, when using different data-augmentation techniques, etc.) [40].

vi) Standards: We need rigorous standards that should be widely accepted by the community (*e.g.*, in dermatological image acquisition) [40].

3 Evaluated Methods

Over the last decade, we have witnessed tremendous improvements in computer vision by using complex deep neural network architectures trained with thousands of images. Solutions based on deep learning have been very successful in the recognition of objects (*image classification*), where handcrafted features were replaced by learned features. In this Section, we explain the following representative architectures that have been evaluated on skin lesion images in our experiments:[1]

- ConvNet: It is the first architecture of Convolutional Neural Network (CNN) in deep learning.[2] It exploits the spatial information of the image using sequential layers that reduce step by step the dimension of the input image. It does not model well the representation of objects with different pose, orientation, or location. It has large size filters and feature extraction of low-level [30].
- AlexNet: It exploits the spatial information of the image using sequential layers. It is wider and deeper (compared with ConvNet's). It can extract low, mid and high-level features. It uses data augmentation to improve the representation of objects [29].
- GoogLeNet: It exploits the spatial information of the image using sequential layers. It introduces the concepts of multi-scale filters. It uses auxiliary classifiers to boost convergence rate [47].
- VGG: It exploits the spatial information of the image using sequential layers. It introduced the concepts of simple/homogeneous architecture and effective receptive field. The kernels are small in comparison with the other ones [46].
- ResNet: It uses residual learning with multi-paths to skips some connections. It mitigates the effect of the vanishing gradient problem [22].
- Wide ResNet: It is ResNet but the bottleneck number of channels is twice larger in every block [54].
- ResNeXt: It adds cardinality to ResNet that provides several transformations at each layer [52].
- DenseNet: It uses multi-paths. It introduces a cross-layer dimension avoiding to relearn of redundant feature-maps [25].
- SqueezeNet: It exploits the feature map using identity and residual mapping [26].

---

[1] The reader is referred to the review on convolutional neural networks in [8].

[2] It has been originally proposed in 1989 for handwritten digit recognition. ConvNet's became more popular in the 2010s s with the introduction of inexpensive hardware such as GPUs (graphics processing units).

- ShuffleNet: It is an architecture with fewer resources developed for mobile devices [34].
- MobileNet: Similar to ShuffleNet, it is an architecture with fewer resources developed for mobile devices [24,43].
- MnasNet: It is a small, fast and accurate CNN model, that includes model latency into the main objective. It is a model that achieves a good trade-off between latency and accuracy [48].
- EfficientNet: It is an architecture, in which the width, depth, and resolution are uniformly scaled using a set of fixed coefficients [49].
- ARLNET: It is a model based on attention residual learning convolutional neural network. It generates attention maps for low layers of the CNN architecture that uses the feature maps learned by high layers [56].
- ViT: Visual Transformer is an adaption of the transformer architecture (a self-attention-based architecture) that is used natural language processing [14].
- ConvNeXt: It is a ConvNet architecture that has been designed using the idea of the transformers [33].

4   Experimental Results

In this Section, we present *i)* the dataset used in our experiments, *ii)* the results obtained by the 50 deep learning methods, *iii)* a discussion of the results, and *iv)* some details of the implementation.

4.1   Dataset

In our experiments, we use the well-known HAM10000 dataset of dermatoscopic images from seven different skin lesion categories [50]. Some images are shown in

Class	Acronym	Name
0	akiec	Actinic keratosis
1	bcc	Basal cell carcinoma
2	bkl	Benign keratosis
3	df	Dermatofibroma
4	mel	Melanoma
5	nv	Melanocytic nevus
6	vasc	Vascular lesion

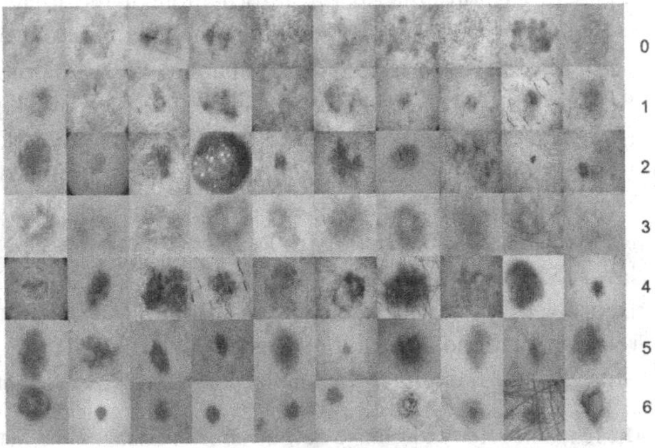

Fig. 2. Some images used in our experiments from HAM10000 dataset. The images belong to seven different classes, as shown at the left.

Table 1. Number of images for training, validation and testing of each class.

| | class → | 0 | 1 | 2 | 3 | 4 | 5 | 6 | |
Subset		akiec	bcc	bkl	df	mel	nv	vasc	Total
Training:	original	210	262	525	70	525	1050	95	2737
	augmented	840	788	525	980	525	0	955	4613
	total	1050	1050	1050	1050	1050	1050	1050	7350
Validation:	original	30	38	75	10	75	150	14	392
	augmented	120	112	75	140	75	0	136	658
	total	150	150	150	150	150	150	150	1050
Testing:	original	30	30	30	30	30	30	30	210
	augmented	0	0	0	0	0	0	0	0
	total	30	30	30	30	30	30	30	210
Total:	original	270	330	630	110	630	1230	139	3339
	augmented	960	900	600	1120	600	0	1091	5271
	total	1230	1230	1230	1230	1230	1230	1230	8610

Fig. 2. Typically, in datasets of skin lesions there are unbalanced classes, *i.e.*, the number of images per class are not distributed uniformly [10]. In our case, the distribution is shown in Table 1: we observe that there are 3339 (original) images in total, an average of $3339/7 = 447$ images per class, with an standard deviation of 393.1 images, however, there is a class with 110 images only (class 3: 'df') and another with 1230 images (class 5: 'nv'). In our experiments, without data augmentation the models are not accurate enough, because they are not able to recognize correctly the under-represented classes.

We decided to separate 30 (original) images per class to testing purposes. Thus, we ensure that our learned classifier is evaluated on original images (with no augmentation in testing subset) uniformly distributed.

To handle the imbalanced classes we use data augmentation by rotating the images in $\pm 90^0$ and 180^0, and by flipping them vertically and horizontally. The idea is to have 1200 images per class for training and validation purposes (that is the maximal number of images of one class, class 5: 'nv'). Thus, if necessary, the number of images is increased up to 1200 images per class using data augmentation as shown in Table 1. From them 87.5% is used for training (*i.e.*, 1050 images per class), and 12.5% is used for validation (*i.e.*, 150 images per class).

4.2   Results

After defining the database, we trained the 50 deep learning models outlined in Sect. 3. Only ConvNet models were trained from scratch. In the other models we used as starting points the weights of models that were trained on ImageNet. In our implementation, the models are learned using the training/validation methodology. That is, in each epoch: *i)* the weights of the model are updated using the training subset, *ii)* the model is evaluated on the validation subset, and *iii)* a performance metrics (*e.g.*, loss function or accuracy) is computed. In case, the performance is not improved after five consecutive epochs, the learning stage is stoped ('early stop'). Finally, we select the trained model of the best performance metrics (on validation subset). The selected model ('best model') is used to evaluate the performance metrics on the testing subset.

Table 2. Results for the 50 models.

Year	#	Method	Parameters				Time/epoch [sec]	Training [min]	Training Accuracy	Validation Accuracy	Testing Accuracy
			Lib*	$\times 10^6$	Features	Epochs					
2010	1	ConvNet 5 × 80 [30]	0	1.0	512	19	73.6	23.3	0.7259	0.6829	0.6048
	2	ConvNet 5 × 128 [30]	0	1.2	1024	31	60.8	31.4	0.7555	0.6152	0.6190
	3	ConvNet 6S × 224 [30]	0	0.4	1024	18	15.9	4.5	0.7306	0.5990	0.5857
	4	ConvNet 6M × 224 [30]	0	1.7	2048	19	20.0	6.3	0.8249	0.6333	0.6286
	5	ConvNet 6L × 224 [30]	0	2.8	2560	18	57.4	17.2	0.8218	0.6371	0.6190
2014	6	AlexNet [29]	1	57.0	4096	19	17.5	5.2	0.9660	0.7314	0.7190
	7	GoogLeNet [47]	1	5.6	1024	10	24.4	3.7	0.9362	0.7581	0.7095
	8	VGG11-bn [46]	1	128.8	4096	19	40.8	12.2	0.9909	0.7790	0.7524
	9	VGG13-bn [46]	1	129.0	4096	10	62.3	9.3	0.9665	0.7790	0.7429
	10	VGG16-bn [46]	1	134.3	4096	9	72.3	9.6	0.9521	0.7686	0.7810
	11	VGG19-bn [46]	1	139.6	4096	17	82.5	22.0	0.9827	0.7743	0.7476
	12	VGG11 [46]	1	128.8	4096	9	36.9	4.9	0.9384	0.7171	0.7333
	13	VGG13 [46]	1	129.0	4096	7	55.5	5.6	0.8267	0.7143	0.7048
	14	VGG16 [46]	1	134.3	4096	20	65.0	20.6	0.9815	0.7371	0.7000
	15	VGG19 [46]	1	139.6	4096	8	74.1	8.6	0.8588	0.7095	0.6571
2015	16	ResNet-18 [22]	1	11.2	512	9	19.7	2.6	0.8946	0.7610	0.7333
	17	ResNet-34 [22]	1	21.3	512	22	26.0	9.1	0.9707	0.7686	0.7429
	18	ResNet-50 [22]	1	23.5	2048	10	42.2	6.3	0.8740	0.7667	0.7429
	19	ResNet-101 [22]	1	42.5	2048	18	66.4	18.8	0.9437	0.7686	0.7619
	20	ResNet-152 [22]	1	58.2	2048	19	92.4	27.7	0.9505	0.7705	0.7381
2016	21	ResNeXt-50 [52]	1	23.0	2048	19	61.2	18.3	0.9653	0.7857	0.7667
	22	DenseNet201 [25]	1	18.1	1920	14	72.1	15.6	0.9958	0.8105	0.7762
	23	SqueezeNet1-0 [26]	1	0.7	512	18	20.6	5.8	0.8156	0.7000	0.6667
	24	Wide-ResNet-50-2 [54]	1	66.8	2048	13	170.2	34.0	0.6996	0.5933	0.5714
2018	25	ShuffleNet-v2-0.5 [34]	1	0.3	1024	8	19.4	2.3	0.7973	0.7381	0.7000
	26	ShuffleNet-v2-1.0 [34]	1	1.3	1024	13	21.2	4.2	0.9590	0.7800	0.7476
	27	MobileNetv2 [43]	1	2.2	1280	17	26.0	6.9	0.9841	0.7943	0.7810
	28	MobileNetv3-S [24]	1	1.5	1024	21	19.0	6.3	0.9799	0.7990	0.7095
2019	29	MobileNetv3-L [24]	1	4.2	1280	19	25.0	7.5	0.9946	0.7924	0.7905
	30	MNasNet1-0 [48]	1	3.1	1280	22	31.0	10.8	0.9894	0.4971	0.5429
	31	EfficientNet-b0 [49]	1	4.0	1280	16	33.2	8.3	0.9765	0.8010	0.7857
	32	EfficientNet-b1 [49]	1	6.5	1280	18	45.2	12.8	0.9876	0.8010	0.7667
	33	EfficientNet-b2 [49]	1	7.7	1408	25	47.4	18.9	0.9946	0.8343	0.7667
	34	EfficientNet-b3 [49]	1	10.7	1536	13	56.9	11.4	0.9539	0.8048	0.7762
	35	EffNet-b0 [49]	2	4.0	1280	22	70.7	25.9	0.8343	0.7842	0.8158
	36	EffNet-b1 [49]	2	6.5	1280	20	63.2	21.1	0.8409	0.7922	0.7524
	37	EffNet-b2 [49]	2	7.7	1408	20	81.4	27.1	0.8430	0.8045	0.7762
	38	EffNet-b3 [49]	2	10.7	1536	14	130.2	41.2	0.8525	0.8226	0.7381
	39	EffNet-b4 [49]	2	17.6	1792	19	326.6	72.2	0.8142	0.7953	0.7429
	40	EffNet-b5 [49]	2	28.4	2048	13	519.6	112.6	0.8147	0.7924	0.7810
	41	EffNet-b6 [49]	2	40.8	2304	18	939.8	281.9	0.8721	0.7857	0.7952
	42	ARLNET-50 [56]	3	23.52	2048	74	60.0	74.0	0.8494	0.7650	0.7466
	43	ARLNET-101 [56]	3	42.51	2048	73	96.0	116.8	0.8773	0.7738	0.7142
	44	ARLNET-152 [56]	3	58.16	2048	96	138.0	220.8	0.9106	0.7821	0.7524
2020	45	ViT-b-16 [14]	1	86.6	768	13	132.7	26.5	0.7433	0.6752	0.6000
	46	ViT-b-32 [14]	1	88.2	768	11	73.7	12.3	0.6035	0.5867	0.5905
	47	ViT-base-patch16 [14]	4	86.4	768	20	212.3	70.8	0.9997	0.8276	0.8190
	48	ViT-base-patch16-in21k [14]	4	86.4	768	10	189.0	31.5	0.9882	0.8343	**0.8429** ←
2022	49	ConvNeXt-tiny [33]	1	27.8	768	11	150.5	25.1	0.9857	0.8276	0.7905
	50	ConvNeXt-small [33]	1	49.5	768	20	213.1	67.5	0.9955	0.8476	0.8190

* Libraries: 0: Own implementation in PyTorch, 1: PyTorch model from `torchvision.models`
2: Library EfficientNet-PyTorch, 3: Library Vipermdl/ARL, 4: Library HuggingFaces

The results are summarized in Table 2, where the accuracy on the training, the validation and the testing subsets are reported. In addition, the number of trainable parameters and the number of features of the last layer of the deep learning architecture are given. Thus, comparison between the approaches can be easily established.

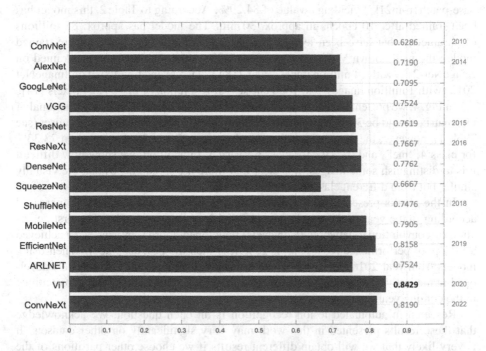

Fig. 3. Accuracy on testing subset for each family of methods. In each bar, the best accuracy for the family is presented.

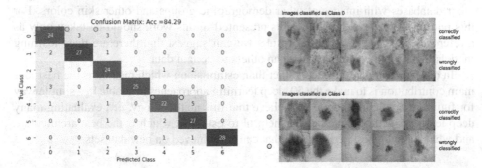

Fig. 4. Confusion matrix. Visually is very difficult to distinguish samples of classes 0, 1 and 2, and classes 4 and 5.

4.3   Discussion

In Fig. 3, we present a summary of the results in which the best performance of each family of models is shown. The bars represent the achieved accuracy on the testing subset. The best accuracy is achieved by (ViT) Visual Transformers (see row #48 'Vit-base-patch16-in21k') yielding a value of 84.29%. According to Table 2, this model has been trained after 10 epochs in approx. 30 min. The model has approx. 85 millions of parameters that have been learned (fine-tuned) using a very powerful pre-trained model, the well-known Vision Transformer (ViT) model that has been pre-trained on ImageNet-21k (with 14 million images, and 21843 classes) and fine-tuned on ImageNet 2012 (with 1 million images, and 1000 classes) at resolution of 224 × 224 pixels [14].

In Fig. 4, we present the confusion matrix for our best model. Ideally, the diagonal of this matrix should be 30, because there are 30 images per class in the testing subset (see Table 1), however, the diagonal numbers are between 22 and 28, *i.e.*, between 73.33% for class 4, 'mel', and 93.33% for class 6, 'vasc'). In addition, we show how difficult it is to distinguish some images: it is clear that there are some images that are visually similar but from different classes.

In the results presented in Fig. 3, we observe how the test accuracy is increased according to the year of the development of the deep learning model. The first generation of convolutional networks (ConvNets) developed approx. in year 2010 achieved a very poor performance (63%, that is 21% less than the best accuracy). When using models from year 2016 we can obtain an accuracy of 78%. Finally, the models developed in the last years are able to obtain more than 80%. This trend is likely to continue in the coming years.

Research in automated lesion recognition is an open question. We acknowledge that these results presented in this work may vary significantly on other datasets. It is very likely that we will obtain different results if we choose other partitions of the database, or if we use other data augmentation techniques, or if we increase the samples of some of the classes. Moreover, the results may be much different if we analyze other databases with images of other demographic groups and other skin colors. For this reason, we believe that the results presented in this work should be taken only as a reference experiment. With our results we can suggest that there are deep learning models that should be more robust than others to certain data.

In our work, in consequence, rather than establishing which method is the best, our main contribution is to make the 50 deep learning approaches available in a simple way for future research in the area. We believe that this methodology, *i.e.*, evaluating many deep learning methods, can be very helpful to establish which is the best architecture and what is the highest performance that can be achieved on new datasets.

4.4   Implementation

The experiments have been implemented in Python using Google Colab.[3] In our Colab Notebooks, the user can run all 50 methods easily on the dataset proposed in Table 1, or on a custom dataset. In our implementation, the training/validation/testing subsets are

---

[3] See https://domingomery.ing.puc.cl/material/.

stored in three different directories. The idea is to use these codes on other skin datasets in a simple way. As shown in Table 2, in our implementation we used five libraries: 0) Sequential models in Pytorch,[4] for the implementation of classic ConvNets, 1) Pre-trained models from Torchvision,[5] 2) EfficientNet-PyTorch,[6] 3) Vipermdl/ARL[7] and 4) VisionTransformer from HuggingFace.[8]

5 Conclusions

In this work, we implemented and evaluated 50 deep learning models on the well-known HAM10000 dataset of dermatoscopic images from seven different skin lesion categories. The approaches were evaluated using the same experimental protocol. In our experiments, the performance of each approach in terms of accuracy and computational time were measured. In addition, the number of trainable parameters and the number of features of the last layer of the deep learning architecture are given. Thus, comparison between the approaches can be easily established. The results showed that the best performance was achieved by a model based on visual transformers with 84.29% of accuracy in the testing subset. We know that these results may vary significantly on other datasets. For this reason, rather than establish which method is the best, the main contribution of this work is to make the 50 deep learning approaches available in a simple way for future research in the area. In the future, we will evaluate this tool on more challenging databases and work on the inclusion of metadata in the models.

Acknowledgments. This work was supported by National Center for Artificial Intelligence CENIA FB210017, Basal ANID and ANID - iHealth, Millennium Science Initiative Program ICN2021_004.

References

1. Al-masni, M.A., Al-antari, M.A., Choi, M.T., Han, S.M., Kim, T.S.: Skin lesion segmentation in dermoscopy images via deep full resolution convolutional networks. Comput. Methods Programs Biomed. **162**, 221–231 (2018)
2. Ashique, K., Kaliyadan, F., Aurangabadkar, S.: Clinical photography in dermatology using smartphones: an overview. Indian Dermatol. Online J. **6**(3), 158 (2015)
3. Attia, M., Hossny, M., Zhou, H., Nahavandi, S., Asadi, H., Yazdabadi, A.: Digital hair segmentation using hybrid convolutional and recurrent neural networks architecture. Comput. Methods Programs Biomed. **177**, 17–30 (2019)
4. Attia, M., Hossny, M., Zhou, H., Nahavandi, S., Asadi, H., Yazdabadi, A.: Realistic hair simulator for skin lesion images: a novel benchmarking tool. Artif. Intell. Med. **108**, 101933 (2020)

---

[1] See http://pytorch.org.
[5] See http://pytorch.org/vision/stable/models.html.
[6] See https://github.com/lukemelas/EfficientNet-PyTorch.
[7] See https://github.com/Vipermdl/ARL.
[8] See https://huggingface.co/google/vit-base-patch16-224.

5. Badrinarayanan, V., Handa, A., Cipolla, R.: SegNet: a deep convolutional encoder-decoder architecture for robust semantic pixel-wise labelling. arXiv preprint arXiv:1505.07293 (2015)
6. Barata, C., Celebi, M.E., Marques, J.S.: Improving dermoscopy image classification using color constancy. IEEE J. Biomed. Health Inform. **19**(3), 1146–1152 (2015)
7. Barata, C., Ruela, M., Francisco, M., Mendonca, T., Marques, J.S.: Two systems for the detection of melanomas in dermoscopy images using texture and color features. IEEE Syst. J. **8**(3), 965–979 (2014)
8. Bhatt, D., et al.: CNN variants for computer vision: history, architecture, application, challenges and future scope. Electronics **10**(20), 2470 (2021)
9. Binder, M., Steiner, A., Schwarz, M., Knollmayer, S., Wolff, K., Pehamberger, H.: Application of an artificial neural network in epiluminescence microscopy pattern analysis of pigmented skin lesions: a pilot study. Br. J. Dermatol. **130**(4), 460–465 (1994)
10. Bissoto, A., Fornaciali, M., Valle, E., Avila, S.: (De) constructing bias on skin lesion datasets. In: IEEE Computer Society Conference on Computer Vision and Pattern Recognition Workshops, pp. 2766–2774, June 2019
11. Brinker, T.J., et al.: Deep neural networks are superior to dermatologists in melanoma image classification. Eur. J. Cancer **119**, 11–17 (2019)
12. Daneshjou, R.: Toward augmented intelligence: The first prospective, randomized clinical trial assessing clinician and artificial intelligence collaboration in dermatology. J. Invest. Dermatol. **142**(9), 2301–2302 (2022)
13. Deda, L.C., Goldberg, R.H., Jamerson, T.A., Lee, I., Tejasvi, T.: Dermoscopy practice guidelines for use in telemedicine. NPJ Digit. Med. **5**(1), 1–7 (2022)
14. Dosovitskiy, A., et al.: An image is worth 16×16 words: transformers for image recognition at scale. CoRR abs/2010.11929 (2020). https://arxiv.org/abs/2010.11929
15. Esteva, A., et al.: Dermatologist-level classification of skin cancer with deep neural networks. Nature **542**(7639), 115–118 (2017)
16. Ferrante di Ruffano, L., et al.: Computer-assisted diagnosis techniques (dermoscopy and spectroscopy-based) for diagnosing skin cancer in adults (2018)
17. Ganster, H., Pinz, A., Röhrer, R., Wildling, E., Binder, M., Kittler, H.: Automated melanoma recognition. IEEE Trans. Med. Imaging **20**(3), 233–239 (2001)
18. Garcia-Garcia, A., Orts-Escolano, S., Oprea, S., Villena-Martinez, V., Garcia-Rodriguez, J.: A review on deep learning techniques applied to semantic segmentation. arXiv preprint arXiv:1704.06857 (2017)
19. Goyal, M., Knackstedt, T., Yan, S., Hassanpour, S.: Artificial intelligence-based image classification methods for diagnosis of skin cancer: challenges and opportunities. Comput. Biol. Med. **127**, 104065 (2020)
20. Hamblin, M.R., Avci, P., Gupta, G.K.: Imaging in Dermatology. Academic Press (2016)
21. Han, S.S., et al.: Evaluation of artificial intelligence-assisted diagnosis of skin neoplasms-a single-center, paralleled, unmasked, randomized controlled trial. J. Invest. Dermatol. **142**(9), 2353–2362 (2022)
22. He, K., Zhang, X., Ren, S., Sun, J.: Deep residual learning for image recognition. CoRR abs/1512.03385 (2015)
23. Heibel, H.D., Hooey, L., Cockerell, C.J.: A review of noninvasive techniques for skin cancer detection in dermatology. Am. J. Clin. Dermatol. **21**, 513–524 (2020). https://doi.org/10.1007/s40257-020-00517-z
24. Howard, A., et al.: Searching for MobileNetV3. CoRR abs/1905.02244 (2019)
25. Huang, G., Liu, Z., Weinberger, K.Q.: Densely connected convolutional networks. CoRR abs/1608.06993 (2016)

26. Iandola, F.N., Moskewicz, M.W., Ashraf, K., Han, S., Dally, W.J., Keutzer, K.: SqueezeNet: AlexNet-level accuracy with 50x fewer parameters and <1MB model size. CoRR abs/1602.07360 (2016)
27. Johr, R.H.: Dermoscopy: alternative melanocytic algorithms - the ABCD rule of dermatoscopy, menzies scoring method, and 7-point checklist. Clin. Dermatol. **20**(3), 240–247 (2002)
28. Kamińska-Winciorek, G., Placek, W.: The most common mistakes on dermatoscopy of melanocytic lesions. Postepy Dermatologii I Alergologii **32**(1), 33–39 (2015)
29. Krizhevsky, A.: One weird trick for parallelizing convolutional neural networks. CoRR abs/1404.5997 (2014)
30. LeCun, Y., Kavukcuoglu, K., Farabet, C.: Convolutional networks and applications in vision. In: Proceedings of 2010 IEEE International Symposium on Circuits and Systems, pp. 253–256. IEEE (2010)
31. Lee, I., Du, X., Anthony, B.: Hair segmentation using adaptive threshold from edge and branch length measures. Comput. Biol. Med. **89**, 314–324 (2017)
32. Liu, Y., et al.: A deep learning system for differential diagnosis of skin diseases. Nat. Med. **26**(6), 900–908 (2020)
33. Liu, Z., Mao, H., Wu, C., Feichtenhofer, C., Darrell, T., Xie, S.: A convnet for the 2020s. CoRR abs/2201.03545 (2022). https://arxiv.org/abs/2201.03545
34. Ma, N., Zhang, X., Zheng, H., Sun, J.: ShuffleNet V2: practical guidelines for efficient CNN architecture design. CoRR abs/1807.11164 (2018)
35. Moreira, D., Alves, P., Veiga, F., Rosado, L., Vasconcelos, M.J.M.: Automated mobile image acquisition of macroscopic dermatological lesions. In: HEALTHINF 2021–14th International Conference on Health Informatics; Part of the 14th International Joint Conference on Biomedical Engineering Systems and Technologies, BIOSTEC 2021, pp. 122–132 (2021)
36. Muñoz-López, C., et al.: Performance of a deep neural network in teledermatology: a single-centre prospective diagnostic study. J. Eur. Acad. Dermatol. Venereol. **35**(2), 546–553 (2021)
37. Navarrete-Dechent, C., Dusza, S.W., Liopyris, K., Marghoob, A.A., Halpern, A.C., Marchetti, M.A.: Automated dermatological diagnosis: hype or reality? J. Invest. Dermatol. **138**(10), 2277 (2018)
38. Pacheco, A.G., Krohling, R.A.: The impact of patient clinical information on automated skin cancer detection. Comput. Biol. Med. **116**, 103545 (2020)
39. Pacheco, A.G., et al.: PAD-UFES-20: a skin lesion dataset composed of patient data and clinical images collected from smartphones. Data Brief **32**, 106221 (2020)
40. Reiter, O., Rotemberg, V., Kose, K., Halpern, A.C.: Artificial intelligence in skin cancer. Curr. Derm. Rep. **8**, 133–140 (2019). https://doi.org/10.1007/s13671-019-00267-0
41. Reshma, G., et al.: Deep learning-based skin lesion diagnosis model using dermoscopic images. Intell. Autom. Soft Comput. **31**(1), 621–634 (2022)
42. Ronneberger, O., Fischer, P., Brox, T.: U-Net: convolutional networks for biomedical image segmentation. In: Navab, N., Hornegger, J., Wells, W.M., Frangi, A.F. (eds.) MICCAI 2015. LNCS, vol. 9351, pp. 234–241. Springer, Cham (2015). https://doi.org/10.1007/978-3-319-24574-4_28
43. Sandler, M., Howard, A.G., Zhu, M., Zhmoginov, A., Chen, L.: Inverted residuals and linear bottlenecks: mobile networks for classification, detection and segmentation. CoRR abs/1801.04381 (2018)
44. Shelhamer, E., Long, J., Darrell, T.: Fully convolutional networks for semantic segmentation. IEEE Trans. Pattern Anal. Mach. Intell. **39**(4), 640–651 (2016)
45. Sidoroff, A.: The role of clinical photography in dermatology. In: Imaging in Dermatology, pp. 5–11. Elsevier (2016)
46. Simonyan, K., Zisserman, A.: Very deep convolutional networks for large-scale image recognition. arXiv preprint arXiv:1409.1556 (2014)

47. Szegedy, C., et al.: Going deeper with convolutions. CoRR abs/1409.4842 (2014)
48. Tan, M., et al.: MnasNet: platform-aware neural architecture search for mobile. In: Proceedings of the IEEE/CVF Conference on Computer Vision and Pattern Recognition, pp. 2820–2828 (2019)
49. Tan, M., Le, Q.V.: EfficientNet: rethinking model scaling for convolutional neural networks. CoRR abs/1905.11946 (2019)
50. Tschandl, P., Rosendahl, C., Kittler, H.: The HAM10000 dataset, a large collection of multi-source dermatoscopic images of common pigmented skin lesions. Sci. Data 5, 1–9 (2018)
51. Vestergaard, M.E., Macaskill, P., Holt, P.E., Menzies, S.W.: Dermoscopy compared with naked eye examination for the diagnosis of primary melanoma: a meta-analysis of studies performed in a clinical setting. Br. J. Dermatol. 159(3), 669–676 (2008)
52. Xie, S., Girshick, R.B., Dollár, P., Tu, Z., He, K.: Aggregated residual transformations for deep neural networks. CoRR abs/1611.05431 (2016)
53. Yacin Sikkandar, M., Alrasheadi, B.A., Prakash, N.B., Hemalakshmi, G.R., Mohanarathinam, A., Shankar, K.: Deep learning based an automated skin lesion segmentation and intelligent classification model. J. Ambient. Intell. Humaniz. Comput. 12(3), 3245–3255 (2021). https://doi.org/10.1007/s12652-020-02537-3
54. Zagoruyko, S., Komodakis, N.: Wide residual networks. arXiv preprint arXiv:1605.07146 (2016)
55. Zakhem, G.A., Fakhoury, J.W., Motosko, C.C., Ho, R.S.: Characterizing the role of dermatologists in developing artificial intelligence for assessment of skin cancer. J. Am. Acad. Dermatol. 85(6), 1544–1556 (2021)
56. Zhang, J., Xie, Y., Xia, Y., Shen, C.: Attention residual learning for skin lesion classification. IEEE Trans. Med. Imaging 38(9), 2092–2103 (2019)

Improving Automated Baggage Inspection Using Simulated X-ray Images of 3D Models

Alejandro Kaminetzky(✉) and Domingo Mery

Department of Computer Science, Pontificia Universidad Católica de Chile,
Santiago, Chile
akp@uc.cl

Abstract. X-ray baggage inspection is essential to ensure transport and border security, as it prevents hazardous objects from entering secure areas. Currently, deep learning is the state-of-the-art approach for automated threat object detection and classification. Proper training of these networks requires substantial data; however, the number of publicly available datasets of X-ray images is limited. To overcome this problem, we propose a method for generating new data by superimposing simulated X-ray images of 3D models onto real baggage X-rays, allowing researchers to train deep neural networks without requiring additional imaging or manual labeling. To validate our proposal, we ran experiments using 3D models of wrenches and the SIXray baggage dataset. The results prove that superimposing synthetic threat objects over a real training subset improves detection performance, with average precision (AP) increasing from 90.2% to 93.7%. As modern object detectors process images in real-time, they prove themselves as a feasible approach for aiding inspectors and even fully automating baggage inspection. Moreover, the novel superimposition and colorization techniques presented in this study can be employed in other areas of X-ray imaging.

Keywords: X-ray baggage inspection · Threat image projection · 3D model X-ray projection · X-ray pseudo-color · X-ray image simulation

1 Introduction

X-ray baggage inspection is widely used in security checkpoints to ensure transport and border security since it reduces the risk of crime, terrorism, and drug smuggling, among other illegalities. Inspectors must quickly analyze complex and cluttered baggage looking for suspicious objects of diverse shapes and materials. As this task requires high focus for long periods, fatigue and distraction have a detrimental effect on the inspectors' detection performance, which is only about 80%–90% [22].

In order to improve the threat detection rate, computer-based inspection methods have been proposed, using traditional computer vision [20] and deep learning [2,3,19] to detect hazardous objects in baggage. The latter has become

© Springer Nature Switzerland AG 2023
H. Wang et al. (Eds.): PSIVT 2022, LNCS 13763, pp. 117–131, 2023.
https://doi.org/10.1007/978-3-031-26431-3_10

the state-of-the-art approach for this task but requires many images for training. This is a problem for X-ray baggage inspection, as there is a lack of publicly available datasets [1, 3, 19].

Sometimes, X-ray images are produced especially for particular studies. Nevertheless, X-ray image acquisition implies a substantial monetary and time investment [19] and is not an option for all researchers. To counter this, studies have proposed using threat image projection (TIP), a technique that superimposes hazardous objects onto baggage images [6, 18, 26, 27]. Using synthetic images "readily enables the introduction of more variability in pose, scale, and prohibited item usage in an efficient and readily available way" [6] and consequently improves detection performance. Simulating new training data by overlaying real threat images is more affordable than generating entirely new datasets but still requires acquiring X-ray images of the threat objects.

In this work, we propose a method that generates new training data by superimposing simulated X-ray images of 3D models onto real baggage X-rays, improving detector performance. Furthermore, our approach requires neither additional manual labeling nor further acquiring of X-ray images, thus allowing researchers to generate new data with the millions of 3D models available online. To the best of our knowledge, this is the first study that uses 3D models for TIP.

The main contributions of this paper are (1) a 3D-model-based X-ray image simulation pipeline that requires no additional labeling or imaging, (2) an algorithm that generates color images from dual-energy grayscale images, (3) a realistic superimposition technique for colored X-ray images, and (4) public availability of all simulation, image generation, and model training scripts.

2   Proposed Method

The proposed method is divided into four main steps: (1) X-ray image generation, (2) colorization, (3) superimposition, and (4) model training. First, X-ray image generation creates grayscale low-energy and high-energy images from 3D models of threat objects. Colorization then uses these image pairs to generate pseudo-color images. Next, superimposition overlays the colored threat object images onto real X-ray images of baggage. Finally, these simulated images are used to train an object detector.

Figure 1 illustrates the algorithm's steps and how they interconnect.

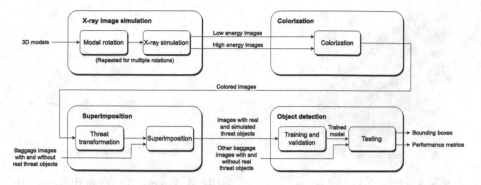

Fig. 1. Block diagram of the proposed method

2.1 X-ray Image Simulation

Instead of overlaying real X-ray images of threat objects, we propose generating these images from some of the millions of 3D models available online.[1] We found numerous models of pistols, shuriken, and wrenches, among other hazardous objects. If enough models cannot be found online, they can be designed from scratch, too.

In order to generate X-ray images of the isolated 3D models, we used aRTist (Analytical RT Inspection Simulation Tool) [4]. It is a paid program but there are free alternatives available, such as Syris [10], py-XVis [16], and xrayscanner.[2] aRTist allows the user to place one or more objects, the X-ray source, and the detector in a 3D space, situating them at any desired position and orientation. The user can select the object's material, the X-ray source's spectrum, and the detector's properties, among other settings.

We designed a script that automates the X-ray image generation process. It rotates the object along two axes, generating a 32-bit float image for each orientation. The rotation range and steps can be adjusted by the user. Figure 2 shows aRTist's virtual scene, and Fig. 3 shows some of the generated images.

---

[1] Some 3D model websites are Sketchfab, Turbosquid, Thingiverse, and Printables.
[2] Available at https://github.com/anthonytec2/xrayscanner.

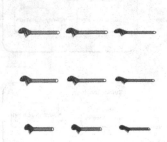

Fig. 2. aRTist's virtual scene

Fig. 3. Wrench X-rays in different orientations

Previous research articles have generated X-ray images of hazardous objects with generative adversarial networks (GANs) [27,31]. However, it has been reported that the generated images are very similar to the ones they were trained with, and the performance gains when training with GAN-generated images are not significant. Our approach generates images of new objects in unseen orientations, resulting in a more diverse training set.

2.2   Colorization

Dual-energy X-ray machines generate pseudo-color images using proprietary algorithms not disclosed to the public. To the best of our knowledge, no articles successfully establish how to generate pseudo-color images from a pair of dual-energy X-rays [32]. Neither have we found non-proprietary scripts or programs that fulfill this task. In our work, we propose a novel methodology for generating colored X-ray images.

Algorithm Overview and Definitions. The colorization algorithm is pixel-wise, meaning that each pixel's output does not depend on its neighbors. We will refer to the low-energy and high-energy input images as I_{LE} and I_{HE}, respectively. The output image will be defined by its hue, saturation, and value (HSV) representation, with its channels being referred to as O_H, O_S, and O_V.

Edge Cases. Some pixels are calculated independently to prevent the subsequent equations from going to infinity.

- If either input pixel is zero, the output pixel is set to black (as all photons were absorbed by the object).
- If the high-energy input pixel is one, the output pixel is set to white (as no photons were absorbed by the object).

Hue. The methods proposed in material determination articles [8,9,11] will help us calculate the output hue. In order to determine the material of an object, these articles present the Q-values. They are dependent on the material's effective atomic number (Z_{eff}) and invariant to the material's thickness (when using a monochromatic X-ray source) [9]. They are defined as follows:

$$Q = \frac{\log I_{LE}}{\log I_{HE}}. \tag{1}$$

The types of materials and their Z_{eff} ranges are chosen arbitrarily, but the three most commonly used are:

- Organic ($Z_{\text{eff}} \in [1, 11)$),
- Inorganic ($Z_{\text{eff}} \in [11, 19)$),
- Metal ($Z_{\text{eff}} \in [19, \infty)$).

The Q-value range for each material is generally determined empirically, as these values depend strongly on each X-ray machine's specifications [8].

Using the equations presented in [8], we can obtain an alternative representation of the Q-value for a particular material:

$$Q = \frac{\log I_{LE}}{\log I_{HE}} = \frac{\tau_{LE}}{\tau_{HE}}, \tag{2}$$

where τ_{LE} and τ_{HE} are the object's mass attenuation coefficients for each energy. They depend on the material's effective atomic number and the photons' energy. These coefficients are experimentally obtained and are currently tabularized in databases such as NIST XCOM [5].

For our colorizer to work for any pair of energies, our proposed method includes a NIST XCOM web scraper[3] that obtains the mass attenuation coefficient for virtually any element and energy. After extracting the data, the colorizer calculates the Q-values of particular elements to determine each material type's boundaries.

Pseudo-color X-ray images generally contain three material colors: orange (organic), green (non-organic), and blue (metal). Additionally, pixels corresponding to air are colored white. The hue is determined as follows:

- If Q is lower than the air-organic threshold, the output pixel is set to white (overriding the subsequent saturation and value calculations).
- Otherwise, if Q is lower than the organic-inorganic threshold, the hue is set to orange (organic).
- Otherwise, if Q is lower than the inorganic-metal threshold, the hue is set to green (inorganic).
- Finally, if Q is higher than or equal to the inorganic-metal threshold, the hue is set to blue (metal).

---

[3] Script that extracts data from a website.

Saturation and Value. Output saturation and value are calculated as follows:

$$O_S = 1 - \left(\frac{i_{LE} + i_{HE}}{2}\right)^3, \tag{3}$$

$$O_V = 1 - \left(1 - \frac{i_{LE} + i_{HE}}{2}\right)^3. \tag{4}$$

These equations generate bright, pale colors for high-intensity input pixels and dark, saturated colors for low-intensity input pixels, resembling the behavior of color images generated by X-ray machines. The resulting color spectrum is shown in Fig. 4, and two examples of colorization are shown in Fig. 5.

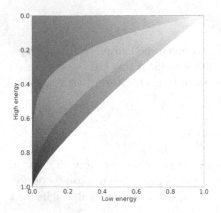

Fig. 4. Output pixels generated by the colorizer for each low-energy and high-energy pixel combination. The input X-ray energies are 50 keV and 150 keV.

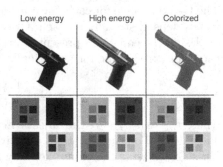

Fig. 5. Grayscale inputs and their respective colorized images. The bottom row shows blocks of different materials (aluminum, iron, titanium, and high-density polypropylene) overlaid over each other. The small blocks are in the same order as the large blocks.

2.3 Superimposition Preparation

Background Masking. This algorithm generates a mask of the baggage so that the subsequent insertion position algorithm places the threat objects only inside the bags. We followed the procedure presented in [6] but slightly modified it to improve the generated masks. The final algorithm is the following:

1. Convert the background image to grayscale.

2. Binarize the image using a threshold slightly lower than the most common pixel value (corresponds to the background).
3. Dilate the mask.
4. Fill small holes.
5. Erode the mask.
6. Close small regions.

Some examples of background images and their respective masks are shown in Fig. 6.

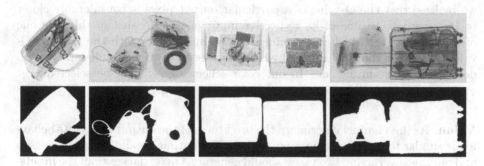

Fig. 6. Examples of background images with their respective bag masks [21,30].

Threat Transformation. In order to increase the threat object variety, we transform the foreground images before overlaying them onto the background X-ray. The steps followed are:

1. Randomly resize the image to a user-defined size range.
2. Rotate by a random angle.
3. Horizontally mirror with a 50% probability.
4. Crop the excess white borders.

Insertion Position Determination. This algorithm randomly generates insertion positions until one where the threat is entirely inside the mask is found. If a valid insertion position is not found after several attempts, the threat is transformed again and slightly shrunk, and the search process is repeated.

Threat Thresholding. In order to remove the threat image's background, we find an optimal threshold using Otsu's method [24]. This adaptive method finds the value that optimally splits the pixels into two classes by minimizing intra-class intensity variance.

2.4   Superimposition

We designed a realistic algorithm for overlaying color X-ray images. Its equations are based on the approximately multiplicative nature of X-ray images [26] and our analyses of simulated images of superimposed objects. This algorithm is performed pixel-wise in the HSV color space, only considering pixels where the threat object is present. The algorithm for each channel is the following:

Hue. When overlaying color images, we do not have information regarding their exact Q-values. However, upon analyzing images of superimposed objects, we realized that the Q-value of a particular output pixel is considerably closer to the greatest Q-value of its respective input pixels. Because of this, the hue of an output pixel will be determined by the input pixel with the greatest Q-value, signifying that the material with the highest effective atomic number will determine the resulting hue. In our color scheme, green will be selected over orange, and blue will be selected over green and orange.

Value. As this channel determines the brightness of the output image, its behavior is similar to grayscale superimposition. The output should be between zero and one, and overlaying two pixels should generate a pixel darker than the inputs. This means that the output value will always be lower than the input values. A simple equation that obeys these restrictions is:

$$V_O = V_{LE}V_{HE}, \tag{5}$$

where V_{LE}, V_{HE}, and V_O are the low-energy, high-energy, and output values, respectively.

Saturation. This channel presents a similar but opposite behavior to the value channel. Here, the output will be between the highest input saturation and one. This behavior can be replicated using Eq. 5 but replacing the variables V with $(1 - S)$, as follows:

$$(1 - S_O) = (1 - S_{LE})(1 - S_{HE}), \tag{6}$$

where S_{LE}, S_{HE}, and S_O are the low-energy, high-energy, and output saturations, respectively.

After reordering, the resulting saturation equation is:

$$S_O = S_{LE} + S_{HE} - S_{LE}S_{HE}. \tag{7}$$

Some existing superimposition algorithms [6] blend the images using a weighted sum. With that method, the brightness of the output pixels will not be lower than the brightness of the input pixels, resulting in synthetic-looking images when one of the inputs is very dark or bright.

We believe our superimposition method is an improvement over existing algorithms, as our approach creates realistic images and obeys the behavior of saturation (output always higher than the inputs) and value (output always lower than the inputs).

Figure 7 shows images generated by our superimposition algorithm.

 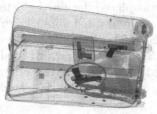 

(a) Simulated wrench over a suitcase [28].   (b) Simulated pistol over a suitcase [21].   (c) Real drill [7] over a plastic container [30].

Fig. 7. Threat objects superimposed over images of various datasets. The overlaid objects are indicated with circles.

2.5 Object Detection

In order to evaluate our method, we trained a modern object detector with the simulated X-ray images. In the subsequent validation and testing stages, it detected these targets on a new set of images, specifying bounding boxes and class probabilities.

In particular, we chose YOLOv5 [12],[4] a state-of-the-art object detection model. Its real-time performance and exceptional accuracy render it an optimal selection for X-ray baggage inspection. Other detectors such as Faster R-CNN [25], SSD [15], and RetinaNet [13] could also fulfill this task, albeit with different results.

Due to the limited number of threat objects, we employ transfer learning, a strategy where the initial weights have already been pre-trained with other targets. This approach is superior to initializing the model with random weights, as pre-trained networks have already learned basic features like edges, shapes, and patterns.

---

[4] Available at https://github.com/ultralytics/yolov5.

3   Experimental Setup

3.1   X-ray Image Simulation

3D Models. We chose wrenches as the threat objects for our experiments, as they are one of the labeled objects of the SIXRay dataset [21]. We selected seven free 3D models and set their material in aRTist to SAE 304 stainless steel.

Rotations. Each wrench was placed flat on the detector and rotated in 22.5° increments. The wrench was fully rotated about its first principal axis for three orientations of the second principal axis: 0°, 22.5° and 45°. Images with rotations of ±67.5°, ±90°, and ±112.5° about the first principal axis were discarded since those rotations self-occluded the wrenches. Sixty images (30 for each energy) were generated per wrench, resulting in 420 simulated images.

Energies. As datasets do not generally include information about the X-ray source's energies, we had to find a pair of energies where the real and simulated objects' opacities looked similar. For these experiments, we selected 100 KeV and 150 KeV monochromatic X-ray sources.

Generated Images. We instructed aRTist to generate 400 × 400 32-bit float images between zero and one. The high bit depth is essential since the colorizer needs high floating-point precision to calculate the Q-values adequately.

3.2   Colorization

X-ray baggage datasets use slightly different hues for each material color (see Fig. 7), so we selected the exact hue based on the dataset used. The colors can also be adapted for datasets that use entirely different colors, like CLCXray [32].

3.3   Superimposition

For the experiments, we used the 8 350 images in SIXRay's [21] "SIXrayP" folder, as all threat objects are labeled [23]. Threats were superimposed over 7 515 images (90% of the total), leaving the rest for testing purposes.

The number of wrenches to overlay was chosen randomly for each background image, based on the following probabilities: 0: 10%, 1: 50%, 2: 30%, 3: 10%. The resulting train and validation sets have a total of 13 704 wrenches, corresponding to an average of 1.82 wrenches per image.

3.4   Object Detection

Data Split. Similar to the procedure followed in [17,27], the images were split into a training, validation, and testing set with an 80%, 10%, and 10% ratio, respectively. The resulting number of images per category is: training: 6 680, validation: 835, testing: 835.

Experiments. Experiments were run on two versions of the same data. One has real and simulated wrenches in its training and validation sets, while the other only has real wrenches. Both experiments use the same non-synthetic images for testing. Running an experiment with only real wrenches allowed us to use its results as a baseline, quantifying the performance improvements that arise from adding fully simulated threat objects.

Training. We trained YOLOv5's largest model, YOLOv5x, for 30 epochs using the default parameters and pre-trained COCO weights [14]. We followed Ultra-lytics' "Tips for Best Training Results" [29] with two exceptions:

- We trained for 30 epochs instead of the recommended 300 to have quicker iterations.
- Due to the limited number of threat objects in the dataset, the baseline training and validation sets have only 3 076 real wrenches, which is fewer than the recommended 10 000 objects per class.

3.5   Implementation

The machines used for each step were:

- **X-ray image simulation:** Windows machine with an Intel Core i5 processor and 8 GB of RAM.
- **Colorization and superimposition:** MacBook Pro with an Apple M1 Pro processor and 16 GB of RAM.
- **Object detection:** Google Colab machine with an Intel Xeon CPU and an Nvidia Tesla T4 GPU.

All python scripts, aRTist scripts, and Google Colab notebooks are available on a public repository.[5] Execution times are presented in Table 1.

Table 1. Execution times

Step	Time per iteration	Iterations	Total time
X-ray image simulation	70 milliseconds	420 images	29.4 seconds
Colorization	1.1 seconds	210 pairs of images	3.9 minutes
Superimposition	120 milliseconds	7515 images	15 minutes
YOLO training	9.17 minutes	30 epochs	4.6 hours
YOLO testing	24.2 milliseconds	835 images	20.2 seconds

---

[5] Available at https://github.com/kaminetzky/axis.

4   Results and Discussion

Table 2 shows how the models performed on the testing set. The reported metrics are precision, recall, and average precision for two intersection-over-union (IoU) thresholds (0.5 and 0.5 to 0.95 with a 0.05 step). The third row exhibits the percentage point increase between experiments.

Table 2. Object detection results

Dataset	Precision	Recall	$AP_{0.5}$	$AP_{0.5:0.95}$
Only real wrenches	93.6%	83.5%	90.2%	74.7%
Real and simulated wrenches	97.2%	91.0%	93.7%	83.5%
Difference	3.6pp	7.5pp	3.5pp	8.8pp

Figure 8 shows complex detections on the testing set and demonstrates how trained models are able to find occluded wrenches.

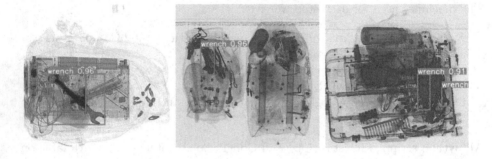

Fig. 8. Examples of complex detections in the testing set

Adding fully simulated threat objects to the training subset improved metrics, increasing precision by 3.8%, recall by 9%, and average precision by 3.9% and 11.8%. These results demonstrate that the proposed method can improve performance when there is limited data for training.

As the testing dataset contains no simulated threats, the results are a realistic representation of real-world performance. In addition, the short inference time (24.2 ms per image) shows that a YOLO detection model could be implemented for real-time detection, analyzing 40 frames per second.

Human-annotated datasets may have improperly placed bounding boxes [32]. This leads to misleading metrics at high IoU thresholds, as the potentially correct predictions will not match the out-of-place ground truths. Datasets may also be missing annotations [23], resulting in worse apparent performance since some accurate detections will be classified as false positives. These issues will cause the metrics to be worse than the actual performance, meaning 100% precision and recall will not always be possible. Nevertheless, this should affect all of the experiments comparably, thus not altering the drawn conclusions.

The results shown in this article are preliminary, and the proposed method's performance will be studied in-depth in a future version of this study. As training and validation loss at 30 epochs are still decreasing, the YOLO model will be trained for longer, resulting in better performance. In addition, we will run experiments training with baggage X-ray images that contain only simulated threat objects, determining if our procedure is applicable when no real X-ray images of a particular object are available. Finally, we will run experiments with additional background datasets and threat objects to verify if the proposed method can be applied to any scenario.

5 Conclusions

This article proposed a novel method that generates data for training deep neural networks by superimposing simulated X-ray images of 3D models onto real data. To our knowledge, no previous studies have used 3D models for TIP. Our approach involves neither manual annotations nor additional X-ray imaging, reducing the time and money investments required for carrying out studies and training threat detection models. The colorization and superimposition techniques presented in this paper could also be used for training inspectors and conducting experiments for other X-ray applications.

We ran preliminary experiments as proof of concept, obtaining considerable performance improvements when adding fully simulated threat objects. This, in addition to YOLOv5's real-time inference capability, demonstrates it is feasible to use our method to aid security operators and even fully automate inspections.

A future version of this article will further analyze our proposed method's performance. The experiments will have longer training times, multiple datasets, and additional threat object types. We will also train with images containing only simulated threats, evaluating the potential for detecting objects not present in X-ray datasets.

Acknowledgments. This work was supported by National Center for Artificial Intelligence CENIA FB210017, Basal ANID, and ANID National Master's Scholarship 2021 N°22211094.

References

1. Akcay, S., Breckon, T.: Towards automatic threat detection: a survey of advances of deep learning within X-ray security imaging. Pattern Recogn. **122**, 108245 (2022)
2. Akçay, S., Kundegorski, M.E., Devereux, M., Breckon, T.P.: Transfer learning using convolutional neural networks for object classification within X-ray baggage security imagery. In: 2016 IEEE International Conference on Image Processing (ICIP), pp. 1057–1061 (2016)

3. Akcay, S., Kundegorski, M.E., Willcocks, C.G., Breckon, T.P.: Using deep convolutional neural network architectures for object classification and detection within X-ray baggage security imagery. IEEE Trans. Inf. Forensics Secur. **13**(9), 2203–2215 (2018)
4. Bellon, C., Jaenisch, G.-R.: aRTist-analytical RT inspection simulation tool. In: Proceedings of the DIR, pp. 25–27 (2007)
5. Berger, M., et al.: XCOM: Photon Cross Section Database (version 1.5). http://physics.nist.gov/xcom. Accessed 30 May 2022
6. Bhowmik, N., Wang, Q., Gaus, Y.F.A., Szarek, M., Breckon, T.P.: The good, the bad and the ugly: evaluating convolutional neural networks for prohibited item detection using real and synthetically composited X-ray imagery. arXiv preprint arXiv:1909.11508 (2019)
7. Caldwell, M., Griffin, L.D.: Limits on transfer learning from photographic image data to X-ray threat detection. J. Xray Sci. Technol. **27**(6), 1007–1020 (2019)
8. Dmitruk, K., Denkowski, M., Mazur, M., Mikolajczak, P.: Sharpening filter for false color imaging of dual-energy X-ray scans. Signal Image Video Process. **11**(4), 613–620 (2017)
9. Duvillier, J., et al.: Inline multi-material identification via dual energy radiographic measurements. NDT E Int. **94**, 120–125 (2018)
10. Faragó, T., Mikulík, P., Ershov, A., Vogelgesang, M., Hänschke, D., Baumbach, T.: Syris: a flexible and efficient framework for X-ray imaging experiments simulation. J. Synchrotron Radiat. **24**(6), 1283–1295 (2017)
11. Firsching, F., Fuchs, T., Uhlmann, N.: Method for dual high energy X-ray imaging with at panel detectors (2006)
12. Jocher, G., et al.: Ultralytics/YOLOv5: v6.1 - TensorRT, TensorFlow Edge TPU and OpenVINO Export and Inference, version v6.1 (2022)
13. Lin, T.-Y., Goyal, P., Girshick, R., He, K., Dollár, P.: Focal loss for dense object detection. In: Proceedings of the IEEE International Conference on Computer Vision, pp. 2980–2988 (2017)
14. Lin, T.-Y., et al.: Microsoft COCO: common objects in context. In: Fleet, D., Pajdla, T., Schiele, B., Tuytelaars, T. (eds.) ECCV 2014. LNCS, vol. 8693, pp. 740–755. Springer, Cham (2014). https://doi.org/10.1007/978-3-319-10602-1_48
15. Liu, W., et al.: SSD: single shot multibox detector. In: Leibe, B., Matas, J., Sebe, N., Welling, M. (eds.) ECCV 2016. LNCS, vol. 9905, pp. 21–37. Springer, Cham (2016). https://doi.org/10.1007/978-3-319-46448-0_2
16. Mery, D.: Computer Vision for X-Ray Testing. Springer, Cham (2015). https://doi.org/10.1007/978-3-319-20747-6
17. Mery, D., Kaminetzky, A., Golborne, L., Figueroa, S., Saavedra, D.: Target detection by target simulation in X-ray testing. J. Nondestr. Eval. **41**(1), 1–12 (2022). https://doi.org/10.1007/s10921-022-00851-8
18. Mery, D., Katsaggelos, A.K.: A logarithmic X-ray imaging model for baggage inspection: simulation and object detection. In: Proceedings of the IEEE Conference on Computer Vision and Pattern Recognition Workshops, pp. 57–65 (2017)
19. Mery, D., Saavedra, D., Prasad, M.: X-ray baggage inspection with computer vision: a survey. IEEE Access **8**, 145620–145633 (2020)
20. Mery, D., Svec, E., Arias, M., Riffo, V., Saavedra, J.M., Banerjee, S.: Modern computer vision techniques for x-ray testing in baggage inspection. IEEE Trans. Syst. Man Cybern.: Syst. **47**(4), 682–692 (2016)
21. Miao, C., et al.: SIXray: a large-scale security inspection X-ray benchmark for prohibited item discovery in overlapping images. In: Proceedings of the IEEE/CVF Conference on Computer Vision and Pattern Recognition, pp. 2119–2128 (2019)

22. Michel, S., Koller, S., de Ruiter, J., Moerland, R., Hogervorst, M., Schwaninger, A.: Computer-based training increases efficiency in X-ray image interpretation by aviation security screeners. In: 2007 41st Annual IEEE International Carnahan Conference on Security Technology, pp. 201–206 (2007)
23. Nguyen, H.D., Cai, R., Zhao, H., Kot, A.C., Wen, B.: Towards more efficient security inspection via deep learning: a task-driven X-ray image cropping scheme. Micromachines 13(4), 565 (2022)
24. Otsu, N.: A threshold selection method from gray-level histograms. IEEE Trans. Syst. Man Cybern. 9(1), 62–66 (1979)
25. Ren, S., He, K., Girshick, R., Sun, J.: Faster R-CNN: towards real-time object detection with region proposal networks. In: Advances in Neural Information Processing Systems, vol. 28 (2015)
26. Rogers, T.W., Jaccard, N., Protonotarios, E.D., Ollier, J., Morton, E.J., Griff-in, L.D.: Threat Image Projection (TIP) into X-ray images of cargo containers for training humans and machines. In: 2016 IEEE International Carnahan Conference on Security Technology (ICCST), pp. 1–7 (2016)
27. Saavedra, D., Banerjee, S., Mery, D.: Detection of threat objects in baggage inspection with X-ray images using deep learning. Neural Comput. Appl. 33(13), 7803–7819 (2021)
28. Tao, R., et al.: Towards real-world X-ray security inspection: a high-quality benchmark and lateral inhibition module for prohibited items detection. In: Proceedings of the IEEE/CVF International Conference on Computer Vision, pp. 10923–10932 (2021)
29. Ultralytics: Tips for best training results. https://docs.ultralytics.com/tutorials/training-tips-best-results/. Accessed 30 May 2022
30. Wei, Y., Tao, R., Wu, Z., Ma, Y., Zhang, L., Liu, X.: Occluded prohibited items detection: an X-ray security inspection benchmark and de-occlusion attention module. In: Proceedings of the 28th ACM International Conference on Multimedia, pp. 138–146 (2020)
31. Yang, J., Zhao, Z., Zhang, H., Shi, Y.: Data augmentation for X-ray prohibited item images using generative adversarial networks. IEEE Access 7, 28894–28902 (2019)
32. Zhao, C., Zhu, L., Dou, S., Deng, W., Wang, L.: Detecting overlapped objects in X-ray security imagery by a label-aware mechanism. IEEE Trans. Inf. Forensics Secur. 17, 998–1009 (2022)

A Wasserstein GAN for Joint Learning of Inpainting and Spatial Optimisation

Pascal Peter[✉]

Mathematical Image Analysis Group, Faculty of Mathematics and Computer Science, Saarland University, Campus E1.7, 66041 Saarbrücken, Germany
peter@mia.uni-saarland.de

Abstract. Image inpainting is a restoration method that reconstructs missing image parts. However, a carefully selected mask of known pixels that yield a high quality inpainting can also act as a sparse image representation. This challenging spatial optimisation problem is essential for practical applications such as compression. So far, it has been almost exclusively addressed by model-based approaches. First attempts with neural networks seem promising, but are tailored towards specific inpainting operators or require postprocessing. To address this issue, we propose the first generative adversarial network (GAN) for spatial inpainting data optimisation. In contrast to previous approaches, it allows joint training of an inpainting generator and a corresponding mask optimisation network. With a Wasserstein distance, we ensure that our inpainting results accurately reflect the statistics of natural images. This yields significant improvements in visual quality and speed over conventional stochastic models. It also outperforms current spatial optimisation networks.

Keywords: inpainting · spatial optimisation · generative adversarial network · Wasserstein distance

1   Introduction

Image inpainting was originally introduced to restore missing or damaged image parts [6,22]. In this classical setting, the known image data is predetermined. However, given the original image, one can instead consider a spatial optimisation problem: finding a fraction of known data that allows a high quality reconstruction of the image with inpainting. These sparse representations, the so-called inpainting masks, have practical applications such as inpainting-based compression [13,26] and adaptive sampling [11]. Therefore, many sophisticated model-based approaches have been proposed for spatial optimisation of inpainting data [5,7,9,10,15,17,21]. However, due to the unique challenges of this problem, solutions are often slow, complicated, or limited to specific inpainting operators.

Recently, some first attempts were made to solve the mask optimisation problem with neural networks [1,11]. However, these approaches have limitations.

© Springer Nature Switzerland AG 2023
H. Wang et al. (Eds.): PSIVT 2022, LNCS 13763, pp. 132–145, 2023.
https://doi.org/10.1007/978-3-031-26431-3_11

From classical methods it is well known that optimal positions for an inpainting mask heavily depend on the inpainting operator [24]. Despite this close connection, existing deep learning approaches do not allow to train a pair of inpainting and spatial optimisation networks, but either train them separately [11] or do not allow learned inpainting at all [1].

1.1 Our Contribution

We propose the first generative adversarial approach for deep inpainting and spatial optimisation. It consists of three networks: an inpainting generator, a mask generator, and a discriminator. The discriminator allows our learned inpainting to approximate the statistics of natural images in terms of a Wasserstein distance, leading to convincing visual quality. Our mask network is the first to generate binary inpainting masks directly. It solves non-differentiability issues with approaches from neural network-based image compression. The combination of these ingredients makes effective joint learning of inpainting and mask optimisation possible.

1.2 Related Work

The selection of suitable known data is highly dependent on the inpainting operator. Only for individual operators such as homogeneous diffusion [16], true optimality statements have been proven [5], but even those can only be approximated in practice. Optimal control [7,9,15] approaches and a recent finite element method [10] offer good results, but are limited to certain operators. In our comparisons, we consider *probabilistic sparsification* (PS) and *non-local pixel exchange* (NLPE) [21] as representatives for classical methods. PS is a stochastic greedy method that gradually removes pixels which increase the inpainting error the least. NLPE is a postprocessing step which moves mask points to the most promising positions of a randomly chosen candidate set. Together, they belong to the current state of the art in quality and are applicable to any deterministic inpainting operator. For a more detailed review of model-based spatial optimisation, we refer to Alt et al. [1].

To the best of our knowledge, only two deep learning approaches for spatial inpainting data optimisation exist so far. The network of Alt et al. [1] differs fundamentally from our approach in that it optimises masks for homogeneous diffusion inpainting, not for a deep inpainting. During training, the mask network feeds a non-binary confidence map for known data to a surrogate network approximating homogeneous diffusion. It requires postprocessing by stochastic sampling to obtain the final binary masks. The adaptive sampling contribution of Dai et al. [11] is closer in spirit to our approach: It combines a mask network *NetM* with a pre-trained inpainting network *NetE*. The authors note that joint training of NetM and NetE did not yield satisfying results due the non-binary output of NetM. We address this in more detail in Sect. 3.1.

A full review of the numerous deep inpainting approaches is beyond the scope of this paper. Most of these [19,20,23,31,32,34–36] focus on classical inpainting problems: Regular shaped regions like squares, circles, text, or free form scribbles are removed from the image. Typically this means that only a modest amount of data is missing (10%–60%). In contrast, sparse spatial optimisation is mostly concerned with much higher amounts of unknown data (>90%) since those are interesting for compression or adaptive sampling purposes. Moreover, optimised known data is often not only extremely sparse, but also does not provide nicely connected regions. Most existing approaches are thus not directly applicable and at the very least, the training procedure must be adapted.

Deep learning methods specifically designed for sparse data are much more rare [28,30]. We explain in more detail in Sect. 2 why we specifically choose Wasserstein GANs [3,30] as a foundation for our approach. Note that none of the aforementioned pure inpainting methods provides the option for data optimisation or has been previously evaluated on optimised known data.

1.3   Organisation of the Paper

After a brief review of Wasserstein GANs in Sect. 2 we introduce our deep spatial optimisation approach in Sect. 3 and evaluate it in Sect. 4. The paper concludes with a discussion and outlook on future work in Sect. 5.

2   Inpainting with Wasserstein GANs

For our data optimisation, we require deep inpainting that is suitable for sparse known data. Vašata et al. [30] have successfully applied *Wasserstein generative adversarial networks* (WGANs) for inpainting on random sparse data. Since WGANs are also mathematically well-founded, they are a natural starting point for our approach. In particular, *generative adversarial networks* (GANs) [14] can be seen as generalisation of classical inpainting techniques that achieve high quality [26] by accurately approximating the statistics of natural images [25].

A GAN relies on two competing networks to generate samples from a target distribution $\mathbb{P}_t$. The *generator* takes a sample from a source distribution $\mathbb{P}_s$ and maps it to a representative of $\mathbb{P}_t$. In our case, $\mathbb{P}_s$ is a uniformly random distribution, and $\mathbb{P}_t$ corresponds to the statistics of natural images. The *discriminator* judges how well the generated representative fits to the target distribution. This creates a minmax problem, in which the generator tries to trick the discriminator in accepting its result as a true sample of $\mathbb{P}_t$.

Unfortunately, GANs tend to suffer from training instabilities due to imbalances between the generator and the discriminator. Arjovsky et al. [3] have shown the large impact of the loss function, which measures the difference between generator samples and target distributions. Using a Wasserstein distance [29] instead of the classical Jensen-Shannon divergence [14] stabilises training, avoids vanishing gradients, and indicates training progress more reliably.

Assume we want to inpaint an image of resolution $m \cdot n$ with k channels with a WGAN [30]. We write its $N := mnk$ pixel values in vector notation as $f \in \mathbb{R}^N$. Data is known at locations where the confidence function $c \in [0,1]^N$

is non-zero, thus providing side information for the generator $g : \left(\mathbb{R}^N\right)^3 \to \mathbb{R}^N$, a parametric function represented by a network. Representing the known data as Cf with a masking matrix $C := \text{diag}(c) \in \mathbb{R}^{N \times N}$, the generator creates the inpainting result $u \in \mathbb{R}^N$ based on the inpainting constraint

$$u(r, c, Cf) := (I - C)g(r, c, Cf) + Cf. \tag{1}$$

The discriminator $d : \mathbb{R}^N \times R^N \to \mathbb{R}$ aims to distinguish the distribution of the reconstruction with the known data as side information $\mathbb{P}(u|c, Cf)$ from the original distribution $\mathbb{P}(f|c, Cf)$, minimising

$$\mathbb{E}_{f \sim \mathbb{P}_t, c \sim \mathbb{P}_c}\left(\mathbb{E}_{r \sim \mathbb{P}_s} d(u(r, c, Cf), c) - d(f, c)\right). \tag{2}$$

Here, f is a sample from the natural image distribution $\mathbb{P}_t$, c a random mask from the distribution $\mathbb{P}_c$, and r a uniformly random seed. $\mathbb{E}$ denotes the expected value which is estimated in practice via the batch mean. To approximate the Lipschitz property required by the Wasserstein distance, the discriminator weights are normalised to 1 in the 2-norm (see [30]). The generator has a combined loss which weights the discriminator opinion with parameter α against a mean absolute error (MAE) in terms of the 1-norm $\|\cdot\|_1$ that attaches the result to the concrete original image f:

$$\mathbb{E}_{f \sim \mathbb{P}_t, r \sim \mathbb{P}_s, c \sim \mathbb{P}_c}\left(-\alpha d(u(r, c, Cf), c) + \|f - u(r, c, Cf)\|_1\right). \tag{3}$$

Vašata et al. [30] use a common hourglass structure for g that successively subsamples the input data, passes it through a bottleneck and upsamples it again to the output (see g in Fig. 1(a)). Skip connections forward data between corresponding scales in this hierarchical network. The building blocks of their architecture are visualised in Fig. 1(b)–(d).

Downsampling in the hourglass is performed by *CBlocks* using 3 parallel convolutions with filter size 5×5, dilation rates 0, 2, and 5, and ELU activation. Their concatenated output is followed by a 2×2 max -pooling, which is the output of the block. Upsampling in *TCBlocks* follows the same principle with transposed convolutions and 2×2 upsampling instead. The parallel dilations increase the influence area of these blocks, which is particularly useful for sparse known data, since it increases the chance to include some reliable pixels in the receptive field of the convolution layers. To restrict the image to the original pixel value range $[0, 1]$, the last transposed convolutional layer has a hard sigmoid activation.

The discriminator follows a simpler downsampling architecture, where *FBlocks* combine 5×5 convolutions (stride 2) with Leaky ReLUs (see d in Fig. 1). For exact details we refer to [30].

3   Learning Masks with Wasserstein GANs

3.1   Learning Binary Masks

Existing networks [1, 11] produce a non-binary confidence map $c \in [0, 1]^N$ during training. Dai et al. [11] have identified this as a major roadblock for joint training

Table 1. Binarisation with Quantisation Operators. Here, ε is chosen uniformly random from $[0, 0.5]$. Among the three different options for binarisation operators [27], we choose hard rounding due to its simplicity and good performance in our practical implementation.

additive noise	stochastic rounding	hard rounding
$b(x) = x + \varepsilon$	$b(x) \in \{0, 1\}$, $P(b(x) = 1) = x - \lfloor x \rfloor$	$b(x) = \lfloor x + 0.5 \rfloor$

of an inpainting and mask networks. The known data Cf obtained in Eq. (1) provides information to the inpainting network that is not available during actual inpainting. Therefore, we need to binarise the mask already during training.

Unfortunately, binarisation is non-differentiable and thus prevents backpropagation. We solve this issue with a *binarisation block* for the last step of our mask generator. In a first step of this block, we apply a transposed convolution with a single channel output, followed by a hard sigmoid activation. We interpret the conversion of this non-binary output $c \in [0, 1]^N$ into a binary mask $b \in \{0, 1\}^N$ as an extreme case of quantisation. Such a discretisation of the co-domain restricts the admissible range of values, in our case just 0 and 1.

In deep compression, non-differentiability is often addressed by choosing representatives of the quantisation intervals according to additive random noise [4]. Theis et al. [27] have investigated different quantisation strategies in neural network-based compression and the impact of quantisation perturbations on training (see Table 1). Compared with additive noise and stochastic rounding they found hard rounding to perform the best. Therefore, we round non-binary confidence values c according to $b(c) = \lfloor c + 0.5 \rfloor$. Following the findings of Theis et al., we approximate the gradient of the binarisation layer by the derivative of a simple linear function for backpropagation.

3.2   Joint Learning of Inpainting Operator and Masks

The overall structure of our joint mask and inpainting WGAN is displayed in Fig. 1. Our new *mask generator* m maps the original $f \in \mathbb{R}^N$ and a uniformly random seed $r \in \mathbb{R}^N$ to a binary mask $b = m(r, f)$. The generator g uses this mask and the known data $Bf := \text{diag}(b)f$ as side information to create the inpainting result u from another random seed. The discriminator loss from Eq. 2 and the generator loss from Eq. 3 ensures that the inpainting respects the statistics of natural images. However, the mask c is replaced by the output b of the mask generator.

Unfortunately, we have no way to obtain training data for the unknown distribution of the binary masks that should be approximated by the mask generator m. This distribution depends on the inpainting operator which is simultaneously trained, thus creating a "chicken and egg" problem. We solve this by indirectly describing the distribution: The mask generator is coupled to the Wasserstein loss of the discriminator and generator, since b influences the

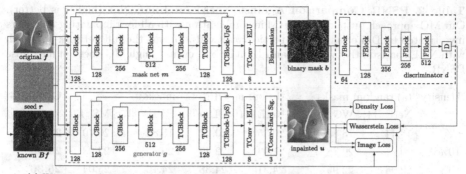

(a) Wasserstein Generative Adversarial Network for Joint Inpainting and Mask Optimisation

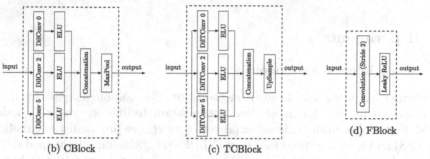

(b) CBlock   (c) TCBlock   (d) FBlock

Fig. 1. Overview over our model structure. The arrows denote forward passes. CBlocks, TCBlocks, and FBlocks denote convolutional, transposed convolutional, and funnel blocks (see Sect. 2). The las TCBlock omits the upsampling layer (indicated by -UpS). TConv denotes transposed convolutions, DConv dilated convolutions, and DTConv their transposed counterpart. All convolutions use filter size 5×5. The numbers in dilated convolution layers indicate the dilation parameter. The block height in (a) visualises resolution and the block width roughly indicates the number of output channels, which is precisely given by the numbers below each block.

inpainting result u. Moreover, we define a *density loss* that measures the deviation of percentage of known pixels $\|b\|_1/N$ from the target density D of the inpainting mask. The following loss is directly imposed on the mask network, weighting the density loss against the inpainting MAE by β:

$$\mathbb{E}_{f \sim \mathbb{P}_t, r \sim \mathbb{P}_s} \left(\left| \|m(r,f)\|_1/N - D \right| + \beta \|f - u(r, m(r,f), Bf)\|_1 \right). \tag{4}$$

The architecture of the generator and discriminator is identical to the one from Sect. 2. The mask generator mostly follows the inpainting generator design. We only replace the last block by the binarisation from Sect. 3.1. Due to the Wasserstein loss, training is straightforward: In each epoch, we update the weights of all three networks with backpropagation. Training remains stable and requires no fine tuning of the balance between generator and discriminator.

Table 2. PSNR Comparison Against NetM on ImageNet (higher is better). Our MG approach outperforms NetM in combination with all four inpainting operators investigated by Dai et al. [11]. In particular, it outperforms the full network approach with NetE consistently by more than 1dB in PSNR, even though MG does not maximise PSNR.

Density	(a) random masks		(b) optimised NetM masks				Our MG
	NetE [11]	WGAN [30]	NetE [11]	CDD [8]	BPFA [37]	MS [12]	
5%	18.44	18.85	20.35	20.22	15.82	20.70	**21.66**
10%	19.94	20.78	21.93	22.42	20.82	22.98	**23.63**
20%	22.06	22.95	24.31	24.38	24.16	25.04	**25.36**

4   Experiments

4.1   Experimental Methodology

We compare against state-of-the-art methods for optimisation of inpainting data. As discussed in Sect. 1.2, most data optimisation techniques are still model-based. Out of the various existing approaches, we choose probabilistic sparsification (PS) and non-local pixel exchange (NLPE) [21], which mark the qualitative state of the art for most inpainting techniques, including the widely-used homogeneous diffusion [16] inpainting. In particular, the diffusion mask network of Alt et al. [1] reaches similar quality as PS on greyscale data. Results on colour images are not available and a corresponding extension would be non-trivial.

Our direct competitor on the neural network side is NetM [11] since it optimises known data for deep inpainting. Therefore, we compare against NetM in combination with all inpainting operators evaluated by Dai et al.- [11]. The numerous pure neural networks for inpainting discussed in Sect. 1.2 only perform inpainting of pre-defined masks and do not perform spatial optimisation. They can therefore not be considered for comparison.

Our neural networks were trained on the same $100,000$ image *ImageNet* subset also used by Dai et al. [11] and the corresponding validation set. Depending on the evaluation set, these were centre-cropped to either 128×128 or 64×64. We used the *Adam* optimiser [18] with learning rate $5 \cdot 10^{-5}$ and a batch size of $b = 32$ for image size 128×128, and $b = 128$ for image size 64×64. The model parameters were set to $\alpha = 0.005$ and $\beta = 1$. For each mask density D, separate networks were trained. We chose the best weights w.r.t. the mask validation loss from Eq. (4) after 1000 epochs. In most cases, this was already reached after roughly 100 epochs.

As evaluation datasets we use the ImageNet test set provided by Dai et al. [11] for the network comparison. For the comparison with NLPE, we use the Berkeley shape database *BSDS500* [2], since it has better public availability and this also demonstrates that our networks transfer well to other natural image databases.

4.2   Comparison Against NetM

We compare against the mask generator NetM [11] on the test set curated by Dai et al. It consists of 1000 images or resolution 64×64. They provide peak-signal-to-noise ratio (PSNR) results of NetM in combination with the corresponding inpainting network NetE and multiple classical inpainting approaches [8,12,37]. Note that NetM is trained to minimise a 2-norm, giving it an advantage over our 1-norm/Wasserstein trained MG in this evaluation. Nevertheless, in Table 2(b), MG outperforms NetM+NetE substantially by up to 1.7 dB.

To verify that this advantage does not only result from using a GAN for inpainting, we also compare the inpainting WGAN [30] to NetE on random masks in Table 2(a). On 5% known data, the WGAN outperforms NetE only by 0.4 dB. Our mask GAN increases this improvement over NetM+NetE to 1.3 dB. This indicates that our mask binarisation and joint training offers an advantage.

Additional inpainting operators in combination with NetM, such as the Bayesian beta process factor analysis (BPFA) [37], curvature-driven diffusion (CCD) [8], or Mumford-Shah (MS) inpainting [12] all yield worse results than our mask GAN. We outperform the best NetM approach by up to 0.96 dB.

4.3   Comparison Against Probabilistic Methods

Probabilistic sparsification (PS) with a non-local pixel exchange (NLPE) as a postprocessing step defines a benchmark for the best results obtainable so far with homogeneous diffusion inpainting. Other methods [1,5,7,9,15] yield comparable or worse quality.

We optimise the stochastic models for mean average error (MAE) since this is also part of the network loss. NLPE uses 5 cycles of $|c|$ iterations. At first glance, in terms of MAE, our mask GAN (MG) is situated between PS and PS+NLPE in Table 3(a). It performs better on sparser masks which are more relevant for e.g. compression applications and comes very close to the NLPE error for 5%. We also evaluate w.r.t. the popular structural-similarity index (SSIM) [33] in Table 3(b). It yields a slightly different ranking, with our mask GAN also outperforming PS+NLPE on the 5% density and very similar values for all methods on 10%.

Since these error measures yield less clear quantitative results than our first set of experiments, we also provide multiple visual examples. Figure 2 demonstrates that our MG excels for low densities which are useful for applications such as thumbnail compression or destructive image acquisition. This holds especially for complex images, for instance the high contrast texture of the zebra, or the house with many small-scale details like the lawn and fence. PS and NLPE need to cluster known data left and right to edges according to the optimality theory of Belhachmi et al. [5]. In regions where this is not possible, they suffer from detail loss and colour bleeding. Sometimes, minimising the MAE with NLPE even leads to a slight deterioration w.r.t. SSIM, since some edges are reinforced while others vanish (see Fig. 2(a) and Fig. 2(b)). In contrast, our approach can

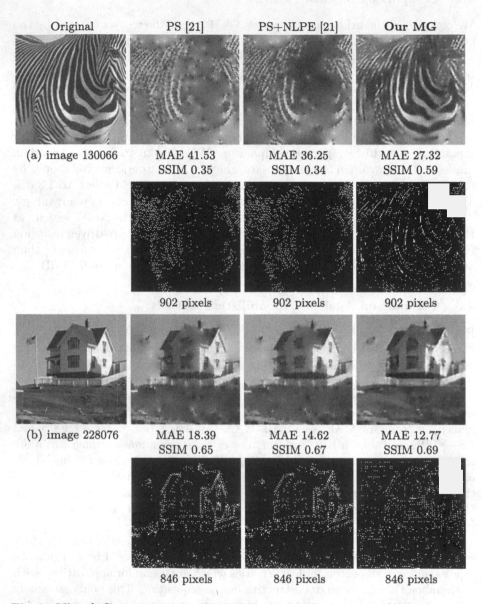

Original   PS [21]   PS+NLPE [21]   **Our MG**

(a) image 130066   MAE 41.53   MAE 36.25   MAE 27.32

SSIM 0.35   SSIM 0.34   SSIM 0.59

902 pixels   902 pixels   902 pixels

(b) image 228076   MAE 18.39   MAE 14.62   MAE 12.77

SSIM 0.65   SSIM 0.67   SSIM 0.69

846 pixels   846 pixels   846 pixels

Fig. 2. Visual Comparison to Probabilistic Methods at ≈ 5% Density on BSDS500. Known data points are marked in white. At this extreme density that might be used for e.g. thumbnail compression or destructive image acquisition, our mask WGAN reconstructs structures from less clustered data. It does not suffer from visual artefacts such as singularities or extreme colour bleeding as PS and NLPE with homogeneous diffusion.

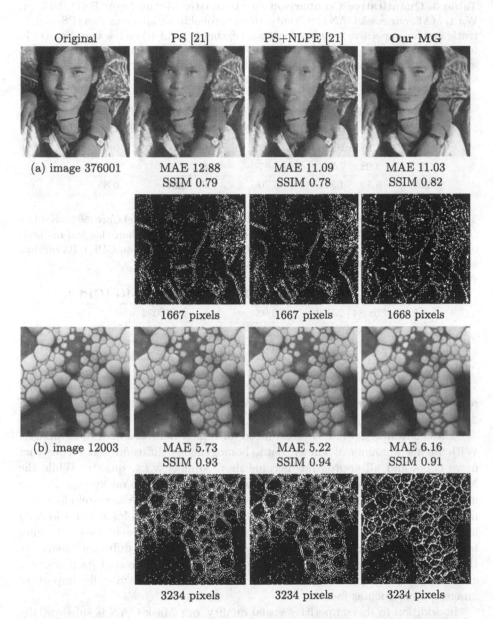

Original   PS [21]   PS+NLPE [21]   **Our MG**

(a) image 376001   MAE 12.88   MAE 11.09   MAE 11.03
                    SSIM 0.79   SSIM 0.78   SSIM 0.82

                    1667 pixels   1667 pixels   1668 pixels

(b) image 12003   MAE 5.73   MAE 5.22   MAE 6.16
                    SSIM 0.93   SSIM 0.94   SSIM 0.91

                    3234 pixels   3234 pixels   3234 pixels

Fig. 3. Visual Comparison to Probabilistic Methods at 10% and 20% on BSDS500. Known data points are marked in white. With increasing density, the quality of all three methods approaches each other. In (a), our MG still benefits from better known data distribution, yielding a more detailed representation of the face. In (b), it produces a similar visual quality as PS and NLPE at a higher error. It does not suffer from singularities, but this is less notable since the quality is overall high.

Table 3. Quantitative Comparison to Stochastic Methods on BSDS500. (a) W.r.t. MAE, our mask GAN (MG) outperforms probabilistic sparsification (PS) consistently and is competitive with non-local pixel exchange (NLPE) on low densities. (b) In terms of SSIM, at low densities the mask GAN slightly outperforms both competitors while remaining competitive for higher densities at significantly reduced computational load (see Table 4).

Density	(a) MAE (lower is better)			(b) SSIM (higher is better)		
	PS	PS+NLPE	**Our MG**	PS	PS+NLPE	**Our MG**
5%	13.98	10.98	11.19	0.69	0.70	0.71
10%	9.08	7.51	8.87	0.80	0.81	0.79
20%	5.19	4.31	6.70	0.90	0.91	0.85

Table 4. Runtime Comparison on 128×128 images with an Intel Core i56660K@3.50 GhZ and a NVIDIA Geforce GTX 1070. Our WGAN is faster than classical methods by several orders of magnitude (factor >400 on CPU or $>12,000$ on GPU). Its runtime is independent of the mask density.

Density	PS	PS+NLPE	**Our MG (CPU)**	**Our MG (GPU)**
5%	58.84	251.28	0.93	0.031
10%	33.89	340.61	0.93	0.031
20%	18.86	389.34	0.93	0.031

reconstruct structural image features from less known data. Therefore, it can distribute the mask pixels much more evenly.

These advantages are less pronounced for higher densities or simpler images. With higher amounts of known data, homogeneous diffusion can reconstruct more edges and all approaches become more similar w.r.t. quality. While the MAE and SSIM scores for high densities are slightly worse on average for our mask GAN in Table 3, its visual quality is competitive. The Wasserstein loss does not lead to the smallest possible quantitative errors, but yields natural looking inpainting results in Fig. 3. In particular, our mask approach does not suffer from the visually unpleasant singularities of homogeneous diffusion inpainting that are clearly visible in Fig. 3(a). Here we can also observe that its more even error distribution often leads to better representations of visually important image content such as faces.

In addition to its competitive visual quality, our Mask GAN is substantially faster than a PS/NLPE conjugate-gradient implementation with relative residual 10^{-6}. On a single CPU core, the speed-up reaches up to a factor ≈ 63 w.r.t. PS and a factor ≈ 419 w.r.t. NLPE. With GPU support, our GAN can be up to $\approx 12,560$ times faster. Faster model-based alternatives to PS exist [5, 10], but so far, they typically require postprocessing to reach the quality of PS+NLPE. Since they use homogeneous diffusion, they also suffer from visual artefacts like singularities. Overall, our network provides a fast solution for sparse data optimisation with a high visual quality.

5 Conclusion and Future Work

We have presented the first adversarial network for joint learning of a generative inpainting operator and a binary mask generator. Based on a mathematically well-founded Wasserstein framework, our inpainting GAN approximates the statistics of natural images, yielding visual improvements over model-based stochastic approaches with homogeneous diffusion. Simultaneously, our approach is faster by several orders of magnitude. It also qualitatively outperforms competing neural networks for spatial optimisation in combination with many inpainting operators.

Currently, we are working on further refinements of both the general framework and the concrete network architecture. Moreover, we plan to evaluate the impact of individual components with an extended evaluation and ablation study in the future. Our model is a step towards fast, visually accurate, and mathematically justified spatial optimisation with deep learning. We hope that it contributes to practical applications such as image compression or adaptive sampling in the future.

Acknowledgements. This work has received funding from the European Research Council (ERC) under the European Union's Horizon 2020 research and innovation programme (grant agreement no. 741215, ERC Advanced Grant INCOVID). We thank Dai et al. [11] for providing their reference dataset.

References

1. Alt, T., Peter, P., Weickert, J.: Learning sparse masks for diffusion-based image inpainting. In: Pinho, A.J., Georgieva, P., Teixeira, L.F., Sánchez, J.A. (eds.) IbPRIA 2022. LNCS, vol. 13256, pp. 528–539. Springer, Cham (2022). https://doi.org/10.1007/978-3-031-04881-4_42

2. Arbelaez, P., Maire, M., Fowlkes, C., Malik, J.: Contour detection and hierarchical image segmentation. IEEE Trans. Pattern Anal. Mach. Intell. **33**(5), 898–916 (2011)

3. Arjovsky, M., Chintala, S., Bottou, L.: Wasserstein generative adversarial networks. In: Precup, D., Teh, Y.W. (eds.) Proceedings of the 34th International Conference on Machine Learning. Proceedings of Machine Learning Research, Sydney, Australia, vol. 70, pp. 214–223, August 2017

4. Ballé, J., Laparra, V., Simoncelli, E.P.: End-to-end optimised image compression. In: Proceedings of the 5th International Conference on Learning Representations, Toulon, France, April 2017

5. Belhachmi, Z., Bucur, D., Burgeth, B., Weickert, J.: How to choose interpolation data in images. SIAM J. Appl. Math. **70**(1), 333–352 (2009)

6. Bertalmío, M., Caselles, V., Masnou, S., Sapiro, G.: Inpainting. In: Ikeuchi, K. (ed.) Computer Vision: A Reference Guide, pp. 401–416. Springer, New York (2014)

7. Bonettini, S., Loris, I., Porta, F., Prato, M., Rebegoldi, S.: On the convergence of a linesearch based proximal-gradient method for nonconvex optimization. Inverse Probl. **33**(5), 055005 (2017)

8. Chan, T.F., Shen, J.: Non-texture inpainting by curvature-driven diffusions (CDD). J. Vis. Commun. Image Represent. **12**(4), 436–449 (2001)

9. Chen, Y., Ranftl, R., Pock, T.: A bi-level view of inpainting-based image compression. In: Kúkelová, Z., Heller, J. (eds.) Proceedings of the 19th Computer Vision Winter Workshop, Křtiny, Czech Republic, February 2014

10. Chizhov, V., Weickert, J.: Efficient data optimisation for harmonic inpainting with finite elements. In: Tsapatsoulis, N., Panayides, A., Theocharides, T., Lanitis, A., Pattichis, C., Vento, M. (eds.) CAIP 2021. LNCS, vol. 13053, pp. 432–441. Springer, Cham (2021). https://doi.org/10.1007/978-3-030-89131-2_40

11. Dai, Q., Chopp, H., Pouyet, E., Cossairt, O., Walton, M., Katsaggelos, A.K.: Adaptive image sampling using deep learning and its application on X-Ray fluorescence image reconstruction. IEEE Trans. Multimedia **22**(10), 2564–2578 (2019)

12. Esedoglu, S., Shen, J.: Digital inpainting based on the Mumford-Shah-Euler image model. Eur. J. Appl. Math. **13**(4), 353–370 (2002)

13. Galić, I., Weickert, J., Welk, M., Bruhn, A., Belyaev, A., Seidel, H.P.: Image compression with anisotropic diffusion. J. Math. Imaging Vis. **31**(2–3), 255–269 (2008). https://doi.org/10.1007/s10851-008-0087-0

14. Goodfellow, I., et al.: Generative adversarial nets. In: Advances in Neural Information Processing Systems, vol. 27, pp. 2672–2680 (2014)

15. Hoeltgen, L., Setzer, S., Weickert, J.: An optimal control approach to find sparse data for Laplace interpolation. In: Heyden, A., Kahl, F., Olsson, C., Oskarsson, M., Tai, X.-C. (eds.) EMMCVPR 2013. LNCS, vol. 8081, pp. 151–164. Springer, Heidelberg (2013). https://doi.org/10.1007/978-3-642-40395-8_12

16. Iijima, T.: Basic theory on normalization of pattern (in case of typical one-dimensional pattern). Bull. Electrotechnical Lab. **26**, 368–388 (1962). in Japanese

17. Karos, L., Bheed, P., Peter, P., Weickert, J.: Optimising data for exemplar-based inpainting. In: Blanc-Talon, J., Helbert, D., Philips, W., Popescu, D., Scheunders, P. (eds.) ACIVS 2018. LNCS, vol. 11182, pp. 547–558. Springer, Cham (2018). https://doi.org/10.1007/978-3-030-01449-0_46

18. Kingma, D.P., Ba, J.: Adam: a method for stochastic optimization. In: Proceedings of the 3rd International Conference on Learning Representations, San Diego, CA, May 2015

19. Liu, G., Reda, F.A., Shih, K.J., Wang, T.-C., Tao, A., Catanzaro, B.: Image inpainting for irregular holes using partial convolutions. In: Ferrari, V., Hebert, M., Sminchisescu, C., Weiss, Y. (eds.) ECCV 2018. LNCS, vol. 11215, pp. 89–105. Springer, Cham (2018). https://doi.org/10.1007/978-3-030-01252-6_6

20. Liu, H., Jiang, B., Xiao, Y., Yang, C.: Coherent semantic attention for image inpainting. In: Proceedings of the 2019 IEEE/CVF International Conference on Computer Vision, Seoul, Korea, pp. 4170–4179, October 2017

21. Mainberger, M., et al.: Optimising spatial and tonal data for homogeneous diffusion inpainting. In: Bruckstein, A.M., ter Haar Romeny, B.M., Bronstein, A.M., Bronstein, M.M. (eds.) SSVM 2011. LNCS, vol. 6667, pp. 26–37. Springer, Heidelberg (2012). https://doi.org/10.1007/978-3-642-24785-9_3

22. Masnou, S., Morel, J.M.: Level lines based disocclusion. In: Proceedings of the 1998 IEEE International Conference on Image Processing, Chicago, IL, vol. 3, pp. 259–263, October 1998

23. Pathak, D., Krähenbühl, P., Donahue, J., Darrell, T., Efros, A.A.: Context encoders: feature learning by inpainting. In: Proceedings of the 2016 IEEE Conference on Computer Vision and Pattern Recognition, Las Vegas, NV, pp. 2536–2544, June 2016

24. Peter, P., Hoffmann, S., Nedwed, F., Hoeltgen, L., Weickert, J.: Evaluating the true potential of diffusion-based inpainting in a compression context. Sig. Process. Image Commun. **46**, 40–53 (2016)

25. Peter, P., Weickert, J., Munk, A., Krivobokova, T., Li, H.: Justifying tensor-driven diffusion from structure-adaptive statistics of natural images. In: Tai, X.-C., Bae, E., Chan, T.F., Lysaker, M. (eds.) EMMCVPR 2015. LNCS, vol. 8932, pp. 263–277. Springer, Cham (2015). https://doi.org/10.1007/978-3-319-14612-6_20

26. Schmaltz, C., Peter, P., Mainberger, M., Ebel, F., Weickert, J., Bruhn, A.: Understanding, optimising, and extending data compression with anisotropic diffusion. Int. J. Comput. Vis. **108**(3), 222–240 (2014). https://doi.org/10.1007/s11263-014-0702-z

27. Theis, L., Shi, W., Cunningham, A., Huszár, F.: Lossy image compression with compressive autoencoders. In: Proceedings of the 5th International Conference on Learning Representations, Toulon, France, April 2016

28. Ulyanov, D., Vedaldi, A., Lempitsky, V.: Deep image prior. In: Proceedings of the 2018 IEEE Conference on Computer Vision and Pattern Recognition, Salt Lake City, UT, pp. 9446–9454, June 2018

29. Vaserstein, L.N.: Markov processes over denumerable products of spaces, describing large systems of automata. Problemy Peredachi Informatsii **5**(3), 64–72 (1969)

30. Vašata, D., Halama, T., Friedjungová, M.: Image inpainting using Wasserstein generative adversarial imputation network. In: Farkaš, I., Masulli, P., Otte, S., Wermter, S. (eds.) ICANN 2021. LNCS, vol. 12892, pp. 575–586. Springer, Cham (2021). https://doi.org/10.1007/978-3-030-86340-1_46

31. Wang, N., Zhang, Y., Zhang, L.: Dynamic selection network for image inpainting. IEEE Trans. Image Process. **30**, 1784–1798 (2021)

32. Wang, W., Zhang, J., Niu, L., Ling, H., Yang, X., Zhang, L.: Parallel multiresolution fusion network for image inpainting. In: Proceedings of the 2021 IEEE/CVF International Conference on Computer Vision, pp. 14559–14568, October 2021

33. Wang, Z., Bovik, A.C., Sheikh, H.R., Simoncelli, E.P.: Image quality assessment: from error visibility to structural similarity. IEEE Trans. Image Process. **13**, 600–612 (2004)

34. Xie, J., Xu, L., Chen, E.: Image denoising and inpainting with deep neural networks. In: Proceedings of the 26th International Conference on Neural Information Processing Systems, Lake Tahoe, NV, pp. 350–358, December 2012

35. Yu, J., Lin, Z., Yang, J., Shen, X., Lu, X., Huang, T.S.: Free-form image inpainting with gated convolution. In: Proceedings of the 2019 IEEE/CVF International Conference on Computer Vision, Seoul, Korea, pp. 4471–4480, October 2019

36. Yu, T,, et al.: Region normalization for image inpainting. In: Proceedings of the AAAI Conference on Artificial Intelligence, New York, NY, vol. 34, pp. 12733–12740, February 2020

37. Zhou, M., et al.: Nonparametric Bayesian dictionary learning for analysis of noisy and incomplete images. IEEE Trans. Image Process. **21**(1), 130–144 (2011)

Rapid On-Site Weed Identification
with Machine Learning

Lihong Zheng[1(✉)], Alex Oczkowski[1], Toufique A. Soomro[2], and Hanwen Wu[3]

[1] Charles Sturt University, Wagga Wagga, Australia
{lzheng,aoczkowski}@csu.edu.au
[2] QUEST, Shaheed Benazirabad, Pakistan
toufique_soomro@quest.edu.pk
[3] NSW Department of Primary Industries, Wagga Wagga, Australia
hanwen.wu@dpi.nsw.gov.au

Abstract. Weed identification is a fundamental step in weed management. Traditional identification based on taxonomic features can be extremely challenging, especially at young seedling stage. It could also take days or months to confirm the identification through various channels, which would mean the loss of prime opportunity to control the weed. Recent advances in computer vision and machine learning have shown great success in various automatic visual detection tasks. It is therefore appropriate choice to capture visual field information and further process it to be able to realize autonomous weed identification promptly. This paper presents a convenient approach that applies image processing and machine learning for quick and accurate weeds identification on-site. Three deep models have been implemented to identify weeds via a smartphone. It is a proof-of-concept study targeting 16 selected most important agricultural weeds in Australia. We believe the proposed approach can help growers make a timely decision to spray the corresponding herbicide to reduce the financial loss annually.

Keywords: Weeds identification · Deep learning · Convolutional neural network (CNN) · MobileNet · Inception · EfficientNet

1 Introduction

Being a major agricultural producer and exporter, Australia's agricultural sector produces a wide variety of crops, fruits, and vegetables that earns a 12% share of GDP according to the Australian Bureau of Statistics. Currently, 61% of Australia's landmass is owned by Australian farmers. Managing farms is not an easy business. Especially, weed control is a critical operation for maintaining crop yield to have a good return at the end of a year. Weeds cost Australian grain growers Au\$3.3 billion annually in expenditure and losses [1] and the rapid

---

Supported by Charles Sturt University research fund.

evolution of herbicide resistance in weeds has threatened agriculture sustainability. To effectively control weeds, correct and rapid identification is critical so that prompt actions can be undertaken to control the "newly-identified" weeds, in particular any new emerging weeds. Mis-identification often occurs in the field even with experienced agronomists, especially when plants are at the seedling stage. Such mis-identification can therefore lead to the use of wrong or ineffective control options such as herbicides, resulting in no or poor control of the weeds in crops. This could cost growers at least $ 20/ha in control cost and another $ 50–180/ha in lost production. The ineffective control will also allow the mature weed plants to set massive amounts of seeds into the soil, which will increase the control cost in the coming years.

The conventional farming practices rely heavily on herbicides. Heavily reliance on herbicides has resulted in more than 500 unique case of resistance in weeds. Moreover, it may introduce potential harmful consequences on the environment. Therefore, how to identify the right type of weeds in a timely manner and spray the corresponding herbicide at the most right time is becoming an important task. Weed cost $708 million to Australian in due to yield loss due and $2,573 million in weed management. Reducing the cost of weed management is one of the grains industry's largest challenges.

Weed identification at the early growth stage contributes to improve herbicide control efficacy. However, while computer vision alongside deep learning has overcome the performance of approaches that use hand-crafted features, there are still some open challenges in the development of a reliable automatic plant identification system. These kinds of system have to take into account different sources of variability, such as growth stages and soil conditions, with the added constraint of the limited size of usual datasets.

There are a number of Weed ID Apps available in the App store, such as Ag Weed ID (75 species) [2], BASF Weed ID App (140 species) [3], Alaska Weeds ID (60 species) [4], Environmental Weeds of Sydney [5], and GRDC Weed ID App: The Ute Guide [6]. All these Apps are in fact electronic weed "photo albums" with manual search functions and can refine the search by using a range of features such as plant type, lifecycle, crop, season and region. The manual search can be a tedious frustrating process and time-consuming, which could discourage the use of the Apps.

However, for several methods developed to identify weeds or plants, such as Weed ID App, LeafSnap, etc., users have to manually compare field weed samples against hundreds of photos in the database when using these Apps. It is a painstaking process to manually go through each photo in order to determine the closest match through naked eyes even though the photos are categorised by plant types. A new method could be further improved and made more automatically, accurate and user-friendly.

Recent advances in computer vision and machine learning have shown great success in various automatic visual detection tasks, from industrial inspection to process control. It is therefore appropriate choice to capture visual field information and further process it to be able to realize autonomous weed identification.

Machine learning is now being broadly used to automatically identify plants through built-in complex algorithms, resulting in the availability of a few generic plant identification Apps, such as Garden Answers Plant ID [7], Plantsnap [8], Pl@ntNet [9]. These generic Apps are developed for instant identification of garden plants, ornamentals, wild plants and other plants in general. A specialised App, the ForestXplorer app [10], is now available for the identification of forest species. However, none is available with a special focus on weeds, particularly weeds in Australia.

This paper presents a new approach to identify weeds through deep learning models with built-in algorithms. Growers, advisors, weed officers, landcare groups and researchers will only need to take a photo of the weed of interest by using their smartphones, and the result will be automatically shown which is the best match of the suspected weed species by our well-trained machine learning model. Such a way making our approach much more user-friendly, more accurate, and time-efficient.

2 Related Work

Recent advance in machine learning gives the computer the ability to learn without being explicitly programmed. In the past decade, the capability of machine learning to analyse big data, to recognise patterns, to train the system to learn from data and to make decisions has seen many successful applications from self-driving cars, speech recognition, web information retrieval, face recognition to a vastly improved understanding of the human genome. Especially in agriculture, machine learning based methods have been applied to weeds identification. Machine learning methods can be categorised into unsupervised, supervised and deep learning based groups. Unsupervised approaches, do not need any ground truth data. For example, Rainville et al. [11] proposed a naïve Bayesian classifier and a Gaussian mixture clustering algorithm to discriminate weeds from crop plants. Haug [12] applied the random-forest decision tree to distinguish crops and weeds based on 15 different types of plant features. Kounalakis [13] developed a code book to represent the images in a linear combination way for weed recognition. While supervised learning methods learn the classification model from some known samples firstly and predict the unknown samples by comparing the similarity mathematically or statistically. A support vector machine-based approach has also been applied to segment crop leaves from weeds with about 90% accuracy [14,15]. The Green-to-green [16] has claimed 95% detection accuracy to identify wild radish in the field. Its trials show savings of up to 80% on chemical purchases are possible.

Nowadays, various deep learning models have been developed for weeds detection. Wu et al. [17] tried to identify soybean leaf diseases in a natural environment by a convolutional neural network (CNN). AlexNet, GoogLeNet, and ResNet were individually used as the backbone for model construction. The results show that the best model with the highest accuracy of 94.29% is based on ResNet. In the parameter settings of the optimal network, the number of iterations and batch size are 1056 and 16, respectively, and the training depth is 140. Wang et al. [18] analysed 11 tomato diseases by using deep convolutional neural networks and object detection models. It used a Faster R-CNN to identify the types of tomato diseases and a Mask R-CNN to detect and segment the locations and shapes of the infected areas. To select the model that best fits the tomato disease detection task, four different deep convolutional neural networks are combined with the two object detection models. The average accuracy of Faster R-CNN reaches 88.53% and Mask R-CNN is 99.64%. In 2016, Mohanty et al. [19] tested 14 crops and 26 diseases in 38 categories of the PlantVillage dataset by using the AlexNet and GoogLeNet networks, respectively. The maximum identification rate reached 99.35%. In 2017, Ramcharan et al. [20] used the Inception v3 network to identify 3 diseases and 2 insect pests of cassava. The recognition rates of brown leaf spot, red mite damage, green mite damage, cassava brown streak disease, and cassava mosaic disease were 98%, 96%, 95%, 98%, and 95%, respectively. In 2018, Ma et al. [21] proposed a deep convolutional neural network to conduct symptom-wise recognition of 4 cucumber diseases with a recognition rate of up to 93.4%. A four-module Deep CNN architecture similar to Lenet5 was used in this paper to detect four cucumber leaf diseases.

In 2019, Geetharamani and Arun Pandian [22] proposed a nine-layer convolutional neural network to identify leaves of 39 plant species, with an average recognition rate of 96.64%. It applied six types of data augmentation methods: image flipping, gamma correction, noise injection, principal component analysis (PCA) colour augmentation, rotation, and scaling, resulting in increased performance of the model. Ding et al. [23] identified three pasture species by using a BP neural network to classify patterns among seven texture features extracted through GLCM (Gray Level Co-occurrence Matrix). An 84.7% of final overall recognition rate has been reported. A weed recognition approach in [24] is proposed by sparse representation classification (SRC). Weeds are recognized by SRC directly without extracting features so that the computing cost and recognition time are reduced. The recognition rate of the proposed algorithm was 94.52%. García-Murillo et al. [25] introduced a sparse-based feature selection approach using the Lasso operator to eliminate noisy features. A trade-off between maximizing the accuracy and minimizing feature dimension has been sought to improve feature discrimination and accuracy in weed/crop discrimination tasks. More recently, Espejo-Garcia et al. [26] proposed a crop/weed identification system that relies on a combination of fine-tuning pre-trained six convolutional networks (Xception, Inception-Resnet, VGNets, Mobilenet and Densenet) with three "traditional" machine learning classifiers (Support Vector Machines, XGBoost and Logistic Regression). A classifier can make fair labels based on extracted deep features. This approach aimed to avoid over-fitting and to obtain a robust and consistent performance. A combination of fine-tuned DenseNet and Support Vector Machine achieved a micro F1 score of 99.29%. Specifically, it proves some heuristics for designing transfer-learning based systems to avoid over-fitting without decreasing performance.

3   Proposed Approach

To address the challenges and issues mentioned before, a framework has been developed to complete the weeds image data processing task. The following Fig. 1 shows the framework of the pipeline. It has a smartphone App based data acquisition, and a ID model development unit, and a fact sheets unit. The following subsections discuss these units individually.

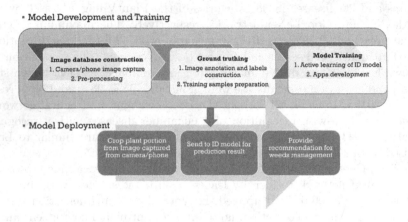

Fig. 1. Proposed Weeds ID Pipeline

Considering the poor internet connectivity in fields remotely, the proposed approach takes the offline version with implementation over a smartphone. Unlike other online Apps, users will need to have an internet connection to upload the captured weeds photo to the image server and download the weed ID information processed by the classification model on the server. It can be attractive from two aspects: 1). The dataset and models are likely to be updated regularly, and 2). It will address the computation and memory limitations smartphones usually face. On the contrary, the offline version will be customised for users with poor or no internet connection. Users will only need to take a photo of the weed of interest and the offline version App will automatically find the best match of the suspected weed species from the pre-built weeds list. Growers often wish to have quick information while they are in the paddock. However, Internet connectivity in the field is still poor and costly in remote areas of Australia nowadays. Therefore, it is more practical if our approach is designed as an offline version of the App with high speed and sound accuracy.

3.1   Weeds Selection and Image Data Acquisition

It has been reported in [1] that the most costly weeds nationally in terms of total yield loss remain annual ryegrass, wild radish and wild oats, with brome grass being the most notable major new weed. Barnyard grass, feathertop Rhodes grass, fleabane and sweet summer grass were found to be most costly in sorghum. Other common weeds include barley grass, wild oat, brome grass, windmill grass, Feathertop Rhodes grass, fleabane, fumitory, wild radish, Indian hedge mustard, marshmallow, common sowthistle, wireweed, Afghan melon, caltrop, turnip weed, bifora, bedstraw/cleavers, etc.

Since 2018, the team has started collecting field samples. Overall there are about 1500 images of 16 weed species, including capeweed, chenopodium album, dadellion, erodium, fleabane(canadian, flaxleaf, tall), fumitory, indian hedgemustard, marshmallow, poppy, prickly lettuce_saligna, prickly lettuce_serriola, shephard purse, sowthistle, and wireweed. Figure 2 shows the distribution of those captured samples of our dataset. Images of the selected weeds have been used for training and testing purposes as shown in the following section of experimental results. Sample photos have been shown in Fig. 3.

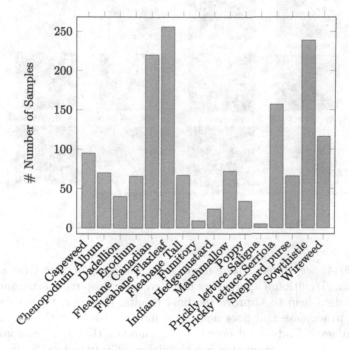

Fig. 2. Distribution Map of All Collections

3.2   ID Model Development Unit

Conventional machine learning-based model consists of three key steps: image pre-processing, feature extraction, training, and classification. Most of the existing weed/plants identification approaches are based on a plain and uniform background which is not feasible in practice. The accuracy decreased when an image is captured in a natural scene. Moreover, most of them use leaf and shape as the dominant features. However, there are no identical leaves in the world. The leaves are often soft and bending or with a twist, which introduced the difficulty of using the conventional approaches. In addition, the shape of leaves typically changes with their age to flowering. Thus, this unit is to apply a deep neural network model to obtain better distinguished patterns of weeds.

Fig. 3. Sample Photos of Sixteen Weed Plants.

Since 2014, deep models have made great successes in object detection and classification. Traditional approaches like increasing deep model size and amount of labelled data help to improve the final results. However, the computational cost tends to increase and does not suit a mobile vision. In this paper, we are working on several advanced deep learning models that suit android devices. These three selected deep models are MobileNet [27], Inceptionv3 [28], and EfficientNet models [29]. We summarise the key ideas of each model firstly, then these models are compared from three key aspects that are the size of the model, the accuracy, and the size of parameters based on the experimental results on three datasets introduced in the section of experiments.

By feeding a good amount of high-quality images to models, the deep models can be trained well to identify a species with a high degree of accuracy. The final step is to assign known weed IDs from the database to the user captured photo according to the result from the well-trained deep models, whose parameters have been learned from training sample previously. Once the models have been developed and validated, they will be transferred to a smartphone platform for more evaluation of their efficiency, complexity and reliability.

a) MobileNet [27]:

The MobileNet model was proposed by Google in 2017. It is a concise network architecture with reduced model size and complexity in a means of replacing the traditional convolution with a depthwise Separable Convolution (DSC). The DSC is a combination of channel-wise depthwise convolutions and point-wise convolutions. In such a way, the model size can be reduced roughly 10 times than the normal convolutional one. For depthwise separable convolutions, MobileNets used two easily tuned hyper-parameters (Width Multiplier and Resolution Multiplier) by trading off a reasonable amount of accuracy to reduce size and latency. So it can build a light-weight, low latency model that suits mobiles and embedded vision applications.

b) Inception V3 [28]:

The Inception v3 model is a 48-layer deep learning network with fewer parameters but similar complexity as VGGNet [30]. The key idea of Inception v3 is that it used factorizing Convolutions to reduce the number of connections/parameters without decreasing the network efficiency. Unlike other models that use auxiliary classifiers to improve the convergence of very deep networks, Inception v3 treats the auxiliary classifiers as a regularizer due that the main classifier of the network performs better if the side branch is batch-normalized or has a dropout layer. Only one auxiliary classifier is used in this model on the top of the last 17×17 layer, instead of using 2 auxiliary classifiers. Moreover, it regularizes the classifier layer by label-smoothing. Furthermore, it attempts to improve the network efficiency by reducing efficiently grid size while expands the filter banks.

c) EfficientNet [29]:

The conventional attempts to improve the accuracy of deep models are to arbitrarily increase the depth or width of a model, or to use larger input image resolution for training and evaluation. However, such approaches usually require tedious manual tuning, and still often yield suboptimal performance. In 2019, EfficientNet was developed as a novel model scaling method that uses a simple compound coefficient to scale up CNNs in a more structured manner. EfficientNet provides higher accuracy than many known models due to its compound scaling, a scaling at not only depth and width, but also resolution. By balancing all dimensions of the network-width, depth, and image resolution- with a fixed set of scaling coefficients, it beats the state-of-the-art accuracy with up to 10x better efficiency (smaller and faster). EfficientNet-D0 is the baseline network of the EfficientNet family. It is a reference model to show the effectiveness of the model scaling. It is similar to the MobileNetV2, but is slightly larger due to an increased computation load.

4   Experimental Results and Discussion

4.1   Experiment Setup

In our experiment, we have run three stages of sample preparation, training and testing.

First, we assemble the dataset of weeds plant images and split them up into separate folders for training and testing. Then, training images are annotated by drawing the bounding box around a plant so that the model can know what part of the image is the plant.

Once the training images have been annotated, we select the proper model(s) to be implemented from the Tensorflow [31] library and fine-tune the hyper-parameters for each model using several benchmark datasets e.g. ImageNet [32].

4.2   Implementation and Results

After that, we start training the model by feeding previously annotated sample images. Depending on the model selected and configuration used, this can take anywhere between 2 h to 3 weeks with our setup (24 GB CPU, 24 GB GPU). Once training is finished, we pack the model into an android compatible format for mobile usage. The following Fig. 4 shows a screenshot of the predicted label of a typical field weed image.

Image name: IMG_2309.JPG
Title: prickly lettuces | Confidence: 0.9903687

Fig. 4. Screenshot of the App Output.

We have evaluated three base deep models with 6 different versions. Moreover, the single-shot multibox detector (SSD) [33], developed by Google in 2016, is running on top of the base networks models (e.g. MobileNet, Inception) to boost deep model computation performance on embedded devices without a significant compensating accuracy. Table 1 has shown the average detection accuracy based on the true label of the weed species we collected. It shows that augmentations help to improve detection accuracy. There is a trade-off between file size and accuracy.

Table 1. Experimental results of different deep models

Model	Average Accuracy	Model Size
SSD_MobileNet V1	76.02%	21.2 MB
SSD_InCeption V2	82.46%	52.3 MB
SSD_InCeption V3	88.56%	99.3 MB
EfficientNet-d0	75.54%	15.8 MB
EfficientNet-d7	**87.75%**	219 MB
EfficientNet-d7x+Augmentations	**91.55%**	322 MB

4.3 Discussion

The photo samples we used in this research are captured in the field under different weather conditions in order to represent the real-time application. There are two main challenges we are facing:

- Low inter-class variance and high intra-class variance. Weed plant images were captured in nature agriculture field settings. Most of the plants are in green color. Color does not make any contribution to the final classification of weeds. It has also been noticed that the complexity of the background is shown in our captured photos. The objects of interest (weed plants) are mixed up with other complicated backgrounds, like barks, stones, etc. A weed plant is mixed up with other neighboring plants or has buddy leaves. Such Complicated backgrounds reduce the detection accuracy. It is necessary to include a background removal step as part of pre-processing and keep the green leaves only as the region of interest (RoI).
- Imbalanced samples with a low number of photos for several weeds species. This pilot research has sourced only about 1500 photos. Some weeds are not very popular in the field during the time we were collecting samples. That leads to a high false detection rate for those types with the low number of samples. We believe that the performance will be improved after having more good training samples.

Thus we include several pre-processing procedures to improve the final results. Firstly, background removal is applied to remove the non-leaf area. Secondly, the imbalance of samples has introduced a huge influence on the final detection results. We apply several data augmentation approaches such as background cut and paste, rotation, flipping, etc. Thirdly, we did padding the images to make sure they were square-shaped, in order to maintain a consistent aspect ratio for the training data. For the weed plants dataset, that appeared to be quite effective at increasing accuracy as the images had varying sizes/aspect ratios. Lastly, we tried refined bounding boxes of the plant as small as possible to rule out the influence of other background information. Obviously, EfficientNet-d7x achieved the best accuracy after introducing the data augmentations. SSD-Inception-v3 is also showing a good performance. In the future, we can ensemble three models by applying the majority voting strategy for better confidence in the final label.

5   Conclusions

In this paper, we have presented our research work on applying a machine learning-based weed identification. Three advanced deep models have been introduced and tested on our captured samples. Data augmentation has lifted the performance of models. The functionality of the App has been initially validated by the project team. It is a proof-of-concept study targeting 16 selected most important agricultural weeds in Australia. Follow-up research could expand to include more agricultural weeds in Australia and the App could be linked to management guidelines for the identified weed species. The App could also be developed to include environmental weeds and invasive weeds such as the Weeds of National Significance during the next phase of the App development. Photos will be taken from fields in different states in order to cover the possible morphological plasticity of each weed species, as the variation in morphology is a challenging reality that creates difficulty for correct identification. High-quality photos at different growing stages from seedling to mature stages will be prepared and stored in the image warehouse. Pictures will include those taken from different views, of different plant parts, combined with close-up images. Leaf, inflorescence/flowers and fruits, single leaves, and whole pictures will be considered. Thus the generalizability of our trained weedsID models will be improved.

Hence, advances in computer vision and machine learning offer a great opportunity to be able to help farmers to gather timely information and make quick action from the perspective of weed control. We believe that the proposed approach can be a good tool for the decision-making of growers. Users will only need to take a photo of the weed of interest and get the result on their smartphones. The App will tell the name of weed, making weed identification much more user-friendly, more accurate, and time-efficient.

References

1. Llewellyn, R., et al.: Impact of weeds in Australian grain production. Grains Research and Development Corporation, Canberra, ACT, Australia (2016)
2. Ag Weed ID. http://www.farms.com/agriculture-apps/crops/ag-weed-id
3. BASF Weed ID. https://itunes.apple.com/au/app/weed-id/id506639384?mt=8
4. Alaska Weeds ID. https://apps.bugwood.org/apps/alaska/
5. Environmental Weeds of Sydney. https://itunes.apple.com/au/app/environmental-weeds-of-sydney/id914766739?mt=8
6. GRDC Weeds ID UTE Guide. https://grdc.com.au/resources-and-publications/apps/weed-id-the-ute-guide
7. Garden Answers Plant ID. http://www.gardenanswers.com/
8. Plantsnap. https://plantsnap.com
9. Pl@ntNet. https://plantnet.org/en
10. ForestXplorer app. https://www.forestry.gov.uk/mobileapp

11. De Rainville, F.-M., et al.: Bayesian classification and unsupervised learning for isolating weeds in row crops. Pattern Anal. Appl. **17**(2), 401–414 (2014)
12. Haug, S., et al.: Plant classification system for crop/weed discrimination without segmentation. In: IEEE Winter Conference on Applications of Computer Vision. IEEE (2014)
13. Kounalakis, T., Triantafyllidis, G.A., Nalpantidis, L.: Weed recognition framework for robotic precision farming. In: 2016 IEEE International Conference on Imaging Systems and Techniques (IST). IEEE (2016)
14. Saha, D., Hanson, A., Shin, S.Y.: Development of enhanced weed detection system with adaptive thresholding and support vector machine. In: Proceedings of the International Conference on Research in Adaptive and Convergent Systems (2016)
15. Murawwat, S., et al.: Weed detection using SVMs. Eng. Technol. Appl. Sci. Res. **8**(1), 2412–2416 (2018)
16. Fulwood, J.: Weed detection technology offers new approach (2019). https://groundcover.grdc.com.au/story/6009959/no-place-to-hide-for-in-crop-weeds/
17. Wu, Q., Zhang, K., Meng, J.: Identification of soybean leaf diseases via deep learning. J. Inst. Eng. (India): Series A **100**(4), 659–666 (2019). https://doi.org/10.1007/s40030-019-00390-y
18. Wang, Q., et al.: Identification of tomato disease types and detection of infected areas based on deep convolutional neural networks and object detection techniques. Comput. Intell. Neurosci. **2019** (2019)
19. Mohanty, S.P., Hughes, D.P., Salathé, M.: Using deep learning for image-based plant disease detection. Front. Plant Sci. **7**(1419) (2016)
20. Ramcharan, A., et al.: Deep learning for image-based cassava disease detection. Front. Plant Sci. **8**, 1852 (2017)
21. Ma, J., et al.: A recognition method for cucumber diseases using leaf symptom images based on deep convolutional neural network. Comput. Electron. Agric. **154**, 18–24 (2018)
22. Geetharamani, G., Pandian, A.: Identification of plant leaf diseases using a nine-layer deep convolutional neural network. Comput. Electr. Eng. **76**, 323–338 (2019)
23. Ding, H., et al.: Study on identification for the typical pasture based on image texture features. In: 2019 Chinese Control and Decision Conference (CCDC) (2019)
24. Zhang, S., Wang, X., Wang, Z.: Weed recognition in wheat field based on sparse representation classification. In: Huang, D.-S., Bevilacqua, V., Premaratne, P. (eds.) ICIC 2019. LNCS, vol. 11643, pp. 511–519. Springer, Cham (2019). https://doi.org/10.1007/978-3-030-26763-6_49
25. García-Murillo, D.G., Álvarez, A.M., Cárdenas-Peña, D., Hincapie-Restrepo, W., Castellanos-Dominguez, G.: Sparse-based feature selection for discriminating between crops and weeds using field images. In: Nyström, I., Hernández Heredia, Y., Milián Núñez, V. (eds.) CIARP 2019. LNCS, vol. 11896, pp. 357–364. Springer, Cham (2019). https://doi.org/10.1007/978-3-030-33904-3_33
26. Espejo-Garcia, B., et al.: Towards weeds identification assistance through transfer learning. Comput. Electron. Agric. **171**, 105306 (2020)
27. Howard, A.G., et al.: MobileNets: efficient convolutional neural networks for mobile vision applications. arXiv preprint arXiv:1704.04861 (2017)
28. Szegedy, C., et al.: Rethinking the inception architecture for computer vision. In: Proceedings of the IEEE Conference on Computer Vision and Pattern Recognition (2016)
29. Tan, M., Le, Q.V.: EfficientNet: rethinking model scaling for convolutional neural networks. arXiv preprint arXiv:1905.11946 (2019)

30. Simonyan, K., Zisserman, A.: Very deep convolutional networks for large-scale image recognition. arXiv preprint arXiv:1409.1556 (2014)
31. Tensorflow. https://www.tensorflow.org/
32. ImageNet. https://image-net.org/
33. Liu, W., et al.: SSD: single shot multibox detector. In: Leibe, B., Matas, J., Sebe, N., Welling, M. (eds.) ECCV 2016. LNCS, vol. 9905, pp. 21–37. Springer, Cham (2016). https://doi.org/10.1007/978-3-319-46448-0_2

Remote Tiny Weeds Detection

Lihong Zheng[1](✉), D. M. Motiur Rahaman[1], Mark Hamilton[2], Remy Dehaan[1],
Felipe Gonzalez[3], Jane Kelly[1], and Hillary Cherry[2]

[1] Charles Sturt University, Wagga Wagga, Australia
{lzheng,mzmotiur,rdehaan,jkelly}@csu.edu.au
[2] NSW National Parks and Wildlife Service, Parramatta, Australia
{Mark.Hamilton,hillary.cherry}@environment.nsw.gov.au
[3] Queensland University of Technology, Brisbane, Australia
felipe.gonzalez@qut.edu.au

Abstract. Weeds cost Australian farmers around $1.5 billion a year in weed control activities and a further $2.5 billion a year in lost agricultural production. Weed management requires a good understanding of weed inventories and distribution for effective management. Nowadays, cutting-edge research provides improved options for remote weed detection, facilitating broader adoption of these transformational technologies like airborne, drones, and satellites, to provide tools to improve weed management in complex environmental and agricultural systems. In this paper, we present our recent research work on applying two deep learning approaches to identify tiny weeds from airborne captured RGB images with the goal of determining feasible approaches for weeds managers. High accuracy and low false-positive have been achieved through convolutional network learning. To address the challenges remote sensing images had, such as low image resolution, high similarity, and a large volume of data, the deep learning-based approach shows superior performance to detect weeds in heterogeneous landscapes. Our findings will enhance remote sensing capabilities in the Australian weed community through knowledge and skills transfer and stimulate the development of applications to process.

Keywords: Remote detection · weed detection · deep learning · VGG19 · Inception v3

1 Introduction

It is estimated that weeds cost Australian farmers around $1.5 billion a year in weed control activities and a further $2.5 billion a year in lost agricultural production [1]. Weed management requires a good understanding of weed inventories and distribution for management to be effective. Hawkweed (Hieracium aurantiacum), one of the 'National Alert List of Environmental Weeds', presents a major threat to primary production and biodiversity across south eastern Australia [2]. Specifically, orange hawkweed is recognised as an 'Agricultural Sleeper

© Springer Nature Switzerland AG 2023
H. Wang et al. (Eds.): PSIVT 2022, LNCS 13763, pp. 159–171, 2023.
https://doi.org/10.1007/978-3-031-26431-3_13

Weed' in Australia (see Fig. 1). It was estimated losses to the Australian grazing industries would be in the order of $48 million pa if this weed were allowed to occupy its potential range.

Fig. 1. Orange Hawkweed Sample Photos: (left) Orange hawkweed flower (right) Orange hawkweed adjacent native

Listed as Prohibited Matter under the NSW Biosecurity Act, orange hawkweed has the potential to seriously degrade Australian ecosystems and be a major cost to the grazing industry even only in the early stages of establishment. Thus these plants must be eradicated from the land once detected. Currently in New South Wales, Australia, orange hawkweed impact on the environment and are mainly located in Kosciusko National Park (KNP). However if its spread is not contained, it has the potential to impact greatly on primary production as well as native vegetation.

Orange hawkweed is a small herb with rosettes 5–20 cm diameter and flowers to 20 mm diameter and up to 40 cm high. It is difficult to be detected especially when not in flower. In the early stage, the eradication program relied solely on humans undertaking ground surveillance, which has achieved impressive results with high cost [3]. However, the flowering period lasts about one week only. Obviously, more hawkweeds can not be identified and treated on time. Hence, there is an increasing need to utilise remote sensing technologies to provide quantitative high-definition inventories of landscapes to improve profitability and sustainability in agricultural and environmental systems for invasive weed management. This can be accomplished through model development and validation of weed distribution and mapping using UAVs (Unmanned Autonomous Vehicles) UAVs for above-ground detection and spatial analysis. The necessary UAVs and sensor technology are now commercially available and capable of spatial resolutions of 2–50 cm. They offer significant advantages over satellite and traditional manned airborne systems because they allow flexibility to collect quantitative data at a very low cost. Nowadays, a drone has been used popularly to survey large areas and small-sized targets. Per hectare survey site usually is covered by approximately 400 photos. Manual photo processing would reduce any benefit gained from the rapid and low-cost survey. With the help of computer vision and machine learning, high-resolution remote sensing data captured by drones can be interpreted well to address weed issues of national significance.

It is envisaged that the machine learning techniques will enhance remote sensing capabilities in the Australian weed management community through transfer of knowledge and skills and subsequent development of applications to process, interpret and use high resolution remote sensing data in order to address weed issues of national significance. To date research has been in progress in this area because the technologies were not sufficiently mature or commercially available at a reasonable cost to allow researchers to collect imagery and develop the image analysis methodologies required for automated and accurate weed mapping.

This paper is organised as follows. Section 2 review current weed remote detection research in . Then we describe the study site and methodology of data acquisition of orange hawkweed in Sect. 3. After that, a couple of machine learning methods are discussed. We present the preliminary results and discussion in the following section. Finally, we conclude the current achievement and explore future research direction and effort for fast and accurate hawkweed detection.

2   Related Work

Sheffield et al. [4] have discussed core weed biosecurity program concepts and considerations for urban and peri-urban areas from a remote sensing perspective and reviewed the contribution of remote sensing to weed detection and management in these environments. Urban and peri-urban landscapes are typically heterogeneous ecosystems with a variety of vectors for invasive weed species introduction and dispersal. This diversity requires agile systems to support landscape-scale detection and monitoring while accommodating more site-specific management and eradication goals. The integration of remote sensing technologies within biosecurity programs presents an opportunity to improve weed detection rates, the timeliness of surveillance, distribution and monitoring data availability, and the cost-effectiveness of surveillance and eradication efforts. A framework (the Weed Aerial Surveillance Program) is presented to support a structured approach to integrating multiple remote sensing technologies into urban and peri-urban weed biosecurity and invasive species management efforts. It is designed to support the translation of remote sensing science into operational management outcomes and promote more effective use of remote sensing technologies within biosecurity programs.

Conventional survey methods for such invasive plants (e.g. field surveys) have time and cost limitations, resulting in a lack of quantitative information about weed distribution in Australia [2,5]. The lack of updated data hampers effective weed management [6]. Remote sensing to survey weeds has been attempted using aerial photography with mixed success [7,8]. Difficulties encountered using satellite imagery included low spatial and spectral resolutions [7,8]. Even with higher spatial resolution, satellite multi-spectral sensors (WorldView, Planet, etc.) have low instrument signal-to-noise ratios (SNR), limiting their use to only large-scale infestations. Analysis using airborne and satellite systems for monitoring can be costly and resolution is not always acceptable [9,10]. Further, previous trials have demonstrated the capacity to deploy active optical sensors in aerial platforms [11]. These systems relied on the ability of the multi-spectral sensor to detect greenness and typically worked well when the weed emergence occurred before the crop developed or weeds were projected above the crop canopy. Where weeds are mixed with other vegetation in heterogeneous situations, multispectral systems are less reliable for the detection and separation of weeds from the desired vegetation. In this paper, we particularly are interested in research work based on UAV RGB images.

The use of remote sensing has been exploited successfully for the detection of hawkweeds during flowering in Australia's Kosciuszko National Park [12]. Many research works have been done for crops/plants/weeds mapping based on UAV images [13–21]. Among them, some professional softwares e.g. ArcMap, Agisoft Metashape, have been used for pre-processing. Authors [17] compared manual and semi-automatic classification methods of UAV images quantitatively to monitor the encroachment process of grassland. [13] uses the gray-level co-occurrence matrix (GLCM)-based texture as a feature to classify crops using the machine learning methods of random forest and support vector machine. A classification tree-based per-pixel segmentation (PPS) method is used in [19] to cut UAV images into vegetation and background pixels. Crops and weeds are differentiated in [16] for targeted weeding. In [14] vegetation skeleton, the Hough transform and the simple linear iterative clustering (SLIC) were used together to detect weeds between crop lines. The average detection accuracy is about 92%. A pipeline process was proposed in [18] for a pixel-wise segmentation of invasive grasses from UAV images acquired in Cape Range National Park, Western Australia (WA), Australia. In total, 342,626 samples were extracted from the obtained data set and labelled into six classes. The average segmentation rate is 96.5% for two types of grass (e.g. Buffel, Spinifex), and a global multiclass pixel-wise detection rate is 97%. [20] conducted weed surveying by analysing pictures taken by a UAV to avoid cloud interference. They used the random forest classifier to differentiate weeds against sugarcane with an overall accuracy of 82%. Moreover, a CNN model was applied to improve the detection by line and achieved overall precision for the beet, spinach, and bean respectively of 93%, 81%, and 69% [21].

It is worth noting that the challenges of hawkweed remote detection are:

1) the hawkweed is a must eradicated species in Australia. It is distributed sparsely. The captured drone images are of low spatial image resolution. It means the individual weed plant of interest is tiny, and may only occupy several pixels.
2) generally there is about 40% overlapped area to guarantee the image quality, which introduces high similarity in the data preparation;
3) The image quality is not good due to the influences from climatic, geological conditions, and flying speed; and
4) the captured images are in a large volume, this needs high computation cost.

All of these introduced the difficulties to the automatic detection model.

3   Methodology

3.1   Study Sites

This research is part of the NSW Hawkweed Eradication Program. A key challenge in this program is delimiting the infestation, particularly across the remote and rugged areas where the infestation occurs. To supplement existing ground surveillance, the weeds experts sought to utilise drone surveying in the orange hawkweed operation as large and remote areas can be surveyed at a low cost. Drones capture colour imagery and a specifically designed algorithm automates the detection process. Since 2016, during peak flowering, field surveys are conducted by using a drone equipped with a high-resolution RGB camera to collect landscape images. In the recent two years, several surveys have been conducted over an area spanning 3200 ha in Kosciuszko National Park and sounds, see the following figure for example survey sites (Fig. 2).

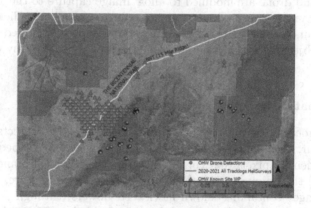

Fig. 2. Map of the Survey Sites Track [22]

3.2   Image Data Acquisition

Drone-based data collection has conducted at the nominated sites over an area. Each site is about 50 ha and approximately 23,500 images are collected per site. The sites have varied conditions including vegetation, access, elevation and surface topography. Sites are selected with the assistance of a dispersal-constrained habitat suitability model and expert knowledge. Surveys have been conducted at the 3 drone sites on Fifteen Mile Ridge in Kosciuszko National Park (Fig. 3).

Survey over large areas generates a significant amount of data. All data were collected with the aim of detecting orange hawkweed infestations as part of the Hawkweed Eradication Program. Helisurveys Pty Ltd collected the imagery

Fig. 3. Drone Operation on a Survey Site

from these three sites. They have a DJI Mavic 600 rotary-wing drone with on-board Sony A7R III 42.4 MP DSLR camera. The drone takes 3 photos a second and flies at a speed of 6 m/s at 30 m high above terrain and constant height is maintained through terrain following afforded by a 1 m digital elevation model. The camera and drone are modified to allow image capture to the specifications required. Imagery is captured at 0.24 cm resolution to allow sufficient pixels of the 20 mm diameter flowers to allow accurate detection. Compared with general RGB-based object detection, the hawkweed flower is a very tiny object to be detected.

3.3   Automatic Detection of Organge Hawkweed

Imagery is processed with a Python script algorithm that detects the flowers through colour, size, shape and hue. An algorithm was developed by Helisurveys [23] to identify pixels that corresponded to the colour of orange hawkweed flowers. Using the unique colour of the flower as the main feature, from a small sample of images containing known hawkweed flowers, through a thresholding based approach. A test version of the software provided an RGB colour detection algorithm that was improved upon once more data was collected, but was robust enough for the initial drone survey. Following Fig. 4 has shown two examples of the detected bounding boxes with hawkweed flower.

A human image culling stage is then employed to verify algorithm detections and dismiss false positives. When more training data was collected and the algorithm improved, previous images and data sets were reanalysed to remove the false positive detection where hawkweed flowers were missed or mislabelled [12]. In this paper, in order to store and process this data quickly and reliably, we have only sampled the image patches where contain hawkweed in a bounding box using the software developed by the HeliSurveys company. The experimental imagery dataset was a part of a greater dataset that of imagery collected in 2020/21. We hence also can benchmark the image patches for the following training procedure described in the following section.

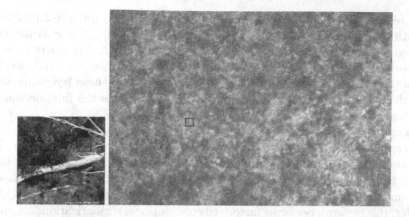

Fig. 4. Detected Hawkweeds in Blue Bounding Boxes (Color figure online)

4 Proposed Deep Models

CNN has been used to analyze images, audio, video, and text data by utilizing deep neural networks. One of the main advantages of CNN is that this can find the right pattern from the training sample (i.e., image) automatically instead of extracting the features manually. CNN consists of hundreds of layers that help to extract rich features from the training samples. Here are the common types of layers i.e., the input layer, convolution layer, pooling layer, flattening process, and output layer. The convolution layer pulls the input samples through a series of filters to represent the a sample into a form that is easier to process without compromising rich features that is required as an input for the next layer. Filters are used to extract trivial features like edges, color, and brightness at an early stage and then, increase the complexity to capture more distinguished features to differentiate and define the required object. In the same way, the pooling layer reduces the spatial size of the convolutional features. It is useful for extracting the most dominant features that are rotational and position invariant and thus maintains the process of effectively training the model. After that, flattening converts the data into a single long feature vector for feeding to the fully connected or dense layer where the features are combined into a wider variety of attributes that make the convolutional network more capable of classifying input samples. Lastly, the final output layer provides the final probabilities for each class.

- VGG19 [24]
  VGG19 is one of the most popular CNN that is 19 layers deep and associate with 16 convolutional layers and 3 fully connected layers. All of them, five sets of convolutional layers in VGG-19 use 3 by 3 filters and the number of filters increases by 2n (where n = 6, 7, 8, 9). The first two sets of the convolution layers have two layers with 64 filters, the second set has two convolution layers with 128 filters, the third set has four convolution layers with 256 filters, and lastly, two sets have 4 convolution layers each with 512 filters. There are also max-pooling layers in between each set of convolution layers

to reduce the size of the input image. These pooling layers have 2 by 2 filters with a stride of 2 pixels. The output of the last pooling layer is flattened, then fed to a fully connected layer with 4096 neurons. The output goes to another fully connected layer with 4096 neurons, whose output is fed into another fully connected layer with 1000 neurons. All these layers are ReLU activated. Finally, there is a softmax layer that makes the final decision by using cross-entropy loss.

- Inception V3 [25]

  Inception V3 is another widely used CNN with 48 layers of depth. This network has a different combination of symmetric and asymmetric building blocks, where each block has multiple branches of convolutions, average or max pooling, concatenated, dropouts, and fully-connected layers. Moreover, this network performs factorized convolutions, regularization, dimension reduction, and parallelized computations which reduces the total amount of computational parameters. This process allows high-quality training for the medium size of the training samples by regularization with batch normalized auxiliary classifiers label smoothing.

  Based on their performance on some bench-marked dataset like Coco, we selected two well-known models i.e., VGG19 and InceptionV3 as the base of our proposed technique.

- Modified pre-trained models:

  Network performance is improved with an increasing convolution layer up to the 8th layer for VGG19 [26]. The experiment was conducted for the network layers between layers 2nd, 4th, 6th, 8th, and 10th [27]. However, the performance of the 10th layer was lowest compared to others. This is due to the vanishing gradient problem of the 10th layer. To address this issue, up to the 10th layer and earlier layers were frozen by fixing the value of the learning rate to 0. Consequently, the trained network stopped updating the parameters and gradients of the frozen layers. This process speeds up network training significantly and improves its performance. Furthermore, freezing initial layers reduces the overfitting problem for any new data if the data sets are small. Generally, the last layer is fully connected. In the proposed method, the fully connected layer from the pre-trained networks is replaced by a new fully-connected layer with two classes i.e., Hawkweed Flower and Without Hawkweed Flower. To learn faster in the new layers compared to the transferred layers, the learning rate factors of the layer have to be set higher (i.e., 8).

  To slow down the learning of the transfer layers that were not frozen, the initial learning rate was fixed to a small value (i.e., 0.0001) by fine-tuning. The trade-off between the high learning rate factors and initial learning rate settings accelerates learning in the new layers, resulting in slower learning in the middle layers, and no learning in the earlier, frozen layers. Then, there is a requirement to fix the number of epochs (i.e., 20) and batch size (e.g., 10) for the training cycle, through a trial-and-error method. Finally, the validation accuracy was computed once per epoch.

5   Results and Analysis

5.1   Training and Testing

As mentioned previously, hawkweeds are distributed very sparsely. Therefore, the number of positive training samples is small. In the proposed technique, we consider 70% (i.e., 39) of the images for training and the rest 30% (i.e.,16) for testing. To monitor the training progress, we recorded average training accuracy, validation accuracy, training loss, and validation losses, as shown in Fig. 5. Besides, to monitor the trend, smooth training accuracy and loss curves are drawn by applying a smoothing algorithm that is less noisy than the un-smoothed curves. The graph shows that the training and validation accuracies improve with increasing the number of iterations, while the training and validation losses saw an opposite scenario. After a certain iteration, both the accuracy and loss are saturated. Based on validation accuracy, the performance of the proposed technique is evaluated in the next subsection.

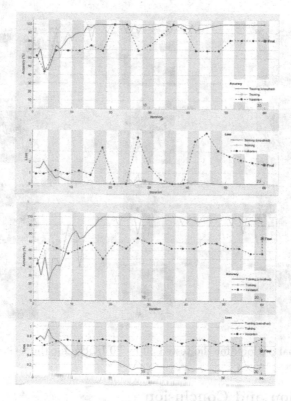

Fig. 5. Graphs of the metrics curves: Average training accuracy, validation accuracy, training loss and validation loss curves of (top) VGG19, & (bottom) Inception V3

5.2   Performance Evaluation

To validate the performances of the proposed methods, we count the number of samples correctly/incorrectly identified into two classes: Hawkweed or Without Hawkweed Flower. The Hawkweed Flower produces almost 100% accuracy except for InceptionV3 (e.g., 90%) among the two classes and models. Only three images were misclassified for both proposed models. A few tested samples for the high-resolution (0.25 cm/pixel) images are shown in Fig. 6 for the VGG19 model where the x and y axes labels represent true and predicted classes respectively. Given that we do not have a large number of hawkweed training samples, we believe the model performance can be improved by increasing the training samples. Moreover, another improvement work can be done by having more different categories like trees, white flowers, rocks, etc. Fine-tuning the Inception V3 network is challenging due to the uncertainty of the performance of the new network. Several methods such as image augmentation, factorised convolutions, regularisation, dimension reduction and parallelised computations can be added to stabilise the performance of the network.

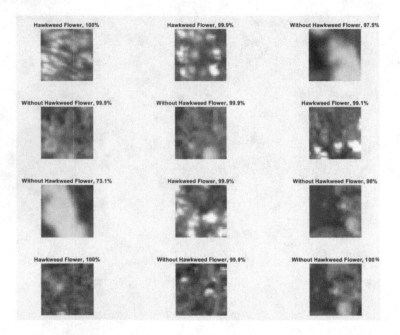

Fig. 6. Visual outlook for the tested 30 by 30 blocks for the VGG19 model.

6   Discussion and Conclusion

Currently, orange hawkweed is identified when the weed is flowering from the spatial resolution (0.24 cm per pixel) UAV RGB imagery and is considered the most effective way of mapping its distribution. The previous method based on color features has shown few false positive detections. This paper investigates the use of image techniques and advanced machine learning approaches that replace conventional approaches like morphology or shape detection including segmentation and texture analysis. Based on previous remote sensing work to detect weeds, we applied and compared two deep learning models to improve the detection accuracy significantly in challenging environments. The success will enhance remote sensing capabilities in the Australian weed community through knowledge and skills transfer and stimulate the development of applications to process.

In this study, Orange hawkweed occurs in very small patches. The size and sparse distribution of Orange hawkweed require very high-resolution spatial imagery resulting in several battles in both the acquisition and processing of data. It is very challenging to highlight the occurrence of hawkweed where significant other green vegetation was also identified using the same settings. With low-resolution images, likely, the similarities between hawkweed and coexisting vegetation at this time of year will lead to any advances in the ability to reduce false positives. To reduce the similarity, it is important to have a thorough understanding of the differences in plant size, growth rate, maturity, structure, and color at certain times of the year such that an optimal time can be determined to aid discrimination between hawkweed and surrounding vegetation. Hence it is an important strategy that collecting imagery at an appropriate time allows maximum separation from surrounding vegetation in maximising classification accuracy in the future.

The paper presents an opportunity to develop a good hawkweed identification platform with new novel detection algorithms capable of mapping weeds and also providing other time-critical information to target and reduce the spread of invasive species (e.g. Cost reduction through the targeted use of pesticides and fertilisers). The innovative methodologies, tools, analysis techniques, and knowledge gained through doing this research will increase the capacity to support weed research activities by other researchers, industry associations, government agencies, and end-users. Advanced machine learning techniques play a critical role in understanding and measuring the complex environments that these weeds occur in as well as the temporal variation that may allow us to optimise our potential detection periods and understand the limitations of the technology for producing weed inventories. Furthermore, Moreover, it may be possible to use a combination of spectral information to highlight where the green vegetation is located. So we will incorporate other types of data and establish a nationally-significant 'model' weed system to explore the limitations of multi-modality data such as RGB, multispectral and hyperspectral technologies across various airborne platforms to detect weeds in heterogeneous landscapes, to determine the best common practice for weeds managers.

Acknowledgement. Authors would like to thank for the grant support from the Australian Department of Agriculture, Water and the Environment (DAWE), would also like to gratefully acknowledge the support of Wendy Menz and Liesl Grant (NPWS) for their assistance in the collection of data at the study site.

References

1. Llewellyn, R., et al.: Impact of weeds in Australian grain production. Grains Research and Development Corporation, Canberra, ACT, Australia (2016)
2. Campbell, M., Weed control in pastures, are we winning?: 1990 CAWSS-Council of Australian Weed Science Societies-oration.-Presented at the Australian Weed Conference (9th: 1990: Adelaide). Plant Prot. Q., **6**(2), 55–63 (1991)
3. Hamilton, M.A., Cherry, H., Turner, P.J.: Hawkweed eradication from NSW: could this be 'the first'? Plant Prot. Q. **30**(3), 110–115 (2015)
4. Sheffield, K., Dugdale, T.: Supporting urban weed biosecurity programs with remote sensing. Remote Sens. **12**(12), 2007 (2020)
5. Pitt, J., Miller, I.: A review of survey techniques for the detection of weeds with particular reference to Mimosa pigra L. Australia and Thailand. Plant Prot. Q. **3**(4), 149–155 (1988)
6. Coutts-Smith, A., Downey, P.O.: Impact of weeds on threatened biodiversity in New South Wales. CRC for Australian Weed Management Adelaide (2006)
7. Thorp, K., Tian, L.: A review on remote sensing of weeds in agriculture. Precision Agric. **5**(5), 477–508 (2004)
8. Lamb, D., Brown, R.B.: PA-precision agriculture: remote-sensing and mapping of weeds in crops. J. Agric. Eng. Res. **78**(2), 117–125 (2001)
9. Rew, L., Cousens, R.: Spatial distribution of weeds in arable crops: are current sampling and analytical methods appropriate? Weed Res. **41**(1), 1–18 (2001)
10. Rew, L.J., Cousens, R.D.: What do we know about the spatial distribution of arable weeds. In: Precision Weed Management in Crops and Pasture: Proceedings of a Workshop (1998)
11. Lamb, D.W., Trotter, M.G., Schneider, D.A.: Ultra low-level airborne (ULLA) sensing of crop canopy reflectance: a case study using a CropCircle^{TM} sensor. Comput. Electron. Agric. **69**(1), 86–91 (2009)
12. Hamilton, M., Matthews, R., Caldwell, J.: Needle in a haystack - detecting hawkweeds using drones. In: 21st Australasian Weeds Conference (2018)
13. Kwak, G.-H., Park, N.-W.: Impact of texture information on crop classification with machine learning and UAV images. Appl. Sci. **9**(4), 643 (2019)
14. Bah, M.D., Hafiane, A., Canals, R.: Weeds detection in UAV imagery using SLIC and the Hough transform. In: 2017 Seventh International Conference on Image Processing Theory, Tools and Applications (IPTA). IEEE (2017)
15. Ajamian, C., et al.: Identifying invasive weed species in alpine vegetation communities based on spectral profiles. Geomatics **1**(2), 177–191 (2021)
16. Lottes, P., et al.: UAV-based crop and weed classification for smart farming. In: 2017 IEEE International Conference on Robotics and Automation (ICRA). IEEE (2017)
17. Oddi, L., et al.: Using UAV imagery to detect and map woody species encroachment in a subalpine grassland: advantages and limits. Remote Sens. **13**(7), 1239 (2021)
18. Sandino, J., et al.: UAVs and machine learning revolutionising invasive grass and vegetation surveys in remote arid lands. Sensors **18**(2), 605 (2018)
19. Hu, P., Chapman, S.C., Zheng, B.: Coupling of machine learning methods to improve estimation of ground coverage from unmanned aerial vehicle (UAV) imagery for high-throughput phenotyping of crops. Funct. Plant Biol. **48**(8), 766–779 (2021)
20. Yano, I.H., et al.: Identification of weeds in sugarcane fields through images taken by UAV and random forest classifier. IFAC-PapersOnLine **49**(16), 415–420 (2016)

21. Bah, M.D., Dericquebourg, E., Hafiane, A., Canals, R.: Deep learning based classification system for identifying weeds using high-resolution UAV imagery. In: Arai, K., Kapoor, S., Bhatia, R. (eds.) SAI 2018. AISC, vol. 857, pp. 176–187. Springer, Cham (2019). https://doi.org/10.1007/978-3-030-01177-2_13
22. Parks, N.N.: Needle in a haystack: finding hawkweed using remote detection (2021)
23. Helisurveys. https://www.helisurveys.com.au/
24. Simonyan, K., Zisserman, A.: Very deep convolutional networks for large-scale image recognition. arXiv preprint arXiv:1409.1556 (2014)
25. Szegedy, C., et al.: Rethinking the inception architecture for computer vision. In: Proceedings of the IEEE Conference on Computer Vision and Pattern Recognition (2016)
26. Ngugi, L.C., Abelwahab, M., Abo-Zahhad, M.: Recent advances in image processing techniques for automated leaf pest and disease recognition-a review. Inf. Process. Agric. 8(1), 27–51 (2021)
27. He, K., et al.: Deep residual learning for image recognition. In: Proceedings of the IEEE Conference on Computer Vision and Pattern Recognition (2016)

Combining Multi-vision Embedding in Contextual Attention for Vietnamese Visual Question Answering

Anh Duc Nguyen[1,2] , Tung Le[1,2(✉)] , and Huy Tien Nguyen[1,2]

[1] Faculty of Information Technology, University of Science, Ho Chi Minh, Vietnam
20C11016@student.hcmus.edu.vn, {lttung,ntienhuy}@fit.hcmus.edu.vn
[2] Vietnam National University, Ho Chi Minh City, Vietnam

Abstract. Visual question answering (VQA) is a challenging vision-and-language task that has recently gained high interest from many researchers. Existing methods adopt the strategy to extract object regional features, which effectively captures the local context of the image, but on the other hand, causes the loss of global context. Motivated by the strength of Vision Transformer, we propose to extract and combine both global and local contextual visual features for to be a Multi-vision Embedding for better image understanding. We also propose a Multimodal Contextual Attention method to adaptively learn the attentional embeddings of different contexts from image and question that are guided by each other. While most VQA models are optimized for the English dataset, few works are accomplished for the Vietnamese language. Hence, in this paper, we perform extensive experiments on a Vietnamese VQA dataset to evaluate and demonstrate the effectiveness of our approach. Our proposed model achieves an accuracy of 60.76% on the test set and outperforms former baseline methods in the Vietnamese language.

Keywords: Visual question answering · Attention mechanism · Vision Transformer · ResNet · BERT

1 Introduction

Computer Vision (CV) and Natural Language Processing (NLP) have made significant breakthroughs in the last decade. Especially, the appearances of attention mechanism [1] are a milestones in both CV and NLP area. Together with the traditional neural networks such as Convolutional Neural Network (CNN) architecture in CV and Long Short-tem Memory in NLP, these attentive approaches improve the performance in most important tasks such as Image Classification [2], Object Detection [3], Machine Translation [4]. With the advancement in both fields, more researchers can effectively solve more complex problems that required the understanding of both vision and language, such as Visual Question Answering (VQA) [5,6], Visual Captioning [7], and Visual Reasoning [8].

© Springer Nature Switzerland AG 2023
H. Wang et al. (Eds.): PSIVT 2022, LNCS 13763, pp. 172–185, 2023.
https://doi.org/10.1007/978-3-031-26431-3_14

Compared to other vision-and-language tasks, VQA is a more challenging task that requires not only a deep understanding separately in image and question but also an efficient method to learn joint feature representations of them in a single framework to predict the correct answer.

Recent works have shown substantial improvement in the VQA task [8–10]. However, most VQA frameworks focus only on VQA in English, there is a lack of datasets for other languages, especially Vietnamese. Khanh et al. [11] introduced ViVQA, a Vietnamese VQA dataset translated from VQA dataset [12] and certain baseline methods but did not achieve reliable results. Motivated by this, we develop our model to enhance the performance of the VQA system in Vietnamese. We evaluate our model on the ViVQA dataset and can outperform the former baselines.

Most modern VQA models hold three major components: (i) image understanding for visual features, (ii) question embedding for textual features, and (iii) fusion of these features as joint feature representations.

For image understanding, early approaches [13,14] used CNN to extract visual features as a feature map, then Anderson et al. [8] proposed bottom-up attention to extracting regional object-level features [15] and gained wide popularity in the VQA community. However, these methods have limitations, while CNN and bottom-up attention can effectively capture the local contextual visual features, they are ignoring the global contexts in an image. Vision Transformer (ViT) [16], a visual Transformer-based architecture [1] originally designed for text-based tasks, is proven to capture more long-range dependencies in visual extraction [17]. To overcome this limitation, we propose to take advantage of both CNN and ViT models to simultaneously attend to both global and local contextual visual features of the image. The combination of our image understanding can obtain more efficiency and performance than a single module.

For question embedding, various methods were applied to extract textual features such as LSTM [18], GloVe [19], etc. In our framework, we try to use the pre-trained BERT model [20], the state-of-the-art method in many NLP tasks, to enhance the question understanding in Vietnamese language.

Beyond the image and question understanding, the most important part of a VQA model is to establish a fine-grained features fusion to align the image and question semantically, which presents the key challenge. Early methods simply used linear fusion such as concatenation, summation, or element-wise product. Recent efforts have shown that the attention mechanism [1] is a powerful method for encoding the relation between visual and textual features. Since the VQA model aims to focus on the specific parts of the image that are relevant to the given question to find the correct answer, simulating the human-like reasoning process. Consequently, we design multi-branch attention that hierarchically fuses both global and local contextual visual features with textual features by leveraging the transformer encoder with top-down attention.

In summary, this paper makes the following contributions: (1) a method to simultaneously learn both global and local contextual visual features of the image; (2) a multi-branch contextual attention fusion that hierarchically integrates visual and textual features; (3) extensive experiments on a Vietnamese VQA dataset to demonstrate the effectiveness and outstanding performance of our model compared with the former baselines.

2 Related Works

Visual Understanding of VQA Models. In VQA tasks, many proposed systems used image features extractor from a single stream: early methods tried to extract features from one or more layers of CNN network such as VGG [21], ResNet [22]; modern approaches used the bottom-up attention [8] which extracts object attended regional proposals from Faster-RCNN [15]. Moshiur et al [23] proposed to jointly attend both object-level and image-grid features to learn objects and scenes context. Recently Vision Transformer [16] and its variants [24,25] open a promising era in Computer Vision, but they seem unpopular in vision-and-language tasks due to its weak inductive bias when training on small datasets. In other domains, many efforts like ConViT [26], Efficient ViT [27] try to combine both CNN network and Vision Transformer to harness both local and global information of an image and achieve competitive results.

Attention Mechanism for Joint Features Representation. In the early stage, many simple techniques were applied for multimodal fusion: concatenation, element-wise product [12]; or bilinear pooling methods [14]. Then attention mechanism became widely used and an important method for learning features fusion. Models [8,13] with attention mechanism adaptively attend to meaningful areas in the image based on the question. Researchers then realized the importance of co-attention to both visual and textual information simultaneously such as: MCAN [9], DMBA [28], etc. To go beyond, certain efforts like ViLBERT [10], OSCAR [5] attempt to embed text and image together as an input sequence, and then feed into a Transformer-based architecture that automatically discovers relations between the two domains.

VQA Datasets for Non-English Language. Recent advancement in VQA task is mostly built based on English datasets. The VQA dataset [12] and Visual Genome [29] are the two most popular datasets in English. Many researchers attempted to build their own datasets in their own languages by two methods [30]: (i) utilize sources like Wikipedia, newspaper, and human annotators to generate question-answer pairs; (ii) translate from existing English VQA datasets into their own language. In Vietnamese, recently, Nguyen et al. proposed ViMMRC [31], a multiple-choice dataset from school supplements of grade, and UIT-ViQuAD [32], a dataset which uses Wikipedia as a data source. Then Khanh et al. [11] proposed ViVQA, a Vietnamese dataset which is translated and adjusted from English VQA dataset [12].

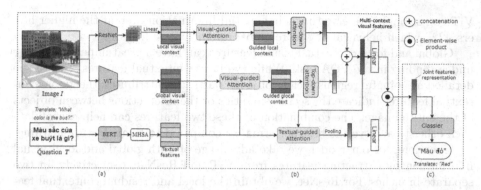

Fig. 1. Overview of our proposed Multi-vision Contextual Attention model

3 Methodology

In this section, we introduce our model architecture for the Vietnamese VQA task. Given an image I and a question T pair, the model will try to predict the best matching answer $\hat{a}$ from the set of candidate answers $\mathcal{A}$:

$$\hat{a} = \underset{a \in \mathcal{A}}{\operatorname{argmax}}\, p(a|I, T, \Theta) \tag{1}$$

where Θ denotes the set of parameters of the model.

The overview of our model is illustrated in Fig. 1, the model consists of 3 main modules: (a) the features extraction networks to learn the image and question understanding; (b) the multi-branch contextual attention fusion to fuse visual and textual features; (c) the classification network to predict the answer.

3.1 Multi-vision Embedding for Image Understanding

Visual features extraction plays a key role in the VQA task, grid features from CNN networks and object regional features from Faster-RCNN [15] are the two most popular techniques. However, these two models heavily depend on convolutional filters to embed visual attributes throughout their layers, where each layer convolves defined regions of the input and passes to the next layer, alias the local receptive fields. This such local connectivity can lead to the loss of global context of the image [33].

Vision transformer (ViT) [16], on the other hand, offers a multi-head self-attention mechanism to learn contextually the relevant information on the image. This mechanism is proven with the same effect as the local receptive field, however, is much more flexible. The flexibility of attention can capture more long-range dependencies information of the overall image, not just bounding to local regions. This results that global contextual information of ViT's receptive field is indeed larger than CNN in lower layers and can maintain that information through the network, while CNN receptive fields grow local to global. This assurance is proven in the recent study of Raghu et al. [17], which established that

ViT can strongly preserve the global spatial information even at the higher layers, [22], which helps gaining more global and attentive features.

Global and local contextual visual features can have a great impact on image understanding in the VQA task. While the local contextual features refer to the detailed meaningful regions such as objects, parts, and attributes; the global contextual features indicate the scene semantics or the interactions between objects of the entire image. The combination of these two features can help consolidate each other to achieve the best performance compared to single feature learning.

Therefore, for our model, we take advantage of both global and local visual information by extracting features from ViT and ResNet, respectively, in two separate branches. For ResNet, we obtain the local and residual contextual features $V_L \in \mathbb{R}^{M \times n_L}$, where M denotes the number of spatial grid locations of the extracted feature map with n_L dimensions. For ViT, we obtain the global and attentive contextual features $V_G \in \mathbb{R}^{N \times n_G}$, where N denotes the sequence length of the visual feature with n_G dimensions. Simplistically, given the input image I, we can formulate as:

$$V_L = ResNet(I) \tag{2}$$

$$V_G = ViT(I) \tag{3}$$

3.2   Question Understanding

By considering the input question T as a sequence of words. We embed these words into textual feature vectors with 768-dimensional using BERT model. BERT [20], which stands for Bidirectional Encoder Representations from Transformers, is a state-of-the-art language model in many NLP tasks, the strength of BERT is its bidirectionality and attention to learn contextual embeddings. BERT divides the sentence into subwords, then maps to a set of embeddings E. Each embedding $e \in E$ is computed by summing: 1) a token embedding e_t, respective to the subword, 2) a segment embedding e_s, indicating which part of sentence the token comes from (in a pair of sentence) and 3) a position embedding e_p, indicating the position of the token in the sentence. The input embeddings E are then passed through a multi-layer Transformer that accumulates a contextual representation of the sentence. As we develop our model especially for Vietnamese, we utilise phoBERT [34], a variant of BERT which is pre-trained intensively on Vietnamese Wikipedia and news corpus, hence phoBERT is efficient for downstream Vietnamese NLP tasks. We can formulate as:

$$Q_T = phoBERT(T) \tag{4}$$

where $Q_T \in \mathbb{R}^{S x 768}$ is output features vector of the input question with length S. After obtaining the question features from phoBERT, we use a Multi-Head Self-attention (MHSA) to enhance the features further. Detail of the MHSA mechanism will be shown in the next section, which now can be expressed as (Fig. 2):

$$Q_{SA} = MHSA(Q_T, Q_T) \tag{5}$$

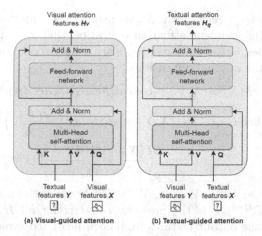

Fig. 2. Two types of Guided Attention modules which are used in our models: (a): Visual-guided attention: to learn the visual features guided by question; (b) Textual-guided attention: to learn the textual attention features guided by image.

3.3   Multi-branch Contextual Attention

Attention in VQA is motivated by how we pay attention to different regions of an image if given the words of a question, and vice versa. Thus, we demonstrate a multi-branch contextual attention fusion to hierarchically integrate contextual features of image and question. Firstly, we introduce a guided self-attention module to learn the attention of global and local contextual visual features guided by the question, then we show how we fuse different contextual features into a joint features representation to predict the best answer.

Guided Attention. The guided attention is inspired by the attention mechanism of Transformer [1]. Given the input features X and Y, the goal of guided attention is to capture the intra-interaction amongst all entities in X guided by Y. Firstly, the attention sub-layer projects the input into query matrix Q, key matrix K, and value matrix V embeddings by three linear projections:

$$Q = X \cdot W^q \qquad\qquad K = Y \cdot W^k \qquad\qquad V = Y \cdot W^v \qquad (6)$$

where $W^q \in \mathbb{R}^{d_x \times d}$, $W^k \in \mathbb{R}^{d_y \times d}$, $W^q \in \mathbb{R}^{d_y \times d}$, are learnable weight matrices; d_x, d_y are dimensions of input X, Y, and d is the common hidden dimension.

Then, by multiplication between each feature of Q and K, we obtain the attention weights matrix for aggregating information from X and Y. Following by normalizing the attention weights with the square root of the hidden dimension d and applying a softmax non-linearity function, we obtain the guided attention weight A by weighted summation over all values V:

$$A = ATT(X, Y) = softmax\left(\frac{QK^T}{\sqrt{d}}\right) V \qquad (7)$$

To get better feature representation, we usually use a multi-head mechanism. Each head is an independent attention operation that runs multiple times in parallel. The independent attention outputs are simply concatenated and linearly transformed into the original dimensions.

$$F = MHSA(X, Y) = concat(head_1, ..., head_H).W^o$$

$$head_h = ATT_h(X, Y) = softmax\left(\frac{Q_h K_h^T}{\sqrt{d_h}}\right) V_h \tag{8}$$

$$= softmax\left(\frac{(XW_h^q)(YW_h^k)^T}{\sqrt{d_h}}\right)(YW_h^v)$$

where $W_h^q \in \mathbb{R}^{d_x \times d_h}$, $W^k \in \mathbb{R}^{d_y \times d_h}$, $W^q \in \mathbb{R}^{d_y \times d_h}$, are the projection matrices of $head_h$; $W^o \in \mathbb{R}^{H*d_h \times d}$ is the projection matrix for all H heads. d_h is the dimensionality of the output features from each head. To avoid the overgrowth of computational cost, d_h is usually set to $d_h = d/H$.

After computing the guided attention features using multi-head attention, skip-connection followed by a layer normalization $LayerNorm(\cdot)$ [35]. is applied to enhance optimization and training stabilization:

$$F' = LayerNorm(MHSA(X, Y) + X) \tag{9}$$

Finally, the guided attention features F' are passed through a pointwise feedforward network (FFN), and another layer normalization with skip-connection is also applied to get the ultimate output H, similar to the Transformer encoder:

$$H = LayerNorm(FFN(F') + F') \tag{10}$$

The $FFN(\cdot)$ consists of two fully-connected layers, each one followed by a ReLU activation function and dropout.

$$FFN(X) = ReLU\{[ReLU(XW_1 + b_1)]W_2 + b_2\} \tag{11}$$

where $W_1 \in \mathbb{R}^{d_{in} \times d_m}$, $W_2 \in \mathbb{R}^{d_m \times d_o}$, $b_1 \in \mathbb{R}^{d_m}$, $b_2 \in \mathbb{R}^{d_o}$ are the parameters, with d_{in}, d_m, d_o are the input, hidden and output dimensions of FFN, respectively.

The final output H should have the same dimensions as the input X. Generally, all above procedures of Guided-attention (GA) module can be formulated:

$$H = GA(X, Y) \tag{12}$$

Multi-context Features Fusion. The guided attention module will apply to both global and local contextual visual features, corresponding to the question, in two different branches. The visual-guided attention will take the input image features as X, question features as Y, and generate the attended global contextual features $H_G \in \mathbb{R}^{N \times n_L}$ and local contextual features $H_L \in \mathbb{R}^{M \times n_G}$. In other words, the output attended visual features will represent the focused regions of the image related to the information in the question.

$$H_L = GA(V_L, Q_{SA}) \tag{13}$$

$$H_G = GA(V_G, Q_{SA}) \tag{14}$$

The output attended visual features H_L and H_G already contain rich information of the image. However, to refine the significant features from the contextual information and fuse them into a multi-context feature representation, an attentional reduction is applied. Attentional reduction is indeed a top-down attention mechanism [8]. It contains the aforementioned FFN layer with hidden and output dimensions of $d_{in}/2$ and 1, a softmax function to generate the attentional distribution, then we take the weighted sum over the visual features. Taking H_L as an example of attended visual features, we can formulate as follows:

$$H_L' = \sum_{i=1}^{M} \alpha_i . h_L^{(i)} \qquad \text{with } \alpha_L = softmax(FFN(H_L)), \qquad (15)$$

where $\alpha_L = [\alpha_1, ..., \alpha_M]$ the learned attention weights.

With the computed attended global and local features of the image, we fuse them into a multi-vision embedding vector by a linear combination:

$$V_{GL} = H_G' \oplus H_L' \qquad (16)$$

The linear combination can be element-wise multiplication, summation, or concatenation. However, we found that the concatenation, which creates a two-glimpse attended visual features vector, can yield better performance.

Visual-and-Textual Features Representation. The multi-vision embedding V_{GL} and the question features Q_{SA} again go through a textual-guided attention module. This textual guided attention is similar to visual guided attention, however, this time, the input X is the textual features and Y is the visual features, thus generates the textual attention features Q_{GA}.

$$Q_{GA} = GA(Q_{SA}, V_{GL}) \qquad (17)$$

This textual-guided attention enhances the question features by focusing on the important words in the question guided by the image.

At this point, we already have two significant visual attended and textual attended features. We need to perform feature fusion to obtain a visual-and-textual features representation J. The visual and textual features vectors are passed through linear projection layers then combined by a Hadamard product. The calculation can be expressed as follow:

$$J = LayerNorm\left(W_a Q_{GA} \odot W_b V_{GL}\right) \qquad (18)$$

where $W_a \in \mathbb{R}^{1024 \times d_a}, W_b \in \mathbb{R}^{1024 \times d_b}$ are the projection matrices, layer normalization is also used to stabilize training.

3.4   Answer Prediction

In the manner of most VQA research, we consider the VQA task as a classification task, the final joint features representation J will be fed into the classifier layer consisting of two fully connected networks, which is actually FFN, then applied a softmax function for final prediction:

$$\hat{p} = softmax(FFN(J)) \tag{19}$$

where $FFN(\cdot)$ used here has the hidden and output dimension of 512 and $|\mathcal{A}|$, which is the number of candidate answers $|\mathcal{A}| = 353$.

3.5   Loss Function

We optimize our model with the cross-entropy loss (CE) as a loss function for training, which is calculated as

$$L_{CE} = -\sum_{i=1}^{|\mathcal{A}|} y_i.log(\hat{p}_i) \tag{20}$$

with y_i is the ground-truth answer, $\hat{p}_i$ is the predicted probability of i-th class.

4   Experiment

4.1   Dataset and Evaluation Metric

Dataset. We experiment our model on a Vietnamese VQA dataset, ViVQA [11]. The images in ViVQA are obtained from the MS-COCO[1] source, the question-answer (Q-A) pairs are translated into Vietnamese by machine translation, and have Vietnamese native speakers tune the sentences to avoid ambiguity. Therefore, the dataset is more accurate and natural than being automatically translated from English, making ViVQA a good-quality one to perform benchmarks in the VQA task for Vietnamese. ViVQA contains $11,999$ Q-A pairs in the train set and $3,001$ Q-A pairs in the test set with a total of $10,328$ images.

Evaluation Metric. By considering the VQA task as classification, we evaluate our model on ViVQA using *accuracy* as the metric.

4.2   Experiment Settings

Model Hyper-parameters. We conduct the experiments to evaluate our model with hyper-parameters as follows. The size of the input image I is reshaped to $224 \times 224 \times 3$, then we extract the global visual features from hidden states of pre-trained ViT-Base's last layer with dimension 197×768, and local visual features from output of Conv5 layer of pre-trained ResNet-34 with features map of $7 \times 7 \times 512$. For the input question, we truncate the question to a maximum length of 20 and do padding with zero vector when its length is less than

---

[1] https://cocodataset.org/.

Table 1. Detail value of training hyper-parameters

Hyper-parameter	Value
No. of epochs	40
Batch size	32
Initial learning rate (LR)	$1e-4$
LR scheduler	linear decay with 5 warm-up epochs
Adam's betas (β_1, β_2)	$(0.9, 0.999)$
Weight decay λ	$1e-5$
Dropout ratio	0.3

Table 2. Comparisons of our model with former baseline methods

Models	Accuracy (%)
Hierarchical Co-Att + PhoW2Vec	34.96
LTSM + PhoW2Vec	33.85
Bi-LTSM + PhoW2Vec	33.97
Our model	**60.76**

20. The extracted question features are obtained from the last hidden states of phoBERT with a dimension of 20×768. In all guided attention modules, we set the number of heads $H = 8$, so the latent dimensionality of each head is $d_h = d/H = 768/8 = 96$; the input, hidden and output dimensions of FFN is $768, 1536, 768$, respectively (Table 2).

Training Hyper-parameters. We trained the model on a machine with a Tesla P100-PCIE-16GB GPU. We use Adamax [36] as the optimizer to update parameters, the other training hyper-parameters are defined detail in Table 1.

4.3   Comparison with Other Methods

As there are few published works on VQA tasks in the Vietnamese. Therefore, we evaluate and compare our model with 3 baseline methods proposed by the authors in ViVQA paper [11]. All three models use ResNet for visual representations and PhoW2Vec for textual features. Each one has a different method for joint features understanding: the first one uses Long Short Term Memory (LSTM) for associative attribute learning between images and questions, the second one enhances by a Bidirectional Long Short Term Memory (Bi-LSTM), and the last one used the Hierarchical Co-Attention [13] method to learn co-attention of both features. Details of the result are shown in Table 3. Undoubtedly, our model outperforms with a much more significant result compared to the former baseline. Our model achieve the accuracy of 60.76% on the test set, which

Table 3. First experiment result on ViVQA test set

Visual extractors	Accuracy (%)
ResNet-34	58.09
ViT-base	59.51
ViT + ResNet	**60.76**

Table 4. Second experiment result on ViVQA test set

Visual features combination	Accuracy (%)
Summation	58.91
Element-wise product	59.50
Concatenation	**60.76**

is approximately 1.5 times better than the best baseline method. This result demonstrates the effectiveness of our proposed method compared to others.

4.4   Ablation Study

To explore the effectiveness of our Multi-vision Embeddings for Contextual Attention learning, we conduct two sets of experiments to study: (1) the better efficiency of extracting both global and local visual features over the single representation, (2) the best linear combination of two guided-attention visual features.

In the first experiment, we train two more models, one using ResNet-34 only and the other one using ViT-base only for image understanding. We compare the results between single visual features and multi-vision contextual features. The evaluation results on the test set are shown in Table 3. We conclude that the combination of both global and local contextual visual features improves the performance and yields a better result than a single representation.

In the second experiment, we train our model with three types of linear combinations of contextual visual features: concatenation, summation, and element-wise product. Results are shown in Table 4, indicating that concatenation is the best choice to combine visual features into a multi-vision contextual representation.

5   Conclusion

In this paper, we proposed a Multi-vision Embedding based on the hypothesis that both global and local contextual features of the image can enhance the visual understanding for VQA task. In addition, the textual features is obtained by phoBERT, a BERT variant for Vietnamese, to learn the attentional embedding of the input question. Based on the extracted visual and textual features, we designed a multi-branch contextual attention fusion that hierarchically integrates visual and textual attention features that guided by each other and fuse them into a multimodal features representation. We also performed extensive experiments on ViVQA, a Vietnamese VQA dataset, to demonstrate the effectiveness and outstanding performance of our model compared to former baselines with the resulting accuracy of 60.67%.

Acknowledgments. This research is supported by research funding from Faculty of Information Technology, University of Science, Vietnam National University - Ho Chi Minh City.

References

1. Vaswani, A., et al.: Attention is all you need. In: Advances in Neural Information Processing Systems, vol. 30. Curran Associates Inc. (2017)
2. Tan, M., Le, Q.: EfficientNet: rethinking model scaling for convolutional neural networks. In: Proceedings of the 36th International Conference on Machine Learning. PMLR, 24 May 2019, pp. 6105–6114 (2019)
3. Li, Y., et al.: Voxel field fusion for 3D object detection. In: Proceedings of the IEEE/CVF Conference on Computer Vision and Pattern Recognition, pp. 1120–1129 (2022)
4. Zhang, S., Feng, Y.: Gaussian multi-head attention for simultaneous machine translation. arXiv preprint arXiv:2203.09072 (2022)
5. Li, X., et al.: OSCAR: object-semantics aligned pre-training for vision-language tasks. In: Vedaldi, A., Bischof, H., Brox, T., Frahm, J.-M. (eds.) ECCV 2020. LNCS, vol. 12375, pp. 121–137. Springer, Cham (2020). https://doi.org/10.1007/978-3-030-58577-8_8
6. Le, T., Nguyen, H.T., Nguyen, M.L.: Multi visual and textual embedding on visual question answering for blind people. Neurocomputing **465**, 451–464 (2021). https://doi.org/10.1016/j.neucom.2021.08.117. ISSN 0925-2312
7. Zellers, R., et al.: From recognition to cognition: visual commonsense reasoning. In: Proceedings of the IEEE/CVF Conference on Computer Vision and Pattern Recognition, pp. 6720–6731 (2019)
8. Anderson, P., et al.: Bottom-up and top-down attention for image captioning and visual question answering. In: Proceedings of the IEEE Conference on Computer Vision and Pattern Recognition, pp. 6077–6086 (2018)
9. Yu, Z., et al.: Deep modular co-attention networks for visual question answering. In: Proceedings of the IEEE/CVF Conference on Computer Vision and Pattern Recognition, pp. 6281–6290 (2019)
10. Lu, J., et al.: ViLBERT: pretraining task-agnostic visiolinguistic representations for vision-and-language tasks. In: Advances in Neural Information Processing Systems, vol. 32. Curran Associates Inc. (2019)
11. Tran, K., et al.. ViVQA: Vietnamese visual question answering. In: PACLIC (2021)
12. Antol, S., et al.: VQA: visual question answering. In: Proceedings of the IEEE International Conference on Computer Vision, pp. 2425–2433 (2015)
13. Lu, J., et al.: Hierarchical question-image co-attention for visual question answering. In: Advances in Neural Information Processing Systems, vol. 29. Curran Associates Inc. (2016)

14. Yu, Z., et al.: Multi-modal factorized bilinear pooling with co-attention learning for visual question answering. In: Proceedings of the IEEE International Conference on Computer Vision, pp. 1821–1830 (2017)
15. Ren, S., et al.: Faster R-CNN: towards real-time object detection with region proposal networks. In: Advances in Neural Information Processing Systems, vol. 28. Curran Associates Inc. (2015)
16. Dosovitskiy, A., et al.: An image is worth 16×16 words: transformers for image recognition at scale. arXiv preprint arXiv:2010.11929 (2020)
17. Raghu, M., et al.: Do vision transformers see like convolutional neural networks? In: Advances in Neural Information Processing Systems (2021)
18. Hochreiter, S., Schmidhuber, J.: Long short-term memory. Neural Comput. **9**(8), 1735–1780 (1997). https://doi.org/10.1162/neco.1997.9.8.1735. ISSN 0899-7667
19. Pennington, J., Socher, R., Manning, C.D.: Glove: global vectors for word representation. In: Proceedings of the 2014 Conference on Empirical Methods in Natural Language Processing (EMNLP), pp. 1532–1543 (2014)
20. Devlin, J., et al.: BERT: pre-training of deep bidirectional transformers for language understanding. arXiv (2019). arXiv:1810.04805, [cs]
21. Simonyan, K., Zisserman, A.: Very deep convolutional networks for large-scale image recognition. arXiv preprint arXiv:1409.1556 (2014)
22. He, K., et al.: Deep residual learning for image recognition. In: Proceedings of the IEEE Conference on Computer Vision and Pattern Recognition, pp. 770–778 (2016)
23. Farazi, M.R., Khan, S.H.: Reciprocal attention fusion for visual question answering. arXiv preprint arXiv:1805.04247 (2018)
24. Bao, H., Dong, L., Wei, F.: BEIT: BERT pre-training of image transformers. arXiv preprint arXiv:2106.08254 (2021)
25. Liu, Z., et al.: Swin transformer: hierarchical vision transformer using shifted windows. In: Proceedings of the IEEE/CVF International Conference on Computer Vision, pp. 10012–10022 (2021)
26. D'Ascoli, S., et al.: ConViT: improving vision transformers with soft convolutional inductive biases. In: Proceedings of the 38th International Conference on Machine Learning. PMLR, 1 July 2021, pp. 2286–2296 (2021)
27. Coccomini, D.A., Messina, N., Gennaro, C., Falchi, F.: Combining efficientnet and vision transformers for video deepfake detection. In: Sclaroff, S., Distante, C., Leo, M., Farinella, G.M., Tombari, F. (eds.) ICIAP 2022. LNCS, vol. 13233, pp. 219–229. Springer, Cham (2022). https://doi.org/10.1007/978-3-031-06433-3_19
28. Yan, F., Silamu, W., Li, Y.: Deep modular bilinear attention network for visual question answering. Sensors (Basel, Switzerland) **22**(3), 1045 (2022). https://doi.org/10.3390/s22031045. ISSN 1424-8220
29. Krishna, R., et al.: Visual genome: connecting language and vision using crowd-sourced dense image annotations. Int. J. Comput. Vis. **123**(1), 32–73 (2017). https://doi.org/10.1007/s11263-016-0981-7. ISSN 1573-1405
30. Chandra, A., Fahrizain, A., Laufried, S.W.: A survey on Non-English question answering dataset. arXiv preprint arXiv:2112.13634 (2021)
31. Nguyen, K., et al.: A Vietnamese dataset for evaluating machine reading comprehension. In: Proceedings of the 28th International Conference on Computational Linguistics, COLING 2020, pp. 2595–2605 (2020). https://doi.org/10.18653/v1/2020.coling-main.233

32. Nguyen, K.V., et al.: Enhancing lexical-based approach with external knowledge for Vietnamese multiple-choice machine reading comprehension. IEEE Access **8**, 201404–201417 (2020). https://doi.org/10.1109/ACCESS.2020.3035701. ISSN 2169-3536

33. Tuli, S., et al.: Are convolutional neural networks or transformers more like human vision? arXiv preprint arXiv:2105.07197 (2021)

34. Nguyen, D.Q., Nguyen, A.T.: PhoBERT: pre-trained language models for Vietnamese. arXiv preprint arXiv:2003.00744 (2020)

35. Ba, J.L., Kiros, J.R., Hinton, G.E.: Layer normalization. arXiv preprint arXiv:1607.06450 (2016)

36. Kingma, D.P., Ba, J.: Adam: a method for stochastic optimization. arXiv preprint arXiv:1412.6980 (2014)

Depth Estimation of Traffic Scenes from Image Sequence Using Deep Learning

Xiaoxu Liu and Wei Qi Yan[✉]

Auckland University of Technology, Auckland 1010, New Zealand
`weiqi.yan@aut.ac.nz`

Abstract. Autonomous cars can accurately perceive the deployment of traffic scenes and the distance between visual objects in the scenarios through understanding the depth. Therefore, the depth estimation of scenes is a crucial step in the obstacle avoidance and pedestrian protection from autonomous vehicles. In this paper, a method for stereo depth estimation based on image sequences is introduced. In this project, we improve the performance of deep learning-based model by combining depth hints algorithm and MobileNetV2 encoder to enhance the loss function and increases computing speed. To the best of our knowledge, this is the first time MobileNetV2 is applied to depth estimation based on KITTI dataset.

Keywords: Deep learning · automatic car · scene depth understanding · depth estimation

1 Introduction

The process of cognizing and assuming environment based on spatial perception is known as scene understanding [1]. A scene, in the context of autonomous cars, is the environment in which the vehicle is presently operating and contains the location, drivers, event, and their interactions [2, 39–42]. In order for autonomous vehicles to be driven safely and smoothly in complex urban traffic environments, the perception and understanding of depth in traffic scenes are of paramount importance [47–50]. Therefore, through robust depth estimation of traffic scene, the autonomous vehicles can become true.

Scene depth information plays an important role in advanced autonomous vehicles. The vehicle-related depth information can accurately perceive the operating environment of the vehicle and obtain the distance between the vehicle and pedestrians or others in traffic environment, so as to realize obstacle avoidance and pedestrian protection functions of autonomous vehicles. Compared with sensors, the driving recorder can obtain the color, texture and other information, the price is relatively low. Therefore, a number of scene understanding tasks are based on the images from driving recorder [43–46].

The performance of depth estimate of traffic scene in autonomous automobile may be improved to further depth recently due to the advancement of deep learning [3].

H. Wang et al. (Eds.): PSIVT 2022, LNCS 13763, pp. 186–196, 2023.
https://doi.org/10.1007/978-3-031-26431-3_15

Additionally, deep learning has the active benefit of transfer learning, which has benefited the training process of multiple traffic scenarios using a variety of pretrained networks and public datasets. Deep neural networks simulate high-level abstraction from the visual data and encode the objects, scenes, and events in motion pictures using an efficient representation in order to comprehend them [4]. As a result, deep learning methods offer special benefits when it comes to detect the depth of a picture.

One of the benefits is the end-to-end nature of deep learning, which, on the theory of a particularly exact recognition of individual situations, produces faster global information processing than standard methods. The deep learning approach can successfully meet the accuracy and real-time requirements for autonomous vehicles that must comprehend the information in complex traffic environments [5, 35–38].

However, for the performance of most depth estimation models based on the KITTI dataset [15–18, 52], we found that the problem of detailed regions in the scene on the predicted depth map is still existing. One of the reasons is that incomplete feature extraction by using encoder [19–22], another is that the network focus is on learning the depth to obtain the local minimum of the reprojection loss in the process of self-supervised learning, which cannot attain the global minimum [31].

Therefore, in this paper, we proffer MobileNetV2 structure as an encoder to transfer fine-grained details from high resolution to low-resolution. At the same time, we employ the depth hints algorithm to compute an alternative depth value and incorporate it into the objective function to obtain a satisfactory result [31].

In this paper, literature review will be presented in Sect. 2, our method will be shown in Sect. 3, our conclusion will be drawn in Sect. 4.

2 Literature Review

We review the outstanding studies of deep learning and depth estimation in this paper. The characteristics of the end-to-end nature in deep learning [6], strong versatility [7], and active mobility [8] have already demonstrated powerful capabilities in traffic depth understanding. Moreover, the layer-by-layer process of deep learning enables the model to better express the information. Therefore, the method based on deep learning has become the standard solution for image depth estimation.

In the past years, there are already heaps of studies related to depth estimation [23–26] based on deep learning in indoor and outdoor scenes. Fully convolutional network is one of the most popular structures in deep learning. The improved fully convolutional network [9] was applied to depth estimation. Different from the previous pretrained network, the fixed fully connected layer is employed to obtain the image-to-image conversion. Iro et al. [9] directly removed the fully connected layer and replaced it with a network having a pretrained network structure to return the high-level features to the same size as the original image. The entire net was regarded as an encoder-decoder process. The advantage is to streamline the parameters to make better use of GPUs. Moreover, the improved network can directly process images with any sizes instead of the fixed size of the network input and output like a normal fully connected network.

By observing the experimental results, FCRN [9] using ResNet-50 performed well in overall depth prediction, but the expression of details is not perfect. Through comparisons, the method [10] can better reflect the detailed information. It is a combination of global and local strategies. This strategy takes use of coarse network to predict the overall trend, and harnesses the fine network to perform local tuning on the overall trend. The depth dimensions obtained by this method are all smaller than the original image. One pixel of the predicted small depth map can represent the overall depth of the current position information, make the RMSE (Root Mean Square Error) smaller, but it will also lose a lot of depth information. This is the reason why it is not as good as FCRN [9] in overall depth estimation, but it handles details and contours better.

Although multilayer neural networks had outstanding performance in depth estimation. However, in the training process of the supervised learning model, it is necessary to obtain in advance the reference standard of the depth value corresponding to a large number of input data as the training samples, so as to carry out the backpropagation of the neural network. However, in reality, it is very costly to obtain the depth information corresponding to the scene. Therefore, a number of studies circumvent the problem of obtaining depth information at a high cost through unsupervised learning methods [27–30].

An unsupervised CNN for single view depth estimation was proposed [11]. The proposed model takes advantage of a structure similar to FCN without the participation of a fully connected layer. The volume of the model is smaller and computing speed is faster. At the same time, the participation of skip-connect ensures the relative integrity of the output feature details. Moreover, this model has the pre-trained network structure as the encoder part, which can achieve relatively good results in the case of insufficient training data.

Based on the model [11], the algorithm and structure were improved. Different from the FCNs, the disparity corresponding to the current feature size for the outermost 4 layers of the decoder part was estimated [12] that passed to the lower layer of the decoder after upsampling. This can ensure that each layer extracts disparity, which is equivalent to conduct a coarse-to-fine depth prediction. Since most models has taken use of bilinear differences, the range of the gradient always comes from the surrounding four coordinate points. The advantage of coarse-to-fine is that the prediction can make the gradient from a coordinate point rather from the current position.

From the perspective of learning methods, the vigorous development of deep learning was driven by large-scale annotated data, supervised learning promotes the development of deep models towards higher and higher performance. However, a large amount of labeled data often requires huge costs, more and more research work has begun to focus on how to improve the performance of the model without acquiring data labels. Hence, there are heaps of studies focusing on self-supervised learning and unsupervised learning for depth estimation.

Pertaining to stereo matching or binocular depth estimation, a device like LiDAR is extremely bulky and expensive, what it can collect is sparse depth information, what we need is a dense depth map; however, devices based on structured light can often only perform depth information annotation in indoor scenes, it is difficult to achieve high annotation quality in outdoor traffic scenes. Therefore, self-supervised learning has received more and more attention in stereo matching.

According to the review of these literatures, in this paper, we introduce a depth estimation model which combines MobileNetV2 and depth hints to achieve high-resolution depth estimation images with lower errors.

3 Our Methods

In stereo matching algorithms based on convolutional neural network, supervised learning is basically a regression method which takes use of smooth L1 loss to calculate the errors between the predicted disparity value and the real disparity value to supervise the learning of the network. For the self-supervised learning, the algorithm mainly outputs labels from the feature of the original image, the features of the disparity map to achieve the purpose of training the deep learning model.

In this study, the loss is calculated by using reconstruction. It is assumed that the left image as a reference image is I_{ij}^l where (i, j) represent the position coordinates of the pixel point. According to the predicted disparity d and the right image I_{ij}^r, the reconstructed left image $\tilde{I}_{ij}^l$ is generated through the warping operation. However, in order to avoid that the reconstructed image has a high loss, we will utilize structural similarity index measure (SSIM) as image quality to comprehensively calculate the photometric errors between the reconstructed image and the original image [32].

$$L = \frac{1}{N} \sum_{i,j} \alpha \frac{1 - SSIM\left(I_{ij}^l, \tilde{I}_{ij}^l\right)}{2} + (1 - \alpha) \left\| I_{ij}^l - \tilde{I}_{ij}^l \right\| \tag{1}$$

where α is the weight of the basic reconstruction loss and similarity loss. Single-scaled SSIM and simplified 3×3 filtering are adopted, α is set to 0.85.

We use U-Net as the basic framework for the deep estimation network and MobileNetV2 as the encoder of the network. The vehicle-related scene images are fed into the deep estimation network and SGM algorithm respectively to calculate the disparity loss, and to compare the magnitude of the two disparity losses produced by the deep estimation network and SGM. Our model will use the disparity with the smaller loss, and eventually generate a depth map by sampler [31]. The workflow is shown in Fig. 1.

190   X. Liu and W. Q. Yan

Although most KITTI-based depth estimation currently employs ResNet as encoder, compared to ResNet using standard convolution to extract features, MobileNetV2 utilizes the combination of depth-wise convolutions with point-wise convolutions can exponentially reduce the time complexity and space complexity. Moreover, in order to suit for depth-wise convolution, the inverted residual block applied by MobileNetV2 can extract features in higher dimensions.

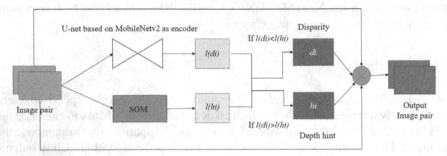

Fig. 1. The network structure of depth estimation based on network architecture and MobileNet v2 module.

To avoid the network gets stuck in a local minimum and fail to seek the global minimum, we employ the Semi-Global Matching (SGM) algorithm to generate a depth hint. We are use of depth hint for regression if the reprojected image generated with depth hint is more accurate than the network estimated [31, 33]. The SGM algorithm sets a global energy function related to the disparity map, composed of the disparity of each pixel to minimize this energy function,

$$E(D) = \sum_{P} \left(C(P, D_P) + \sum_{q \in N_p} P_1 I\big[\big|D_P - D_q\big| = 1\big] + \sum_{q \in N_p} P_2 I\big[\big|D_P - D_q\big| > 1\big] \right)$$

$$(2)$$

where D is the disparity map, p and q are the pixels in the image, N_p is the adjacent pixel point of the pixel point P_d, $C(P, D_P)$ is the cost of the pixels if the disparity of the current pixel is D_P, P_1 and P_2 are penalty coefficients, which are applicable if the disparity value in the adjacent pixels of pixel P and the disparity difference of P is equal to 1 and greater than 1, respectively.

The steps of the SGM algorithm are listed as follows:

Step 1 (Pre-processing): Employ Sobel operator to process the source image, map the image processed by the Sobel operator to a new image, and obtain the gradient information of the image for subsequent calculation costs.

Step 2 (Cost calculation): Use the sampling method to calculate the gradient cost of the pre-processed image gradient information and apply the sampling method to calculate the SAD cost of the source image.

Step 3 (Dynamic planning): There are four paths by default, and the parameters P1 and P2 of path planning are set and SAD Window size.

Step 4 (Post-processing): There are four parts: Uniqueness detection, sub-pixel interpolation, left-right consistency detection, and connected area detection.

We apply the root mean squared error (RMSE), absolute relative error and squared relative error with the 1.25 as the threshold as the evaluation methods.

$$ABsRel = \frac{1}{N} \sum \frac{|d_i - d_i^*|}{d_i} \tag{3}$$

$$SqRel = \frac{1}{N} \sum \frac{|d_i - d_i^*|^2}{d_i} \tag{4}$$

where d_i and d_i^* are the ground truth and predicted depth at pixel i and N is the total number of pixels.

$$RMSE = \sqrt{\frac{1}{m} \sum_{i=1}^{m} |d_i - d_i^*|^2} \tag{5}$$

where d_i is the real depth information, d_i^* is the predicted depth value, and m is the total number of pixels.

4 Experimental Results

We run the experiments based on the KITTI dataset which consists of calibrated stereo video registered to LiDAR measurements of a city, captured from a moving car. We totally obtained 1,000 data points for training and testing as shown in Fig. 2. The dataset is split into training set and test set at a ratio of 7:3, the resolution of the training images are all 320 × 1024.

In this experiment, we apply depth hints as a substitution of depth ground truth [31]. If the loss using depth hints is smaller than the network using ground truth for regression, we reply on depth hints to optimize the network.

The result shows in Fig. 3 that the model is able to well identify the distance in the scene. Moreover, the boundaries of vehicles, walls, traffic light and other objects displayed in the output images are of high definition. The depth information of the main objects in the color maps are also relatively high. In our preliminary experimental results, RMSE is up to 4.083.

In order to ensure the stability and reliability of our network, we take use of Root Mean Squared Error (RMSE), Absolute Relative Error (AbsRel), and Squared Relative Error (SqRel) as evaluation metrics to compare the performance of the networks with different encoders when training the same data set as shown in Table1. The results show that the MobileNetV2 encoder performs better than ResNet-18 and ResNet-50 based on all three evaluation methods with and without using depth hints. In the case of employing the MobileNetV2 as the encoder, the network with depth hints outperforms the other networks. This may indicate that in this dataset, MobileNetV2 combined with depth hints is able to achieve outstanding performance.

Fig. 2. The original RGB images as the training data

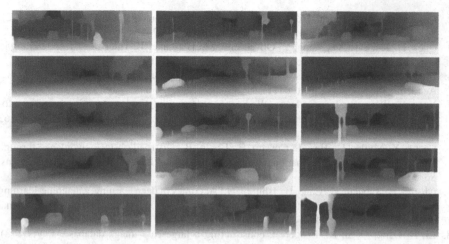

Fig. 3. The depth estimation of traffic scenes with color maps at pixel level (Brighter colors indicate closer distances, darker colors show greater distances)

Table 1. Comparisons of multiple deep neural networks

Training modality	AbsRel	SqRel	RMSE
ResNet-18	0.132	0.86	4.518
ResNet-50	0.121	0.777	4.467
MobileNetV2	0.115	0.736	4.293
ResNet-18 + depth hints	0.131	0.81	4.384
ResNet-50 + depth hints	0.120	0.726	4.395
OURS **(MobileNetV2 + depth hints)**	**0.112**	**0.702**	**4.083**

5 Conclusion

We initially demonstrate a MobileNetV2 method combined with depth hints to infer high-resolution depth maps from 2D images. Through comparisons, we see that in this dataset, MobileNetV2 combined with depth hints performed better than other encoders. At present, the RMSE of this model has reached 4.083.

In the near future, in order to expand this work, we will generate a depth information data set of traffic scenes in New Zealand and conduct depth estimation of traffic scenes based on this data set. Moreover, we will further optimize this algorithm to obtain a higher resolution depth estimation map

References

1. Li,Y., Tong, G., Yang, J., Zhang, L. Peng, H.: 3D point cloud scene data ac-quisition and its key technologies for scene understanding. Laser Optoelectron. Prog., 040002 (2019)

2. Liu, L., et al.: Deep learning for generic object detection: a survey. Int. J. Comput. Vis. **128**(2), 261–318 (2019). https://doi.org/10.1007/s11263-019-01247-4
3. Chen, H., Engkvist, O., Wang, Y., Olivecrona, M., Blaschke, T.: The rise of deep learning in drug discovery. Drug Discovery Today **23**, 1241–1250 (2019)
4. Husain, F., Dellen, B., Torras, C.: Scene understanding using deep learning, pp. 373–382. Academic Press, Cambridge (2017)
5. Yang, S., Wang, W., Liu, C., Deng, W.: Scene understanding in deep learning-based end-to-end controllers for autonomous vehicles. IEEE Trans. Syst. Man Cybernet. Syst. **49**, 53–63 (2019)
6. Lecun, Y., Muller, U., Ben, J., Cosatto, E., Flepp, B.: Off-road obstacle avoidance through end-to-end learning. In: International Conference on Neural Information Processing Systems, pp. 739–746 (2005)
7. Ohsugi, H., Tabuchi, H., Enno, H., Ishitobi, N.: Accuracy of deep learning, a machine-learning technology, using ultra-wide-field fundus ophthalmoscopy for detecting hematogenous retinal detachment. Sci. Rep. **7**(1), 9425 (2017)
8. Li, F., Deng, J., Li, K.: ImageNet: constructing a largescale image database. J. Vis. **9**(8), 1037–1038 (2009)
9. Laina, I., Rupprecht, C., Belagiannis, V., Tombari, F., Navab, N.: Deeper depth prediction with fully convolutional residual networks. In: International Conference on 3D Vision (3DV) (2016)
10. Eigen, D., Fergus, R.: Predicting depth, surface normals and semantic labels with a common multi-scale convolutional architecture. In: IEEE International Conference on Computer Vision, pp. 2650–2658 (2014)
11. Garg, R., B.G., V.K., Carneiro, G., Reid, I.: Unsupervised CNN for single view depth estimation: geometry to the rescue. In: Leibe, B., Matas, J., Sebe, N., Welling, M. (eds.) ECCV 2016. LNCS, vol. 9912, pp. 740–756. Springer, Cham (2016). https://doi.org/10.1007/978-3-319-46484-8_45
12. Godard, C., Aodha, O., Gabriel, J.: Unsupervised monocular depth estimation with left-right consistency. In: IEEE CVPR, pp. 270–279 (2017)
13. Ranftl, R., Lasinger, K., Hafner, D., Schindler, K., Koltun, V.: Towards robust monocular depth estimation: Mixing datasets for zero-shot cross-dataset transfer. IEEE Trans. Pattern Anal. Mach. Intell. **01**, 1 (2020)
14. Miangoleh, S.M., Dille, S., Mai, L., Paris, S., Aksoy, Y.: Boosting monocular depth estimation models to high-resolution via content-adaptive multi-resolution merging. IEEE CVPR, pp. 9685–9694 (2021)
15. Zhao, C., Sun, Q., Zhang, C., Tang, Y., Qian, F.: Monocular depth estimation based on deep learning: an overview. Sci. China Technol. Sci. **63**(9), 1612–1627 (2020). https://doi.org/10.1007/s11431-020-1582-8
16. Ochs, M., Kretz, A., Mester, R.: SDNet: semantically guided depth estimation network. In: Fink, G.A., Frintrop, S., Jiang, X. (eds.) DAGM GCPR 2019. LNCS, vol. 11824, pp. 288–302. Springer, Cham (2019). https://doi.org/10.1007/978-3-030-33676-9_20
17. Darabi, A., Maldague, X.: Neural network based defect detection and depth es-timation in TNDE. NDT E Int. **35**, 165–175 (2012)
18. Zama Ramirez, P., Poggi, M., Tosi, F., Mattoccia, S., Di Stefano, L.: Geometry meets semantics for semi-supervised monocular depth estimation. In: Jawahar, C.V., Li, Hongdong, Mori, Greg, Schindler, Konrad (eds.) ACCV 2018. LNCS, vol. 11363, pp. 298–313. Springer, Cham (2019). https://doi.org/10.1007/978-3-030-20893-6_19
19. Repala, V.K., Dubey, S.R.: Dual CNN models for unsupervised monocular depth estimation. In: Deka, Bhabesh, Maji, Pradipta, Mitra, Sushmita, Bhattacharyya, Dhruba Kumar, Bora, Prabin Kumar, Pal, Sankar Kumar (eds.) PReMI 2019. LNCS, vol. 11941, pp. 209–217. Springer, Cham (2019). https://doi.org/10.1007/978-3-030-34869-4_23

20. Honauer, K., Johannsen, O., Kondermann, D., Goldluecke, B.: A dataset and evaluation methodology for depth estimation on 4D light fields. In: Lai, S.H., Lepetit, V., Nishino, K., Sato, Y. (eds.) ACCV 2016. LNCS, vol. 10113, pp. 19–34. Springer, Cham (2017). https://doi.org/10.1007/978-3-319-54187-7_2

21. Liu, F., Shen, C., Lin, G.: Deep convolutional neural fields for depth estimation from a single image. In: IEEE Conference on Computer Vision and Pattern Recognition, pp. 5162–5170 (2015)

22. Dan, X. et al. Multiscale continuous CRFs as sequential deep networks for monocular depth estimation. In: IEEE Conference on Computer Vision and Pattern Recognition, pp. 5354–5362 (2017)

23. Liu, J., Li, Q., Cao, R., et al.: MiniNet: an extremely lightweight convolutional neural network for real-time unsupervised monocular depth estimation. ISPRS J. Photogrammetry Remote Sens. **166**, 255–267 (2020)

24. Hu, J., Zhang, Y.Z., Takayuki, O.: Visualization of convolutional neural networks for monocular depth estimation. In: International Conference on Computer Vision, pp. 3869–3878 (2019)

25. Ding, X., Wang, Y., Zhang, J., et al.: Underwater image dehaze using scene depth estimation with adaptive color correction. In: OCEANS, pp.1–5 (2017)

26. Torralba, A., Aude, O.: Depth estimation from image structure. IEEE Trans. Pattern Anal. Mach. Intell. **24**, 1226–1238 (2002)

27. Song, W., et al.: A rapid scene depth estimation model based on underwater light attenuation prior for underwater image restoration. In: Pacific Rim Conference on Multimedia, pp.1–9 (2018)

28. Rajagopalan, A., Chaudhuri, S., Mudenagudi, U.: Depth estimation and image restoration using defocused stereo pairs. IEEE Trans. Pattern Anal. Mach. Intell. **26**, 1521–1525 (2014)

29. Chen, P., et al.: Towards scene understanding: unsupervised monocular depth estimation with semantic-aware representation. In: IEEE Conference on Computer Vision and Pattern Recognition, pp. 2624–2632 (2019)

30. Watson, J., Firman, M., Brostow, G.J., Turmukhambetov, D.: Self-supervised monocular depth hints. In: IEEE International Conference on Computer Vision, pp. 2162–2171 (2019)

31. Godard, C., Aodha, O.M., Brostow, G.J.: Unsupervised monocular depth estimation with left-right consistency. In: IEEE Conference on Computer Vision and Pattern Recognition, pp. 270–279 (2017)

32. Hirschmuller, H.: Stereo processing by semiglobal matching and mutual information. IEEE Trans. Pattern Anal. Mach. Intell. **30**(2), 328–341 (2008)

33. Godard, C., Aodha, O.M., Firman, M., Brostow, G.J.: Digging into self-supervised monocular depth estimation. In: IEEE International Conference on Computer Vision, pp. 3828–3838 (2019)

34. Liu, X., Yan, W.Q.: Traffic-light sign recognition using capsule network. Multimed. Tools Appl. **80**(10), 15161–15171 (2021). https://doi.org/10.1007/s11042-020-10455-x

35. Liu, X., Yan, W.: Vehicle-related scene segmentation using CapsNets. In: IEEE IVCNZ (2020)

36. Liu, X., Neuyen, M., Yan, W.Q.: Vehicle-related scene understanding using deep learning. In: Cree, Michael, Huang, Fay, Yuan, Junsong, Yan, Wei Qi (eds.) ACPR 2019. CCIS, vol. 1180, pp. 61–73. Springer, Singapore (2020). https://doi.org/10.1007/978-981-15-3651-9_7

37. Liu, X.: Vehicle-related Scene Understanding Using Deep Learning. Master's Thesis, Auckland University of Technology, New Zealand (2019)

38. Mehtab, S., Yan, W.: FlexiNet: fast and accurate vehicle detection for autonomous vehicles-2D vehicle detection using deep neural network. In: ACM ICCCV (2021)

39. Mehtab, S., Yan, W.: Flexible neural network for fast and accurate road scene perception. Multimed. Tools Appl. **81**, 7169–7181 (2021). https://doi.org/10.1007/s11042-022-11933-0

40. Mehtab, S., Yan, W., Narayanan, A.: 3D vehicle detection using cheap LiDAR and camera sensors. In: IEEE IVCNZ (2021)
41. Yan, W.: Computational Methods for Deep Learning: Theoretic Practice and Applications. Springer, Berlin (2021)
42. Yan, W.: Introduction to Intelligent Surveillance: Surveillance Data Capture, Transmission, and Analytics. Springer, Berlin (2019)
43. Gu, Q., Yang, J., Kong, L., Yan, W., Klette, R.: Embedded and real-time vehicle detection system for challenging on-road scenes. Opt. Eng. **56**(6), 06310210 (2017)
44. Ming, Y., Li, Y., Zhang, Z., Yan, W.: A survey of path planning algorithms for autonomous vehicles. Int. J. Commercial Veh. **14**, 97–109 (2021)
45. Shen, D., Xin, C., Nguyen, M., Yan, W.: Flame detection using deep learning. In: International Conference on Control, Automation and Robotics (2018)
46. Xin, C., Nguyen, M., Yan, W.: Multiple flames recognition using deep learning. In: Handbook of Research on Multimedia Cyber Security, pp. 296–307 (2020)
47. Luo, Z., Nguyen, M., Yan, W.: Kayak and sailboat detection based on the im-proved YOLO with transformer. In: ACM ICCCV (2022)
48. Le, R., Nguyen, M., Yan, W.: Training a convolutional neural network for transportation sign detection using synthetic dataset. In: IEEE IVCNZ (2021)
49. Pan, C., Yan, W.Q.: Object detection based on saturation of visual perception. Multimed. Tools Appl. **79**(27–28), 19925–19944 (2020). https://doi.org/10.1007/s11042-020-08866-x
50. Geiger, A., Lenz, P., Urtasun, R.: Are we ready for autonomous driving? The KITTI vision benchmark suite. In: Proceedings of the IEEE Conference on Computer Vision and Pattern Recognition (CVPR), pp. 3354–3361 (2012)

Author Index

© Springer Nature Switzerland AG 2023
H. Wang et al. (Eds.): PSIVT 2022, LNCS 13763, pp. 197–198, 2023.
https://doi.org/10.1007/978-3-031-26431-3

Printed in the United States
by Baker & Taylor Publisher Services